CHENG-ZHU CONFUCIANISM IN THE EARLY QING

SUNY series in Chinese Philosophy and Culture
Edited by David L. Hall and Roger T. Ames

CHENG-ZHU CONFUCIANISM IN THE EARLY QING

Li Guangdi (1642–1718) and Qing Learning

On-cho Ng

STATE UNIVERSITY OF NEW YORK PRESS

Published by
State University of New York Press, Albany

Printed in the United States of America

For information, address State University of New York Press,
90 State Street, Suite 700, Albany, NY 12207

Production by Cathleen Collins
Marketing by Dana E. Yanulavich

Library of Congress Cataloging-in-Publication Data

Ng, On-cho.
Cheng-Zhu confucianism in the early Qing : Li Guangdi (1642–1718) and Qing learning / On-cho Ng.
p. cm. — (SUNY series in Chinese philosophy and culture)
Includes bibliographical references and index.
ISBN 0-7914-4881-9 (alk. paper) — ISBN 0-7914-4882-7 (pbk. : alk. paper)
1. Li, Kuang-ti, 1642–1718—Views on Neo-Confucianism. 2. Neo-Confucianism.
I. Title. II. Series.
B127.N4 N44 2001
181′.112—dc21

00-039477

10 9 8 7 6 5 4 3 2 1

Contents

ACKNOWLEDGMENTS

The pursuit of a project, and indeed scholarship in general, means the constant incurring of intellectual debts. Receiving instruction, help, encouragement, and inspiration from colleagues and mentors is perhaps one of the most satisfying aspects of the life of an academic, whose companionship and interaction with texts constitute a rather solitary existence otherwise. It is therefore a great pleasure to have the opportunity to offer my thanks and gratitude to those kind and generous souls who have over the past few years provided guidance and assistance. John Henderson, most generous with his time, read the entire manuscript and proffered words of wisdom that helped revise my thinking, clarify my arguments, and strengthen my thesis. Moreover, he has never failed to be supportive of my various scholarly ventures, having been a patient reader and gentle critic of many of my unworthy writings.

My participation in the International Conference on the Hermeneutic Traditions in Chinese Culture, held in October 1996 at Rutgers University, proved to be very helpful in the eventual production of chapter five. In that forum, I presented a paper that began my engagement with contemporary theories of hermeneutics. Comments from colleagues at that gathering, especially those from John Berthrong, Chung-ying Cheng, Kai-wing Chow, and Longxi Zhang, helped formulate and sharpen my comparative perspective of Confucian exegesis and Western hermeneutics. Daniel Gardner, most knowledgeable on the topic of Confucian commentaries and hermeneutics, kindly critiqued the penultimate draft of chapter five and contributed to its improvement. An earlier and shorter version of this chapter appeared as "Negotiating the Boundary between Hermeneutics and Philosophy in Early Ch'ing Ch'eng-Chu Confucianism: Li Kuang-ti's Study of the *Doctrine of the Mean* (Chung-yung) and Great Learning (*Ta-hsueh*)," in Kai-wing Chow, On-cho Ng, and John B. Henderson, eds., *Imagining Boundaries: Changing Confucian Doctrines, Texts and Hermeneutics* (Albany: SUNY Press, 1999). Thanks are due to SUNY Press for allowing reuse of the material.

I am grateful to members of the Regional Seminar in Neo-Confucian studies at Columbia University, especially the co-chairs in 1993, Anne Birdwhistell and Conrad Schirokauer, who invited me to present a paper in March of that year. That paper turned out to be the basis of chapter one. I also owe University of Hawaii Press a word of thanks for permission to reprint parts of my article, "*Hsing* (Nature) as the Ontological Basis of Practicality in Early Ch'ing Ch'eng-Chu Confucianism: Li Kuang-ti's (1642–1718) Philosophy," *Philosophy East and West* 44.1(January 1994):79–109. Chapter four is a much expanded and revised version of that published piece. It should be mentioned that the research and writing of the article was facilitated by a grant from the Research and Graduate Studies Office of the College of Liberal Arts at Penn State University, which made possible a reduction in my teaching load in 1992. A library travel grant from the Center for Chinese Studies at the University of Michigan in the same year was also helpful in the completion of the article, which sowed the seeds for this book.

The role of two senior scholars in my intellectual growth must be gratefully acknowledged. Daniel W. Y. Kwok, my first and perennial teacher in Chinese intellectual history, has never stopped being a mentor, a cheerleader, and a muse. Hoyt Cleveland Tillman, whose excellent scholarship on Song Confucianism never ceases to instruct, has over the past decade been an unfailing supporter of the kind of work that I do, giving me much-needed confidence and inspiration in my exploration of the Qing Confucian tradition. Encouragement and ideas were received from a host of other kind scholars while I was working on this project: the late Charles Wei-hsün Fu, Professors Wm. Theodore de Bary, Benjamin Elman, P. J. Ivanhoe, Lynn Struve, and Yü Ying-shih. Professor Ivanhoe has especially been kind enough to read quite a few of my publications. His various comments have influenced the formulation and development of some of my thinking in this book. Last but not least, I am particularly grateful to Roger Ames for initially welcoming and encouraging my submission of the original manuscript to this series that he co-edits. Needless to say, I am solely responsible for whatever shortcoming and demerit readers may discern in my work.

On a more personal note, my wife, Mary Ann Maslak, who has herself not long ago entered the professoriate, deserves much credit in putting up with my habit of writing late at night, and most important, in bringing much joy and happiness to our life together. I am also much obliged to members of my blues-jazz band, The Irreconcilable Differences, who allow me to assume the roles of lead vocalist and guitarist. Their musical comradeship introduces a welcomed noisy diversion in my quiet life of scholarship.

INTRODUCTION

This is a history of ideas. The exercise of the logic of such a history involves both the disciplines of philosophy and intellectual history. The former demands a thick description of any claims and ideas regarding ultimate truths and first principles; the latter begs the situation of those claims and ideas in the context of a particular time and space. If the concentration on the lofty wisdom of philosophy sometimes leads to self-absorption in ideas, neglecting the direction of surrounding events or failing to judge their meaning afterward, the intervention of history rescues ideas from the condescension of essentialism and generality. Accordingly, this study of Li Guangdi (1642–1718), a devout follower of the Cheng-Zhu school of Confucianism in the early Qing and a powerful official in the court of the Kangxi emperor (r. 1662–1722), examines and explores his thought with reference to the larger intellectual developments in the Ming–Qing transition. It identifies the genealogy of Li's philosophic affiliation and sorts out the issues that led him to the views he propounded and defended. Li's adventures of the mind, what he thought, felt, and said, unfolded in the context of the intellectual currents that animated sixteenth- and seventeenth-century China.

The general contour of this context has often been traced in the historiography of the Ming–Qing transition as follows. The late Ming and early Qing intellectual contestations apparently led to the diminution of the Song–Ming *daoxue* (learning of the Way) of moral speculative philosophy (*yili zhi xue*). This tradition came to be generally and generically labeled as *Songxue* (Song learning) in the Qing, and it faced the challenge of concrete and practical learning. There was the rise of the so-called *jingshi* (practical statecraft) scholarship focusing on the study of institutions, history, and governance, coupled with the emergence of *Hanxue* (Han learning), concentrating on the exegetical and philological probing of classical texts.[1] The genesis of such an interpretation of the developments of Qing learning and thought actually owes much to the appropriation of the utterances of the eminent early Qing savants, who deplored abstruse metaphysical speculation and vacuous moral introspection that appeared to be pervasive among the Ming literati. For instance, Gu Yanwu (1613–1682) lamented, "It is a matter of great regret to me, that for the past hundred odd years, scholars have devoted so much discussion to the mind and human nature, all of it vague and quite incomprehensible."[2] Likewise, Wang Fuzhi complained, "In recent times . . . theory of intuitive knowledge has been just like this. It is identical with Buddhism in that it would . . . refuse to believe in knowing and seeing. . . . When reckless doctrines prevail, all shame and modesty disappear."[3]

By the mid-Qing period in the eighteenth century, when evidential scholarship (*kaozheng xue*) based on a critical and empirical methodology became dominant, Song–Ming learning increasingly came to be categorized as a monolithic *type* of moral discourse, impractical, speculative, and feckless. Qian Daxin, for example, opined, "Since the Song and Yuan when success in the civil service examination was determined by [one's understanding of] the meaning of the classics, the teachings of one master had been adhered to. Even impertinent ideas were carelessly included and discussed as parts of the same teachings. All those who were empty, loose and wanting in scholarship could label themselves as masters of the classics. . . . This problem indeed reached its extreme in the Ming."[4] Similarly, Cui Shu (1740–1816) contended that most of the Song Confucians "concerned themselves with questions of the nature and principle of things and with moral philosophy. . . . By Ming times scholarship had grown increasingly heterodox and it became so that if one hoped to write anything important he had to be conversant with Ch'an [Zen] doctrines."[5] Thus, Song learning, that is, learning of both the Song and Ming, came to be typecast as recondite and impractical, at odds with the prevailing intellectual temper of the Qing world, aloof from the mainstream.

Consequently, in later historiography, the content, spirit, and purport of Qing intellectual history seemed to have been exemplified by the production of three major nineteenth-century compilations: the *Huangchao jingshi wenbian* (Anthology of Essays on Statecraft in the Qing) of 1827, the *HuangQing jingjie* (Classical Exegeses in the Qing) of 1829, and its sequel, the *HuangQing jingjie xubian* (Further Classical Exegeses in the Qing) of 1886–1888. The authorial visions of these monumental anthologies ipso facto became meshed with later readers' perspectives, yielding a historiography that sees statecraft and classical exegesis as the defining twin forces of the Qing epoch from the seventeenth to nineteenth centuries. It is small wonder that in the early part of the twentieth century, commentators such as Liang Qichao (1873–1929) and Hu Shi (1891–1962) regarded

Qing learning as exclusively practical in intent and pegged to textual glossing of classical texts. They readily saw Qing learning as a drastic rupture from the Song–Ming antecedent, which was apt to dwell on the ultimate, the interior, and, worse still, the abstract.[6]

As is well known, this thesis of cataclysmic disjunction is no longer tenable in light of the scholarship produced in subsequent decades. The late Qian Mu (1895–1990), for instance, writing in the 1930s, had already suggested that while the seventeenth century ushered in a new phase in Chinese intellectual history, Song learning remained the dominant tradition in which scholars were versed, and continued to serve as the yardstick by which scholarly accomplishments were measured.[7] Yü Ying-shih, more specifically, defines the principal animus of Qing learning in terms of the fruition of "intellectualism," the time-honored way of *dao wenxue* (following the path of inquiry and study) that inhered in the Confucian tradition. The Qing product was the consequence of the unraveling of the "inner logic" of Confucianism since the Song times toward the "intellectualist" pursuit of the classics, as opposed to the other (by no means antithetical) Confucian way of *zun dexing* (honoring the heaven-endowed virtuous nature), moral introspective self-cultivation. Yü in fact faults the Qing scholars themselves and the modern-day epigones for constructing a narrow, and therefore incomplete and distorted, concept of Song learning. Yü explains that Song learning should not be identified exclusively with "metaphysical speculation on the Confucian *Tao*." Rather, it should be defined broadly. Yü refers to the Song scholar Liu Yi (1017–1086), who proclaimed that Song learning encompassed "substance" (*ti*), "function" (*yong*), and "literary expression" (*wen*).[8] Indeed, the variegated and multifaceted nature of "the learning of the Way" (*daoxue*), ranging from speculative philosophy, through cultural values, to the advocacy and formulation of sociopolitical policies, has been admirably explicated by Hoyt Cleveland Tillman.[9] In any event, Yü Ying-shih's point is that Song learning, conceived as a multifarious tradition, was alive and well in the Qing period, although by then, it had fully developed the inherent "intellectualist" orientations.

Benjamin Elman, instead of seeing the fruition of this "intellectualism" in terms of its continuity with Song learning, propounds a thesis that apparently stresses disjunction. To him, a "revolution of discourse" occurred in the seventeenth and eighteenth centuries, propelled and fueled by a "shared epistemological perspective" among the early and mid-Qing literati. This epistemological revolution was the consolidation and maturation of the *kaozheng* (literally, the search for and investigation of evidence) movement, marked by evidential, empirical, and critical approaches to learning, especially the textual and philological plumbing of the classics. Eventually, as Elman contends, this "rigorous and critical approach to the Classics awakened a critical consciousness that jeopardized the classical claim to unquestioned authority."[10] Despite his rather sanguine depiction of the subversive consequence of the Qing *kaozheng* movement, Elman nevertheless reminds us, time and again, that, as with the Song–Ming Confucians, the Qing *kaozheng* scholars sought to locate "a bedrock of timeless order." The goal was to retrieve the moral Way (*dao*) of the ancient sages that inhered in the classics. While it is true that the classics came to be rigorously studied and at times even historicized as historical documents or condemned as apocryphal texts, the ideal of the authentic classics as the repository of universal truths remained intact. Elman provides us with ample examples of this Qing conviction in the perennial value of the classical Way.

For instance, Wang Mingsheng (1722–1798) maintained that "The Classics are employed to understand the Tao." Dai Zhen claimed that "the Classics provide the route to the Tao."[11] The Way that Wang and Dai celebrated and sought was not the Buddhist or Taoist Way; it was the same Confucian Way that the Song–Ming Confucians honored. Thus, as He Youshen has pointed out, because of their same fundamentalist goal of seeking the true teachings of the sages, the Song learning of moral principles and the *kaozheng* scholia of textual dissections were intimately related. Their difference was a matter of contigent strategy, the means, not ultimate aim, the end.[12] Moreover, as Elman notes, the epistemological revolution was after all an incompleted and truncated one, since in the early nineteenth century there was what he calls the "Han- and Sung-Learning syncretism." Once again, there was much talk of, and much store placed in, meanings and principles (*yili*); *kaozheng* immersion in the texts and other artifacts came to be viewed by many as finicky and pedantic.[13] This syncretism could not have been possible had Song learning not been an integral and vital, albeit eclipsed, part of the Qing intellectual universe.

Others have, in their own ways, underscored the persistence and relevance of the so-called Song learning in the Qing intellectual world. Tu Wei-ming, for one, contends that if Qing learning, as "a distinctive mode of scholarship," was in general a "critique" of Song learning, it was nonetheless intimately filiated with the Song tradition, "especially the legacy of Chu Hsi."[14] Thomas Metzger has also remarked that "in the Ming–Ch'ing period, the Cheng-Chu school was both a living intellectual movement and the official ideology of the state."[15] He Yousen urges us to temper our view of those early Qing savants—Gu Yanwu (1613–1682), Huang Zongxi (1610–1695), Wang Fuzhi (1619–1692), and Yan Yuan (1635–1704)—as personifications of the trends of practical and concrete learning by an appreciation for their continued allegiance to Song learning. From them, He admits, we certainly hear strictures on the abstractness of moral-metaphysical speculation, but such criticism was specifically directed at the failure on the part of many late Ming literati to embrace the goals of learning for practical ends, be they sociopolitical betterment or ethico-cultural elevation. But the early Qing scholars did not disavow what they considered to be worthy elements in Song–Ming learning. As He points out, Gu Yanwu saw himself as a Cheng-Zhu follower while Huang Zongxi considered himself a transmitter of Lu-Wang teachings, although both expressed their aversion toward empty philosophizing about the ultimate substance. They did not assail Song–Ming learning per se, but rather attacked their contemporaries' fatal flaw of ignoring the proper Confucian ends, namely, bringing reflective intelligence to bear on state and society.[16]

Most recently, Kai-wing Chow has proffered an overview of the development of Song learning, specifically the Cheng-Zhu school, from the mid-seventeenth to early nineteenth century, by focusing on its four fundamental concerns or elements: the definition of the core of the classics, the treatment of Buddhism, the apprehension of the moral principles of the classics, and the study of rituals. Chow argues that Cheng-Zhu learning, by engaging these principal concerns, constituted a dynamic and unfolding intellectual force. As with those Qing scholars arguing for practical statecraft and critical evidential scholarship, the Song learning partisans sought to reinvent and purify the Confucian tradition.[17]

It seems clear that any nuanced portrayal of Qing learning should perforce recognize its continuity with the Song–Ming tradition. Yet Song learning, broadly defined, has seldom been a focused subject of inquiry in the intellectual history of the Qing. The historiography of the Ming–Qing transition has often simply presented Song learning narrowly as metaphysical speculation on the moral *dao*, equating it with vacuous and jejune discourse on the ultimate. To the extent that the influential scholars of the age tended to emphasize the practical, the concrete, and the instrumental, Song learning associated with the introspective and speculative was judged to be out of joint with the epochal climate of thought. Moreover, as a result, this historiography is by and large unconcerned with philosophy and philosophical argument. In short, to construe Song learning narrowly as something bereft of practical import, at odds with the Qing zeitgeist, and to ignore the philosophical dimensions of the Ming–Qing intellectual transition, is to produce a picture that is wrong in both detail and principle. First, as regards detail, Song learning was in fact a vital force, by no means aloof from the intellectual orientations of the time. Second, as regards principle, it is difficult to understand intellectual shifts if we do not seek to comprehend the fundamental philosophical concerns and perspectives that were the underpinnings of the altered worldviews. These two issues warrant some investigation as an effort to properly locate and define the roles of Song learning in the Qing intellectual universe.

With regard to the issue of including accurate details in a picture of Qing thought, one obvious fact should be pointed out: the Cheng-Zhu school of Song learning was the court-sanctioned orthodoxy. As early as 1645, the interpretations of Cheng Yi (1033–1107), and especially those of Zhu Xi (1130–1200), were declared the canon of the examination curricula.[18] By the reign of the Kangxi emperor, Cheng-Zhu learning received ardent patronage from the throne. The offspring of Cheng Yi and his brother, Cheng Hao (1032–1085), and Zhou Dunyi were awarded chairs of the Five Classics. Zhu Xi's tablet was inducted into the temple of Confucius, ensconced among those of the ten Confucian disciples.[19] Moreover, the Cheng-Zhu school of Song learning was by no means an ossified academic canon embraced merely because of its orthodox status. Far from being isolated from the epochal emphasis on practicality, it was actually a dated reflection of, and active contributor to, the intellectual content and temper of the early Qing. Some scholars have adumbrated its vital and timely nature. Yamanoi Yu, for example, has identified a transitional phase of development in the seventeenth century, between the Ming "learning of the mind-heart" (*xinxue*) of the fifteenth and sixteenth centuries and the Qing "evidential textual scholarship" (*kaozheng xue*) of the eighteenth century. The transition was marked by the emergence of the "learning of practical governance and utilitarian statecraft" (*keisei chiyô no gaku*), which had three strains: practice (*jissen*), technical skills (*gijutsu*), and classical and historical studies (*keishi*). Associated with the first strain, according to Yamanoi, were none other than the Cheng-Zhu partisans and those scholars who sought to achieve a synthesis between Cheng-Zhu and Lu-Wang. They spurned pedantic study, rote memorization, and feckless speculation on nature and mind-heart. Instead, they stressed the realization and practice of morals in everyday living. Some wrote directly on various aspects of sociopolitical-economic management, such as government, agriculture, and military affairs. They brought to the fore those ideas in the Confucian "learning of the mind-heart" that stressed active self-cultivation and direct engagement with society. In a nutshell, Yamanoi sees a special focus on practicality and action in the writings of the Cheng-Zhu followers.[20]

The late Wing-tsit Chan also argued that the tenor of the early Qing Cheng-Zhu learning was consonant with the call for the practical and concrete. It "put matters of practical concern ahead of matters of abstract interest . . . ; there was also the deliberate effort to avoid empty speculation."[21] An elegant illustration was the compilation of the *Xingli jingyi* (Essential Ideas of [the Cheng-Zhu School of] Nature and Principle) by our protagonist, Li Guangdi, under imperial aegis. As Chan showed, even a cursory look at the contents of this work reveals the deliberate axiological effort of mitigating the importance of abstruse metaphysical speculation in favor of enhancing the value of active engagement with the experiential world. Chan concluded that to ignore Cheng-Zhu learning in the early Qing is to distort the nature of seventeenth-century Chinese thought.[22]

One of the more recent observations on the early Qing Cheng-Zhu learning can be found in Wm. Theodore de Bary's 1989 monograph on the development of the philosophic lineage of the Neo-Confucian official orthodoxy, which he calls the "Learning of the Mind-and-Heart." His central thesis is that there was unmistakable continuity from the Song to the Qing in the historical unfolding of this "Learning of the Mind-and-Heart." The same enduring core ideas and premises—the central notions of *xin* (the mind-and-heart), *xinfa* (the message/method/measure of the mind-and-heart), and the *daotong* (tradition)—remained throughout the temporal passage from the sixteenth century down to the nineteenth century. Although it is not de Bary's goal to dissect specifically the lineaments of the early Qing manifestation, he nevertheless pinpoints its particular qualities. He suggests that the Learning of the Mind-and-Heart in this period demonstrated certain concerns that corresponded to "a more general trend in the early Ch'ing toward practical learning and evidential inquiry," contributing "significantly to the larger Ch'ing trend toward critical scholarship and to a fundamentalism that emphasizes basic moral and intellectual values instead of philosophical speculation or religious aspirations."[23]

Thus, it seems clear that any picture of early Qing thought must include Song learning, particularly the orthodox Cheng-Zhu school, as a crucial and integral detail. To lend this detail additional depth and clarity, we may in fact further show that such orientations and emphases had their roots and origins in the Confucian tradition. After all, the growing Qing preoccupation with direct philological engagement with classical texts and other forms of evidential studies was the manifestation and development of what Yü Ying-shih calls "Confucian intellectualism," as pointed out earlier. A host of other scholars, such as John Henderson, Steven Van Zoeren, and Daniel Gardner, have also pointed to the paramount importance of exegesis in the Confucian project of learning.[24] On the question of the practical and utilitarian import of Confucian learning, one needs only to glance at those works by authors such as Hoyt Cleveland Tillman, Hao Chang,

Wm. Theodore de Bary, and Chung-ying Cheng. They all point to the persistence of the ethos of practicality in the Confucian *daoxue* tradition; the quest for moral transformation of humanity and society was complemented by the concern with curing sociopolitical-institutional maladies.[25] Tillman, for instance, duly reminds us that utilitarian cogitation on policies and measures aimed at the betterment of state and society was one of the three key elements of the Confucian discourse, apart from speculative philosophy and cultural values.[26] In brief, early Qing Cheng-Zhu Song learning had a definite pedigree; its quotidian utilitarianism and textual classicism were very much the indigenous products of its history and culture. Cheng-Zhu learning drew from the motifs of the original structure, and in the process struck notes harmonious with the intellectual tone and tenor of the early Qing age.

However, the mere addition of this central detail of Cheng-Zhu Song learning does not quite succeed in portraying the entire picture of early Qing thought. For in principle, intellectual shifts are undergirded by shifts in some fundamental philosophical perspectives, if not positions.[27] To align early Qing thought almost exclusively with practical and classical learning comes close to reading philosophical pondering out of the intellectual life of the time. Thus to get the picture right in principle, it should be posited that in the early Qing, Song learning's stress on practical and concrete learning not only did not exclude metaphysical speculation but actually stemmed from it. By probing the fundamental first principles of reality, Song learning built an ontological edifice that justified and legitimated the pursuit of practicality in the experiential world. It was a way of thought that encapsulated the view that knowledge of ultimate reality led to practical action. In other words, practicality, and the disposition toward concrete learning, through philosophical rendering acquired cogency as ontological truths, and in the workaday world, they became experiential goals. By practical is here meant the endeavor to establish experience as the locus and means for apprehending reality and testing truths in everyday living, with keen awareness of the importance of function and utility.[28] Therefore, this study of early Qing Cheng-Zhu Confucianism as represented by Li Guangdi, by paying due attention to its philosophical arguments and import, seeks to provide a philosophical angle from which to view the Ming–Qing intellectual transition.

To be sure, the Cheng-Zhu philosophical speculation was not pursued in a temporal vacuum or spatial isolation. It was not, to use the words of Karl Jasper, "suprahistorical . . . in the realm of a single, unbroken presence, . . . in a timeless area of human kinship."[29] Rather, the very meaning of the early Qing Cheng-Zhu philosophy hinged on the early Qing issues it was designed to address—the negative repulsion of vacuous introspection and the positive pursuit of practical knowledge. These very issues were in turn seen to be intimately related to the predominance and popularity of Lu-Wang learning in the late Ming, especially Wang Yangming's destabilization of the meaning of nature (*xing*) by defining it as beyond good and evil. Thus, in the late Ming, there had already emerged a philosophical bone of contention. The Cheng-Zhu partisans' goal was to restructure and reformulate Song learning by reasserting human nature as the ontological basis of ultimate reality. Thus, if Cheng-Zhu learning was a dated reflection of, and active contributor to, the ethos of practicality in the early Qing, it was so because of its direct engagement with one of the central philosophical issues of the time. Therefore, any comprehensive view of the Ming–Qing intellectual transition and the resulting constitutive elements of Qing learning should include the philosophical dimensions. Specifically, in examining the complex intellectual changes in seventeenth-century China, one cannot lose sight of the literati's reexamination of the question of *xing* that began in the late sixteenth century.

In the late Ming, scholars of the Cheng-Zhu persuasion preoccupied themselves with the plumbing of the meaning of *xing* (nature). It was an agonistic response to the perceived ethico-moral degeneration perpetrated by the latter-day followers of Wang Yangming. This corruption was ultimately traced back and attributed to the flawed teachings of the master himself, specifically his idea of the mind-heart (*xin*), the fundamental substance (*benti*), as beyond good and evil. Many thought that the key to combating the futility of abstract introspection, and to affirming the sense of right and wrong, lay in the redefinition of the constitution of human nature and humanity. *Xing* must be shown to be inexorably good, specifying the substance of morality. In turn, this good substance must be realized in actions. Hence the pivotal role of effort (*gongfu*) and its intimate relation with fundamental substance; the latter could not be some transcendental entity capable of sudden self-enlightenment or self-realization in the absence of concrete efforts. Hence also a keener appreciation of *xing* as holistic, integrally and inseparably consisting of both moral (*yili*) and material (*qizhi*) natures; the cognitive, affective, and conative must be identified with the innate moral essence in *xing*.

Such late Ming and early Qing philosophical pondering, albeit metaphysical in its inception and substance, offers no metaphysical comfort and consolation, in the sense that humanity is accorded a universal authority by being underwritten and guaranteed by the natural order of *xing*. Rather, it points ineluctably to effort. The metaphysical certitude of *xing* is inexorably mediated and expressed by practice and action. Thus, the Ming–Qing intellectual transition characterized by the stress on solid and concrete learning was simultaneously informed by a fundamental philosophical question—what is nature?—and animated by a pragmatic philosophical position—drawing out the practical implications for quotidian living and learning of the very idea of the goodness of human nature. Therefore, this very philosophical dimension of the Ming–Qing intellectual shift is the point of departure for this study of seventeenth-century Cheng-Zhu thought.

Our focus on the Cheng-Zhu school notwithstanding, it is only fair to note that the Lu-Wang camp was by no means an idle bystander as Qing thought and learning began to take shape. As we shall see, not surprisingly, Li Guangdi and the Cheng-Zhu partisans lambasted the Lu-Wang followers and their teachings, blaming them for empty speculation, doctrinal confusion, and philosophical blundering, all of which contributed to ethico-moral degeneration. But such criticism, as sectarian parti pris, is to be expected. It is important to state that reporting faithfully and accurately Li's and others' invectives against the Lu-Wang scholar, as this study aims to do, is not tantamount to suggesting that the former were correct in their attribution of blame and error to the latter. The fact of the matter was that the early Qing Lu-Wang sectarians, together with their Cheng-Zhu counterparts, shared the epochal ethos of practicality and utility. The prime example was of course Huang Zongxi (1610–1695), whose advocacy of practical learning is common knowledge and needs no special introduction here. It is well known, for instance, that his *Waiting for the Dawn: A Plan for the Prince* (Mingyi daifang lu) is a bold interrogation of the principles of good government.[30] His other major work, *Mingru xue'an* (Records of Ming Scholars), is a systematic intellectual history of the Ming dynasty, in which he famously proclaimed: "The mind-heart has no fundamental substance (*benti*). What it accomplishes through its effort and activity (*gongfu*) is fundamental substance."[31]

Huang was not alone.[32] His teacher Liu Zongzhou (1578–1645) had already begun to reformulate some of Wang Yangming's philosophical tenets in order to bring into sharp relief the practical and activist demands that inhered in Wang's teachings. As I reveal in chapter one, Liu probed the nature of fundamental substance (*benti*) with reference to its immanence and inherence in quotidian function and normal activity. The innate knowledge of the good (*liangzhi*) was never separate from the knowledge gained through seeing and hearing (*jianwen*). To Liu, there could not be knowledge in the absence of things.[33] Another early Qing Lu-Wang sympathizer, Li Yong (1627–1705), pronounced, "If we regard the illumination of the Way and the preservation of the mind-heart as substance, and the ordering of the world and the harnessing of things as function, then this substance is the authentic substance, and this function is the concrete function."[34] The Lu-Wang school in fact continued to evolve in response to the changing intellectual climate, so much so that in the eighteenth century, Li Fu (1675–1750) engineered what Chin-shing Huang describes as a "philological turn" of Lu-Wang Confucianism as *kaozheng* scholarship began to blossom.[35]

One last prefatory question remains to be answered: Why Li Guangdi? Why is he chosen as the representative Cheng-Zhu figure of the early Qing? To the extent that Cheng-Zhu learning was both an intellectual persuasion and a state orthodoxy, the life and thought of Guangdi afford us the opportunities to explore its various manifestations. At the same time that he was a high-ranking and trusted official in the Kangxi court, a mandarin upholding the orthodoxy, he was a thinker committed to the ethico-moral philosophical project taught by Zhu Xi. As a spokesperson for the court-promoted orthodoxy, he was, as mentioned above, entrusted with the court-sponsored task of compiling the *Xingli jingyi* (Essential Ideas on Nature and Principle), the definitive synoptic text that supposedly summarized the main teachings of the Cheng-Zhu school. He was also given the responsibility of editing the complete works of Zhu Xi. In addition, he served as the emperor's tutor on the Confucian classics. He was, in short, "the most important figure in the formulation of the official orthodoxy of the Ch'ing," as Wm. Theodore de Bary describes him.[36] As an avowed student of Cheng-Zhu learning, he wrote profusely and pondered deeply within the philosophical matrices of his acknowledged Song intellectual forebear. However, Guangdi was no slavish rehasher of established and received ideas. Being a bona fide, disinterested thinker in search of knowledge and truth, he viewed the original Cheng-Zheng philosophy not as immutable truths but as a set of tools that he employed to make sense of his own experiences. While he embarked on the purposeful activity of thinking with the view to addressing the problems of his time, he arrived at his own philosophical position with its own *idée maîtresse* : the intrinsically good human nature.

By looking at the life and thought of this seventeenth-century follower of Zhu Xi, we may gain some insights into how a philosophical discourse was formed in the early Qing. Allegiance to a sectarian tradition did not mean servile restatement of inherited beliefs. Rather, Cheng-Zhu learning, as it was embraced by Guangdi, was a timely system of thought aimed at reevaluating the individual, state, and society, offering reformulated views of that which had validated the life of his community. As such, it does not deserve the relative historical obscurity in which it has been mired. Guangdi was not simply an editor of Confucian texts or a court official with a Confucian outlook; he was also a genuine thinker who critically sought to develop and expand the original Cheng-Zhu philosophical structures. Moreover, what he had to say illuminated some of the central intellectual concerns and problems of his time.[37]

While it may be ascertained that Guangdi's thought developed out of, or was a response and related to, the particular historical setting of discourses and debates, we must also resist the temptation to reduce the meaning of his ideas to a specific context, especially his life. The birth certificate of ideas and the conscious intents of authors may not always be found in personal lives.[38] To put it another way, while it may be surmised that Guangdi's personal life influenced his writing and thought, I have found little evidence that would enable me to directly and confidently interpret his works in those terms. One is on surer ground if one's contextualist search, as it were, is confined to the intellectual milieu, as I have attempted to show. Indeed, with regard to the stimuli to philosophical contemplation on the part of a thinker, the major sources of inspiration are previous or contemporary works, and not necessarily one's own provincial experiences. Therefore, the value, validity, relevance, and genealogy of Li Guangdi's thought are best interpreted in light of the early Qing intellectual temper and the received store of Cheng-Zhu ideas. It should also be pointed out that as a historian of ideas, I am simply seeking to explicate and make intelligible Guangdi's ideas, and accordingly, I will by and large refrain from any internal criticism of his thought in terms of our philosophical standards. To demand from him the clarity and rigor that he had no intention of meeting, and of which he had no knowledge, is to be anachronistic and ahistorical. Li Guangdi is worth studying for what he *had* to say. For what he said was temporally and spatially indexical, the distinct voice of a time and place: seventeenth-century China.

ONE

A Philosophical Dimension of the Ming–Qing Intellectual Transition

Conceptions of Human Nature (Xing)

> Man is declared to be that creature who is constantly in search of himself—a creature who in every moment of his existence must examine and scrutinize the conditions of his existence. In this scrutiny, in this critical attitude toward human life, consists the real value of human life.
>
> —Ernst Cassirer, *An Essay on Man*

Conceptions of human nature (*xing*) in the Confucian tradition, particularly Neo-Confucianism (or *daoxue*, learning of the Way), were not meant to be merely piecemeal philosophical analyses of a problem of humanity. They were propounded as doctrines that responded directly to questions of ultimate reality. For human nature was often construed as the whole of reality. As one eminent contemporary interpreter of Confucianism, Mou Zongsan, explains, "*Xing* is that which flows down from the reality mandated by Heaven and is fully embodied in the self." The locus of transcendence is therefore found in self-awareness and the moral-ethical deeds that stem from such awareness: "Since nothing is outside of the 'reality of the self's nature' (*xingti*), the cosmic order is the moral-ethical order; the moral-ethical order is the cosmic order." Mou contends that this holistic conception of the profound self as the site of transcendence is absent in the West. Hence his coining the term *xingti*, the reality of the self's nature, to denote the Confucian sense of the absolute located in the individual self. *Xing* cannot be adequately translated as "nature," "essence," "substance," "being," or "reality," because these words all fail to connote the meaning of the self as the "moral creative reality."[1]

If we may generalize, there is, in the Confucian scheme of things, the certainty that the universe embodied and manifested in the authentic nature of the self is enlivened with moral inclinations, even though the world which humanity confronts every day is fraught with uncertainties and demands ceaseless acts of doing good.[2] Thus, within the Confucian definition of the vital reality, there is, to borrow Ortega y Gasset's argument, a "certainty of faith" (*creencia*) in our nature's innate goodness or moral creativity. *Creencias* are ideas and conceptions of reality that have become identified with reality; they are, as Ortega told us, "not ideas which we *have*, but ideas which we *are*."[3] Insofar as the conception of *xing* as the encapsulation of heaven's nature does not have the tentative quality as a mere explanation of reality, any formulation of human nature is an engagement with ultimate reality as it is. Such conception is no longer simply a contingent statement of truth, but a collective faith, a part of reality with which Confucians must reckon. As a result, Confucian cogitation on human nature is ineluctably a self-referential activity—discourses on *xing* are ideally instances of *xing*'s own meaning. Not unlike the Socratic dictum that philosophy often explains what is already known, in Confucian terms, to learn is to bring to light what the authentic self already knows.[4] Every thought and every act that follow are at once involved in presumptions of the fundamental reality of our nature. Learning is practice; knowing is acting.[5] To the extent that epistemology is ontology, pursuing false learning, such as misconstruing the nature of human nature, means not only misrepresenting the truth of reality; it is also a violation and corruption of reality itself. For in the process of learning to know *xing*, we are also turning inward to and cultivating our nature, and in so doing, we are at once humanizing and cosmicizing our very own being.

Consequently, when the latter-day followers of Wang Yangming in the late Ming expounded the idea of nature's being beyond good and evil, they were seen by many Confucian literati not only as exponents of ideas but as destroyers of *creencias*, of parts of reality. Such destruction was readily evidenced by the increasingly palpable process of dynastic weakening, a consequence of the misapprehension of human nature, which in turn led to spiritual degeneration and moral anarchy among the scholars. As scholars sought to extirpate the flawed understanding of human nature that bred the spiritual-psychological plague of ethicomoral chaos and the sociopolitical scourge of dynastic decline, they also positively reformulated a view of human nature in order to renew the unalienable *creencias* underlying the Confucian order. To combat moral uncertainty, they began with the reassertion of the certainty of faith in human nature as the innately good moral creative reality. To forestall pure philosophizing about *xing*, they further reaffirmed it as the inexorably good ontological foundation of state and society. Knowing nature involved the simultaneous working out of its practical potentialities. No person, even with the heaven-endowed virtues and power, was an eternal person, as it were. One had to constantly act in concert with the changing circumstances as one sought to know and contemplate truth and reality.

This chapter has three tasks. First, it examines the late Ming polemics on the nature of *xing*, demonstrating how the notion of *xing* as being beyond good and evil was conceived as a fundamental assault on the Confucian *creencia* of *xing* as good. The fundamental issues that defined the polemics were well reflected in two revealing debates in the late Ming, one between Zhou Rudeng (1547–1629) and Xu Fuyuan (1535–1604), and the other between Gu Xiancheng (1550–1612) and Guan Zhidao (1536–1608), which incited a good deal of intellectual exchanges among a host of scholars. Second, this chapter shows that in vigorously restoring goodness as the quintessence of *xing*, the late Ming and early Qing scholars established a philosophical agenda that ascertained the ontological centrality and primacy of *xing*. An investigation of the main items on this agenda helps us establish some principal motifs that enlivened and dominated intellectual discourse at the time. Third, by way of conclusion, it may be suggested that the Ming–Qing intellectual transition might well have turned on a meta-practical fulcrum. The advocacy for practicality and concreteness, which is customarily ackowledged to be a major characteristic of the intellectual shift, might have a root in the philosophical agenda that was premised on the meta-ethical creativity of *xing*.

Xu Fuyuan's "Nine Scrutinies" versus Zhou Rudeng's "Nine Explanations"

Huang Zongxi (1610–1695), in his *Records of the Ming Scholars* (Mingru xue'an), described a debate between Zhou Rudeng and Xu Fuyuan that took place in the midst of a series of conferences attended by many prominent scholars in 1592 in Nanjing. The exchange started with Zhou's exposition, in one meeting, on *Verifying the Way in Tianquan* (Tianquan zhengdao) by Wang Ji (1498–1583), Wang Yangming's pupil. Zhou's purpose was to underscore the text's primary thesis that fundamental reality was beyond good and evil. The following day, Xu presented an essay entitled "Nine Scrutinies" (Jiudi), listing nine ways in which the tenability of Wang Ji's idea could be challenged, arguing that ultimate nature was indisputably and inexorably good; whereupon Zhou issued a point-by-point rebuttal in his "Nine Explanations" (Jiujie). Lively discussions apparently ensued among the scholars as a result of the Zhou–Xu exchange.[6] One may reasonably surmise that the two essays and the controversy they generated reflected some of the central philosophical concerns of the time, which centered around the basic question of the nature of *xing*.

Xu's nine "scrutinies" (*di*) of the nature of *xing* may be summarized as follows:[7]

1. The classics all hammer home the message that *xing* is good. The notion that nature is neither good nor bad stems from Gaozi's original flawed understanding, which was effectively refuted by Mencius. Therefore, to embrace this false doctrine is to violate what has been clearly transmitted in the classics.

2. The existence of goodness in the universe is a law of nature: "Within the universe, that which is upright is good, and that which is partial is evil. As with ice's being clear and charcoal's being black, they cannot be altered with one's opinion." Just as heaven and earth have their virtuous aura, and sun and moon their pure brightness, so too humanity has its genuine mind-heart, and affairs their correct principles. If there is neither good nor evil, then people will not know how to act.

3. Goodness is ontological substance, expressed variously by the sages as "centrality" (*zhong*), "ultimacy" (*ji*), "humaneness" (*ren*), "rightness" (*yi*), "propriety" (*li*), "wisdom" (*zhi*), and "trustworthiness" (*xin*). Goodness is the name for that which is "upright, pure and flawless." Goodness inheres universally in humanity's mind-heart. If there is no goodness, then there is no "profound root of all-under-heaven."

4. The effort (*gongfu*) of self-cultivation, as defined by the *Great Learning*, is based on the conviction that "human nature is innately good." Its aim is "the return to the beginning of one's nature." If things, knowledge, the will, and the mind-heart, mentioned in the *Great Learning*, are all neither good nor bad, effort will have no secure point of departure. Moreover, the classics' teachings are not devised only for those with average and low intelligence, but for everyone. Unfortunately, there is the prevailing idea among scholars nowadays that if one is endowed with "sharp intelligence," then "one knows without having to learn." Here, Xu is referring to Wang Yangming's idea that people may be demarcated into two types when Wang elucidates his so-called four maxims (*siju jiao*) in

response to the queries of his two best disciples, Wang Ji and Qian Dehong (1497–1574). Wang claims that those with sharp intelligence can dispense with earnest effort and "gain understanding straight from the source," while those less well-endowed will have to follow specific paths and assume definite tasks in order to remove the obstacles in the recovery of original substance.[8] Xu contends that the notion of nature's being beyond good and evil eviscerates the *Great Learning*'s clear teaching on systematic and painstaking cultivation. It breeds contempt for solid learning in the name of a putative transcendent intelligence.

5. The consolidation of both the ethico-moral and sociopolitical orders depends on the good natural disposition of the people: "The ancients sages' upholding age-old teachings and tending to the education of the people are entirely dependent on the existence of the good natural disposition of the multitude." It is because of the indestructible disposition of people's goodness that rulers can "enlighten the dull, tame the violent, change habits and alter customs, and overthrow meanness so as to return to honesty." To say that there is neither good nor evil is to disregard the naturally good disposition of the people.

6. Moral cultivation is rigorous. Confucius told us that "in studies, he started from below and got through to what was up above, that he was fond of antiquity and was quick to seek its knowledge, that he forgot to eat and forgot to sleep [while learning], and that there was this pursuit which did not stop with the end of one's life." With such an earnest attitude, Confucius exhorted us "to restrain ourselves in order to return to propriety." But scholars nowadays, instead of hard and steady work, "wish to realize the principle of instantaneous enlightenment in non-goodness."

7. There is a crucial difference between criticizing one for doing good deliberately and espousing the categorical idea that there is no goodness. The *Classic of Documents* does state that "the indulgent consciousness of goodness destroys that very goodness," cautioning one not to boast of goodness. It is also true that "if good is done with deliberation, it is good that is crude." Nonetheless, authentic goodness that requires no intentional enlargement is immanent everywhere all-under-heaven. One cannot jump to the conclusion that because contrivance to do good is undesirable, there is no goodness as such at all.

8. Wang Yangming's various ideas, especially the famous "four maxims," can be reconciled with the notion of *xing* as innately good. Wang's thought, particularly the idea of "extending innate knowledge of the good to the utmost," is not at odds with traditional Confucian teaching. Wang himself explicitly states that "there is no nature that is not good, and so there is no knowing that is not good." His first maxim that

"there is no distinction of good and evil in the original substance of the mind-heart" simply refers to the state of profundity and silence of the mind-heart before its issuance. As for the other three maxims—"when the will becomes active, there is the distinction between good and evil"; "knowing good and evil is innate knowledge of the good"; "to investigate things is to do good and remove evil"—they are the initiation of cultivational efforts. Wang's pupils have distorted the master's original teachings when they thoughtlessly assert that "the mind-heart, the will, knowledge and things [that emanate from the mind-heart] are all beyond the descriptions of good and evil."

9. Wang Ji is the prime example of one who distorts Wang Yangming's ideas: "[Wang Ji] took the doctrines of 'four nonbeings' and 'four beings' as two methods of teaching. His contemporary, Qian Dehong, was not convinced." Wang was wrong in creating the doctrine of the "four nonbeings" in response to his teacher's "four maxims." This doctrine not only sees the original substance of the mind-and-heart as beyond good and evil, but also regards the will, knowledge, and things as transmoral, thereby nullifying the good-evil distinction. Countering Wang's doctrine of "four nonbeings" is Qian Dehong's antipodal theory of "four beings" (*siyou*), also issued in response to the master's "four maxims." Qian argues that although the original mind-heart is neither good nor evil, there is also a mind-heart trammeled by bad habits and customs, and so in our ordinary everyday thoughts, a clear sense of good-versus-evil does exist. It is therefore crucial that one constantly investigate things, extend knowledge, make the will sincere, and rectify the mind-heart. According to Wang Ji, after he and Qian had put forth their respective interpretations of the "four maxims," the master revealed that he had two ways of teaching, one for those endowed with sharp intelligence (*ligen*), the other for those with "dull intelligence" (*dungen*); the former would be taught in accordance with the dictum of the "four nonbeings," the latter the doctrine of the "four beings."[9] In actuality, this dual approach based on the division of humanity was Wang Ji's own fabrication. His doctrine of the "four nonbeings" not only consigns Yangming's solid endeavor to the realm of incorporeality, but also violates what the classics teach.

The gist of Zhou Rudeng's point-by-point rebuttal, in the form of "nine explanations," may be presented as follows:

1. "Beyond good and evil" (*wushan wu'e*) really "means that doing good and removing evil have no traces. Doing good and removing evil can only be genuine when there is the realization that there is neither

good nor evil." The "ultimate authenticity" (*zhicheng*) and "highest good" (*zhishan*) expounded by the sages refer to the "original substance" that defies dichotomization. Although in the classics, the word "good" (*shan*) often appears in the context of the good-evil polarity, "the good which is ultimately manifested in the mind-heart's nature is the good which is not pitted against evil." Hence the *Great Learning*'s usage of the term "highest good" (*zhishan*). The word "highest" (*zhih*) is added to distinguish the transcendent primal good from the ordinary good. When Mencius states that "human nature is good," he is already talking about the posterior good.

2. "Uprightness" and "partiality" are descriptions and views created by individuals. They have nothing to do with rules of the universe. The attributes of the various things that Xu pinpoints do not, in themselves, constitute goodness. Xu's discussion on the essence of human nature is crude, since it is reduced to reward and punishment, and rigid prescription of what and what not to do. Authentic human nature is above such ordinary conceptual and behavioral constraints.

3. In equating the mind-heart with the great vacuity, Xu correctly identifies the nature of ultimate reality, namely, that it does not rest in anything as such. But since Xu refuses to give up the label of goodness, he eventually has to abandon the idea that the mind-heart is vacuous. Once the supremely vacuous mind-and-heart is reified as "centrality," "ultimacy," "humaneness," and so forth, it is rendered into a thing and loses its essential connection with "that which is before the manifestation [of feelings]" (*weifa*).

4. Zhou defines the word "good" in the statement "Human nature is innately good." Such good is the "highest good." Evil arises as a result of the misapprehension of this highest good. To return to the beginning of one's nature means not losing the mind of an infant. "Since an infant's mind has no evil, how could there be goodness?" Zhou asks. Earnest moral efforts refer simply to illuminating the highest good which is the infant's mind.

5. The naturally good disposition means the absence of the deliberate intent to do good and evil. People cannot be truly persuaded to do good, and customs and habits cannot be genuinely transformed by those who seek to convince others with their own goodness. These people do not know that the "root [of reality] is beyond good, [they] rashly formulate views on goodness, abandoning this and adopting that, holding onto this and letting go of that." In history, there was no dearth of good men embroiled in "factional strife" (*tanggu*) and involved in the implementation of the "new policies" (*xinzheng*). Despite their good intentions, havoc was wreaked. Therefore, we should listen to Wang Yangming, who correctly

defines our original substance as beyond good and evil. The ancient sage-kings and dynasties understood this, and were able to forge their glorious rule through "policies that are subtly quiet (lit. 'having neither sound nor color')" and "customs that are free from kingly coercion."

6. Wang Yangming never ceased to teach cultivation, for the attempt to understand the two words of "beyond evil" (*wu'e*) easily consumed a lifetime of demanding effort. Moreover, "since there is neither evil nor good, one's cultivation has no trace, which is genuine cultivation." Confucius's moral exhortation boils down to "self-reflection" (*zisi*); only in introspection of our own being can authentic cultivation proceed. In short, it is Wang Yangming who transmits the genuine teachings of Confucius.

7. Xu's own classical references speak for themselves and prove beyond doubt the validity of the idea of nongoodness.

8. Xu fails to comprehend the holistic oneness of the original substance of the mind-heart. Hence his distinguishing the preissuance state of the mind-heart from its postissuance state. Zhou here affirms Wang Ji's doctrine of the "four nonbeings" (*siwu*): the mind-heart in its original state is nonbeing, in that it transcends good and evil; consequently, the good-evil distinction also becomes irrelevant in the three entities of the will, knowledge, and things. To the extent that the mind-heart, the will, knowledge, and things are "nonbeings," reality can only be intuited and realized through the spontaneous awakening of the mind-heart. Wang Ji's idea of the four nonbeings captures the key to Wang Yangming's final teaching.[10] Xu perverts Wang's thought by reducing it to mundane and artificial effort.

9. The division of people into two grades began with Confucius and not Wang Yangming. The so-called two different methods with two different languages are really one. The doctrine of the "four nonbeings" encapsulates "what the thousand sages have transmitted." In Confucius's idea of "absence of will and absence of the self" (*wuyi wuwo*), as well as Cheng Yi's notion of "absence of sentiments and absence of the mind" (*wuqing wuxin*), one discerns the central message of nonbeing as the ultimate being. Moreover, specifying ways of cultivation is not the way of the sages: "Although the sages, in establishing their teachings, did concoct prescriptions for specific maladies, when the malady is cured, the prescriptions are gone. There is after all no specific method."[11] In other words, there is a core self, a basic and essential unity of innate capabilities that is above and beyond the world of appearance, and therefore, its realization cannot be achieved by any specified method.

This exchange shows that in the late Ming, some scholars, such as Xu Fuyuan, repudiated the prevalent idea of a nature that transcends the normative categories of good and evil. They sought to redefine the goodness of human nature as an absolute truth that could be meaningfully reconciled with history, culture, and society. The goodness of *xing* demanded social fulfillment by way of rigorous individual efforts, thereby serving as the foundation of the ethical and sociopolitical orders. *Xing* was a philosophical issue, the first principles of which had been distorted and perverted by Wang Yangming and his latter-day followers. Xu Fuyuan and others strove to restore a clear notion of human goodness as the foundation for purposeful moral-ethical individuation.

Gu Xiancheng versus Guan Zhidao

In 1598, after Gu Xiancheng, the famous Donglin scholar, had been dismissed from office, he initiated a series of scholarly meetings in the Erquan Academy in the Suzhou area. A friendly but earnest debate on the question of human nature again erupted among the scholars. The themes of this round of discussions may be glimpsed from the exchanges between Gu Xiancheng and Guan Zhidao,[12] a Lu-Wang partisan who was an active participant in these conferences. As one sympathetic to Cheng-Zhu learning, Gu began with the premise that human nature was inexorably good, while Guan adhered to Wang Yangming's dictum that the original substance of the mind-heart was beyond good and evil. Details of their divergent opinions are recorded in a two-part essay that Gu penned, "Questions on the Doubtful, Part One" (Zhiyi shang) of 1598 and "Questions on the Doubtful, Part Two" (Zhiyi xia) of 1599.[13] This essay was in turn collected in a larger work by Gu, devoted entirely to the problem of human nature, *A Treatise on Corroborating Human Nature* (Zhengxing bian), published in 1600.[14]

Guan Zhidao, associated with the Taizhou school in the Lu-Wang camp, was steeped in the late Ming intellectual trend of syncretizing the "Three Teachings."[15] For him, the imperative issuing from the pondering over *xing* is the understanding of the interconnectedness, and indeed oneness, of the "Three Teachings." His defense of Wang Yangming's idea of nature's being beyond good and evil begins with a confirmation of its respectable provenance. To begin with, it can be traced back to Zhou Dunyi's (1017–1073) discourse on the Great Ultimate (*taiji*): "It may be said that Master Wang pinpoints the original substance of the mind as beyond good and evil so as to renew Master Zhou's [idea of] the Great Ultimate."[16] In turn, Zhou's conception of ultimate reality as the "Great Ultimate" is the product of "the blending with the Two Teachings [i.e., Taoism and Buddhism], precisely tracing the origin of the Great Ultimate to the 'Ultimate Nothingness' (*wuji*)."[17] Guan explicates human nature in terms of the Great Ultimate, conceived as the ultimate nonbeing:

> Human nature is the Great Ultimate; goodness and evil are yin and yang. Yin must be juxtaposed with yang, and goodness must be juxtaposed with evil. To say that nature has goodness but not evil is the same as saying that the Great Ultimate has yang but not yin. To talk of the Great Ultimate is to talk of the primal state where yin and yang are not yet distinguished; to talk of the authentic nature is to talk of the very beginning when goodness and evil are not yet demarcated. To characterize nature as good is to force a name [on it]. Therefore Cheng Hao said, "When Mencius claimed that nature was innately good, he was referring to the development of the origin, which was good." This goodness is the *Great Learning*'s "highest good." The highest good is beyond good. As good cannot be named, so too evil cannot be named. [Nature] ought to be intuitively apprehended in the state before its manifestation (*weifa*).[18]

Guan postulates that "the goodness-evil distinction comes from the yin-yang dichotomy." But yin-yang and goodness-evil are not the ultimate; they are posterior to the Great Ultimate, which has "no opposite" (*wudui*). Human nature also has "no opposite." Even Mencius's "good nature" pits "humaneness" (*ren*) against "inhumaneness" (*buren*), and so it is really the "nature of sentiments" (*qing zhi xing*) and not the "nature of nature" (*xing zhi xing*). In the final analysis, there is only the Ultimate Nothingness or the Great Ultimate, in which even "the incipience of yin and yang is no more," and where virtues such as "humaneness, rightness, propriety and wisdom find no settled place." What the *Changes* calls "the creative origin" (*qianyuan*) and what the *Great Learning* calls "the highest good" refer exactly to this state of nonopposition.[19]

Guan, following Cheng Hao, affirms fundamental nature as supremely "tranquil" (*jing*). It also defies description: "Cheng Hao says, 'Humanity by nature is tranquil at birth. The state prior to it cannot be discussed.' Once human nature is discussed, it is no longer human nature." Goodness and evil, Guan states, "become active while responding to things; they are the desires (*yu*) of human nature, not nature itself. That humanity is born in tranquility is heaven's nature. Although it embodies the incipience of goodness and evil, it does not yet function as material nature in things. This is the real appearance of heaven's nature."[20] In short, ontologically speaking, the supremely tranquil human nature, as the manifestation of the Great Ultimate or heaven's nature, is ineffable. To summon the categories of good and evil is to introduce an inappropriate caesura that shatters the original oneness of *xing*.

Gu Xiancheng counters by first suggesting that Guan may have glossed over the complexity of the cosmological realities of the Great Ultimate and yin-yang. There are two ways of understanding the yin-yang duality as expounded in the *Changes*. First, yin-yang is a holistic dyad in which the two forces coexist in complementary and mutual reinforcement. Second, yin and yang are also constantly in contention, distinctly separate. When Guan interprets human nature in terms of the Great Ultimate, he never does clarify the meaning of the yin-yang duality. Rather, Guan simply argues that insofar as the Great Ultimate has both yin and yang, characterizing human nature as good is tantamount to saying that the Ultimate has only yang but not yin. Gu maintains that yin-yang, seen as a complementary whole, is the Great Ultimate itself, which embodies only goodness. But if yin and yang are regarded to be in tension, then yang is goodness, which must be upheld, and yin is evil, which must be curbed. Whichever is the case, there is still the indisputable distinction between goodness and evil. It is specious reasoning on Guan's part to claim that once nature is ascertained to be good, one may then logically say that the Great Ultimate has only yang, thereby detracting from the profound wholeness of the Great Ultimate.[21]

According to Gu, when Zhou Dunyi equates the Great Ultimate with Ultimate Nothingness, he aims not at synthesizing the tenets of the Three Teachings. Rather, "Master Zhou, by linking the Ultimate Nothingness to the Great Ultimate while discoursing on yin-yang and the Five Agents, seeks to illustrate the so-called common root of substance and function. From discussing yin-yang to saying that the Great Ultimate is originally the Ultimate Nothingness, [he wants to] reveal that there is no separation between the conspicuous and the subtle." In other words, ultimate reality is far from nothingness; yin-yang and the Five Agents are concrete entities. Moreover, Guan should not say that before the appearance of the yin-yang polarity, there is this supreme nothingness which explains the absence of good or evil in humanity:

> According to Master Zhou, "Through movement, the Great Ultimate creates yang; through tranquility, yin is created. Movement and tranquility alternate and serve as each other's root, engendering the separation of yin and yang. The two modes are thus established." The so-called separation of yin and yang speaks to the [distinction of the] two modes. Therefore, it is quite proper to say that before the establishment of

> the two modes, yin and yang are not separated. But can it be said that there is neither yin nor yang before the separation of yin and yang? If it is said that there is neither yin nor yang before the separation of yin and yang, then what sort of things are [the activities] from movement to tranquility, and from tranquility to movement? It is dubious to use it to prove that human nature is beyond good and evil.[22]

Gu concedes that indeed human nature is the Great Ultimate, and that this fundamental reality is universally uniform in character: "In heaven, it is heaven; on earth, it is earth; in humanity, it is humanity. It is not two. Therefore, it is that which precedes the birth of humanity; it is that which acts in response to things." But the classics and the sages have taught one clear fact: human nature, as manifestation of the one ultimate reality, is inherently good.[23]

Gu faults Guan Zhidao for bifurcating goodness into the goodness of "unifying substance" (*tongti*), in which good and evil are dissolved, and ordinary goodness of the "diverse myriad" (*wanshu*), where there is a stark sense of good and evil. The former is seen as "the profound virtue of great transformation"; the latter as "the small virtue of separate dissemination." With such bifurcation, Guan places even the cardinal virtues of humaneness, rightness, propriety, and wisdom in the realm of the diverse myriad, since their very existence inevitably presumes the existence of their opposites. To Gu Xiancheng, such polar conception of *xing* is highly perilous. For once the ethico-moral norms are relegated as small virtues, our normal sense of the difference between right and wrong will become diluted. Dwelling on transcendent goodness means in effect the assertion of the autonomous subject, and this boundless human self-assertion, in the absence of reference to the normatively good, will only lead to the destruction of the common world and public reality of accepted moral living. To halt any further slide toward the annihilation of the normative sense of goodness, Gu affirms that there is only one pervading goodness.[24]

The Xu–Zhou and Guan–Ku debates, in and of themeselves, may not be seminally remarkable since they displaced no philosophical matrices of their intellectual forebears and provided no truly new insights on the question of *xing*. Yet the debates were indexical phenomena, in that they revealed some scholars' preoccupation with *xing* as a central concern of their day. Their agonistic quest to explore and explicate nature constituted a clear motif in the Ming–Qing intellectual transition. As a generation of late Ming and early Qing literati came to look askance at the latter-day developments of Lu-Wang learning, seeing in it the ontological roots of the existential woes of dynastic decline and social chaos, they urged the reaffirmation of *xing*'s innate goodness as the indisputable ultimate grounding, the *sensus communis,* for individual moral action, forging a philosophical agenda in the late sixteenth and early seventeenth centuries.

The Philosophical Agenda of *Xing* in the Late Ming and Early Qing

The late Qian Mu, in his classic work, *The History of Chinese Learning in the Past Three Hundred Years* (Zhongguo jin sanbainian xueshushi), has identified the contents of the philosophical agenda that arose in the late Ming. The principal item on that agenda was the nature of *xing*. Many scholars initially became preoccupied with this question as a response to the ethico-moral degeneration supposedly brought on by the latter-day followers of Wang Yangming. Eventually, some of them traced the problem back to the errant teachings of the master himself. Many repudiated Wang's idea of the mind-heart, or the fundamental substance (*benti*), as beyond good and evil. They asserted that *xing* was inexorably good and that it specified the substance of morality. But this substance must be realized by actions in the experiential world. Hence the emergence of the second and related item on the philosophical agenda: the mutuality of fundamental substance (*benti*) and effort (*gongfu*). The conviction was that substance was not some transcendental entity, capable of sudden self-enlightenment or self-realization in the absence of concrete efforts. Concomitant with this view was the notion of a holistic nature, which established the third item on the agenda. As *xing* was accepted to be an integrated whole, the distinction between moral (*yili*) and material (*qizhi*) natures was deliberately blurred. The cognitive, affective, and conative were increasingly identified with the innate moral essence in *xing*.[25]

In the early seventeenth century, there was thus a coherent set of issues that engaged a generation of Confucian literati. To illustrate these core questions, it is helpful to examine more closely Gu Xiancheng's thought and also pinpoint the central philosophical views of several roughly contemporaneous scholars: Gao Panlong (1562–1626), the Donglin stalwart; Liu Zongzhou (1578–1645), the grand synthesizer of Song-Ming metaphysics; Chen Que (1604–1677), Liu's disciple; and Huang Daozhou (1585–1646), who according to Huang Zongxi's *Record of Ming Scholars,* belonged to the group of "miscellaneous scholars" whose scholarly affiliations were ambiguous.[26] Such a sampling of dramatis personae may provide a broad representation of the diverse branches of learning in the late Ming which displayed an overt interest in metaphysical discourse. Needless to say, to refract their thoughts through the philosophic agenda outlined above is not to say that the thinkers in question were uniform in their thought. It is to suggest that there was a general *Problematik* to which all of them submitted in one way or another.

Reassertation of the Goodness of *Xing*

A generation of scholars, beginning with the Donglin scholars, reasserted the primacy of the goodness of human nature and repudiated the idea of fundamental human substance as "beyond good and evil."[27] We have already seen how Gu Xiancheng, in his debate with Guan Zhidao, propounded this central idea. In the same year (1600) that Gu's *A Treatise on Corroborating Human Nature* appeared, he recorded in his notebook the statement that the "fundamental principle" (*zongzhi*) of his learning was the conviction in the innate goodness of human nature:

> It may be asked [of me:] "Those who discourse on learning in recent times often establish a fundamental principle. How come you alone do not have one? You earnestly claim that human nature is good. Is it not your fundamental principle?" I will reply, "I have been contemplating this for some years now, and after repeated thinking in many ways, [I feel that] nothing is as good as the two words of '*xing shan*' (good nature). If one can thoroughly understand even one point here, one gains one point of moral strength; if one can thoroughly understand two points here, one gains two points of moral strength. One who understands completely its entirety is a sage."[28]

Gu's junior Donglin associate, Gao Panlong, agreed. In his essay "Discourse on the Mind-Heart and Nature" (Xin xing shuo), Gao posits that human nature, as substance, is prior to the mind-heart: "Even though it can be said that the mind-heart and nature are one, they must not be confused with each other. . . . The function of the mind-heart can be described, but the substance of the mind-heart cannot. Nature is the substance of the mind-heart."[29] Elsewhere, Gao underscores the ontological centrality of *xing* by pointing to the principal tenet of the *Doctrine of the Mean* (Zhongyong): "What is centrality (*zhong*) and what is commonality (*yong*)? It is the nature of human beings; it is heaven's decree (*tianming*). Speaking in terms of universal developments, it is heaven; speaking in terms of individual beings, *xing* is heaven."[30] Human nature is also the epistemological foundation: "Any discussion of learning must have as its basis [the issue of] human nature. Any discussion on human nature must have as its basis the recovery of human nature."[31] This *xing*-cum-heaven is thus the ultimate substance in humanity. As such, Gao maintains, it is definitely good (*shan*), not beyond good and evil. Gao clearly states that "goodness is *xing*. Without goodness, there is no *xing*. I regard goodness as *xing*; others regard goodness as [something] external [to *xing*]."[32] "Goodness" comes with "the birth of humanity." It is the "beginning" (*yuan*), "the beginning and source of growth endowed in all beings."[33] In fact, in an effort to further establish the unalienable goodness of *xing*, Gao goes on to assert that goodness is the very foundation of all beings. Goodness, he argues, is in fact prior to *xing*: "Goodness is the change generated by the creation and reproduction of beings. There is goodness and then there is *xing*. Scholars do not understand goodness, and so they do not know *xing*."[34] In contending that goodness is not only *xing* but is antecedent to it, Gao seeks to forestall any suggestion that nature can be anything but good.

Liu Zongzhou, who was sympathetic to Wang Yangming's ideas but also studied with Xu Fuyuan, so remarked when talking about the debate between his teacher and Zhou Rudeng: "I, in my career, have always admired and followed Master Xu. As for the teachings of Master Zhou, I look at his door and dare not enter." Liu declares that "the Way and principle of heaven-and-earth" are nothing but the fact that "they are good and devoid of evil." He rejects Wang Yangming's credo that "the substance of the mind-and-heart is beyond good and evil." Liu's logic is that any "talk of the existence of goodness" inexorably means the exclusion of evil, and any "talk of the absence of evil" confirms the existence of goodness. In fact, this logical linkage inheres in Yangming's own belief that "the removal of human desires is at once the preservation of heaven's principle." Therefore, it is erroneous to say that "the moment when mistakes and flaws have been thoroughly cleansed is not the moment when the highest good is fully realized."[35] Any "discussion on the fundamental substance" must lead to the inescapable conclusion that "it has only goodness but not evil."[36]

Liu regards this substance as both *xing* and the will (*yi*). He refers to the *Doctrine of the Mean* in an effort to expound the innate goodness of *xing*. As nature is good, any act that follows this nature is good. In fact, "what is called the good nature can only be seen in the Way of following nature (*shuaixing*). The Way mentioned in the *Mean* is but the five ultimate ways [i.e., the Five Relationships]. Is there anything that is not good in the five ultimate ways?" It is highly significant that Liu's conception of the good nature embodies the corresponding act of following nature. He explains the *Mean*'s dictum that one cannot depart even for one moment from the Way of following nature: "As human nature is regarded as good, the Way is also regarded as good. Therefore, one cannot depart from it." The act of following nature is integrally a part of nature. To suggest the contrary is to suggest that "there is no water in the [act of] drinking water, or that there is no book in [the act of] reading a book." Although it is quite true that depending on the reader, the act of reading may not lead to the complete comprehension of a book, the act itself should not be blamed. Liu thus asserts that "to follow [nature] is precisely nature, and nature is the Way."[37]

As both T'ang Chün-i and Tu Wei-ming have shown, Liu Zongzhou also construes the fundamental human substance as *yi*, the absolutely good will. In T'ang's words: "Liu's insistence on the ultimacy of goodness is very much like the thought of thinkers in the Tung-lin school. . . . Liu did not merely stress the priority of good in the ethical sense; he also had ontological statements about the status of good in the original mind, and connected the 'good' with the innermost part of mind which is a 'will' having its source in an unseen Heaven."[38] In Tu's words, this will, in the deep recess of one's being, is "the ontological substance" of "vigilant solitariness" (*shendu*), one's "heaven-endowed nature" that was "solitary, unique and absolute."[39] In his essay, "Reading the *Great Learning*" (Du Daxue), Liu Zongzhou conceives the absolutely good human nature as the will and vigilant solitariness:

> The way of the *Great Learning* is merely the authentication of the will. The endeavor of authenticating the will is merely being vigilantly [in tune with] solitariness. . . . The will is the final resting place of ultimate goodness. . . . To talk of the priority of authenticating the will over the extension of knowledge is to show people precisely that the aim of the way to arrive at the ultimate is to dwell on the highest good. Outside of the will, there is no goodness. Outside of solitariness, there is no goodness.[40]

Toward the end of his life, in a 1643 essay, "A Discourse on the Innate Knowledge of the Good" (Shuo liangzhi), Liu addresses Wang Yangming's famous "four maxims" as transmitted by Wang Ji, and expresses once more his disagreement with the idea of human nature as beyond good and evil. Yangming's notion of innate knowledge of the good, as it is located in the scheme of the "four maxims," is fundamentally at odds with the original teachings of the *Great Learning*. This canonical text, Liu again tells us, teaches the Way of authenticating the will, which requires the effort of investigating things, the ultimate goal of which is to rest in the highest good. To rest in the highest good is to extend exhaustively the innate knowledge of the good. Self-critically, Liu faults his own elucidation as one marred by circuituous verbiage. But at least it connotes the fundamental substance of the will as a holistic seamless web of mutually reinforcing and correlating elements. By contrast, the "four maxims" fragment the reality of the ultimate substance and thus distort the ontological status and meaning of innate knowledge of the good.

Liu raises two major objections. First, the opening maxim affirms the substance of the mind-and-heart as beyond good and evil. The next maxim then asserts that good and evil arise with the movement of the will. Innate knowledge of good appears only in the third maxim. Liu asks, "Since it is only after the emergence of good and evil that there is knowledge of good and knowledge of evil, knowing is thus the servant of the will. In what way then is knowing good innate? . . . Although the original substance is beyond good and evil, yet it knows good and evil. Knowing is thus merely a posterior faculty of the mind-and-heart. In what way then is knowing good innate?" In other words, within the "four maxims," innate knowledge of the good is consigned to a second-order existence.

Second, Liu asks, "Since the *Great Learning* clearly refers to the resting in the highest good, from where does evil come?" Far from being transmoral "nonbeings," as Wang Ji has defined them, the four entities of the "mind-heart (*xin*), will (*yi*), knowledge (*zhi*), and things (*wu*)" must be defined in terms of the "highest good (*zhishan*)." Liu also rejects the inconsistent explanation that the distinction between good and evil applies only to those with dull intelligence. All these "various contradictions" began with Yangming's fractured conception of the will, the faculty of knowing, and finally the mind-heart: "Because Yangming wrongly conceives the meaning of the word 'will,' he cannot avoid moving forward and seek the good in knowing. Because [he] roughly conceives the meaning of the word 'knowing,' he cannot avoid withdrawing into and seeking the essential in the mind-and-heart. Even without waiting for a refutation of Wang Ji, that these various contradictions are not the principles of the *Great Learning* can be known."[41]

In a letter written in the same year, Liu presents his holistic view of the mind-heart as the undifferentiated fundamental substance, which is absolutely good, devoid of evil. The will, knowledge, and things are but varying manifested states of fundamental substance, that is, the one and only mind-heart. Liu here refuses to regard the will as the "issuance" (*fa*) of that which is "preserved" (*cun*) in the mind-heart. For to do so is to create a false dichotomy. Instead, Liu proffers this interpretation of the interrelation between the inextricably linked mind-heart, will, knowledge, and things:

> There is but one mind-heart. When speaking of it as the preservation of that which is primary, it is called the will. When speaking of it as the illumined awareness of the preservation of that which is primary, it is called knowledge. When it returns to the highest good with the illumined awareness that there is good but not evil [in fundamental substance], it is called things. Only after knowing this will do we realize the intricate marvel that the learning of the mind-heart has one root.[42]

Thus, Liu Zongzhou spares no analytic pains in rejecting the four maxims and reaffirming the goodness of humanity, whether it be construed as human nature or human will.

Chen Que, Liu's pupil, spells out the idea of goodness of *xing* in many of his writings, for it is foundational to his anthropology. In a two-part essay on human nature, "An Explication on Human Nature" (Xingjie), Chen claims that Confucius and Mencius have said the final words on nature. Confucius's statement, "By nature, human beings are similar," according to Chen, "is uttered from the fundamental vantage point of goodness."[43] Mencius then laid bare the explicit fact that nature is universally good in all humanity: "Mencius's idea is that the nature of a good person is no doubt good. But even the nature of a wicked person is also nothing but good. [The problem is that one] fails to do good. [It is not that one is] unable to do good."[44] Chen points out that the term "original substance" (*benti*) does not exist in the classics. What can be found in the sages' words is the notion of nature as good. In other words, human nature is the ultimate ontological substance. Chen Que thus concludes: "Human nature is the substance, and goodness is the substance of human nature."[45]

Similarly, Huang Daozhou, taking his cue from the *Classic of Changes*, sees the heaven-endowed goodness of nature as the origin of all things: "The *Changes* says, 'That which continues it [i.e., the Way] is goodness, and that which completes it [i.e., the Way] is nature.' Goodness is that which continues heaven-and-earth, and nature is that which completes the myriad things. . . . Goodness is the cause of which the myriad things are born."[46] Humanity is grounded in the inexorable and infinite "good consciousness" (*shannian*): "The point of departure for the sages and the universe is the good consciousness. This good consciousness, in heaven, is the brilliant mandate, which is described as incessant. In humanity, it is the ultimate sincerity, which is described as ceaseless. Incessancy and ceaselessless refer precisely to its eternality."[47]

Heaven-conferred *Xing* as the Locus of Action

By reaffirming the innate goodness of human nature and by making it the ontological center of gravity, the host of scholars we examined restored the self as the domain in which moral action and practice must unfold. In other words, the ontology of the absolutely good nature would have to move on the experiential fulcrum of practice, so that fundamental substance (*benti*), or nature, was in constant commerce with effort (*gongfu*). Indeed, many of the late Ming and early Qing thinkers sought to arrest the tendency toward the recondite. They were deliberately combating the perceived twin-evils of latter-day Wang Yangming learning: the first, moral-ethical uncertainty prompted by the idea of "beyond good and evil"; the second, vacuous introspection prompted by the faith in a pure void, and luminous original substance capable of sudden self-enlightenment. The perceived inseverable nexus between fundamental ontological substance and experiential efforts thus emerged as a major *Problematik*. In the essay "Criminal Words" (Zuiyan), Gu Xiancheng took the lead in attacking unsavory learning that undermined cultivation and effort:

> The idea that the fundamental substance of the mind-heart is beyond good and evil in its original state degenerates readily into the conclusion that it is but one emptiness. . . . With emptiness, everything is liberated, no longer bridled and obstructed. The clever delve into [this idea] and take delight in it, accordingly making such a statement on its behalf: "The harm wrought by the blight of principles (*li*) is worse than that wrought by the blight of desires (*yu*)." As a consequence, it is said, "Humaneness and propriety are fetters and handcuffs; the rites and laws are coarse sackcloths; the daily utilities are worldly entanglements; adhering to proper conduct merely gives occasion for talk; to reflect on things as they arise is to chase after contingent circumstance; to be contrite and to change is to be trapped in the wheel of life; to begin learning from below so as to reach the top is to be *déclassé*. To polish virtue and improve behavior, and to be fearlessly upright is to be willful in one's pursuits." In confusion, everything becomes muddled. There is no way for discrimination anymore.[48]

In other words, flying in the face of accepted norms and behaviors, the notion of human nature as beyond good and evil breeds a topsy-turvy world where conventions and protocols are subverted. Every effort is seen as unnecessary and superfluous. Gu finds it highly reprehensible that many of Wang Yangming's latter-day disciples, hiding behind a distorted view of Wang's idea of " innate knowledge of the good," forge the peculiar epistemology that because of the presence of such knowledge, one "knows without thinking and becomes capable without learning," so much so that "even one bit of effort need not be exerted." These are "lies" that "wreak great havoc all-under-Heaven." Gu reminds them that Wang pointedly adds the word *zhi* (to extend to the utmost) before the term *liangzhi* (innate knowledge of the good), thereby underscoring the fact that one "must solidly and steadfastly extend [it] before innate knowledge of the good can be realized."[49]

Gu illustrates the inseparability between the ontological and experiential in terms of the well-known polarities of *benti* (fundamental substance) vis-à-vis *gongfu* (effort). "Fundamental substance and effort are originally one. Therefore, scholars regard goodness of human nature as the principle, advocating doing good and removing evil," Gu opines.[50] The sages' learning focuses precisely on "doing good and removing evil. To do good is to realize that which is immanent; to remove evil is to extirpate that which is originally non-existent. It is so with regard to fundamental substance; it is so with regard to effort. It is nothing but to exhaust the one [goal]."[51] Even an ardent Wang Yangming follower like Luo Hongxian (1504–1564), according to Gu, has expressed his great discomfort with those who "talk all day long about fundamental substance and do not discuss effort, thinking that once effort is mentioned, the Way will be excluded."[52] Gu equates fundamental substance with the "innately good nature" (*xing shan*), and effort with the "careful mind" (*xiaoxin*).[53]

In fact, Gu names his study the "Studio of the Careful Mind" (*Xiaoxin zhai*) to remind himself of the necessity for ceaseless, meticulous effort in realizing and fulfilling the fundamental good nature. He has in mind in particular the reckless approach of some of his contemporaries, who blithely bypass effort and claim instantaneous identification with ultimate reality. Ku uses a medical analogy by way of explanation: "To bring to the fore the two words of '*xiaoxin*' is to prescribe medicine according to the illness."[54] Using another analogy, Gu suggests that fundamental substance is like a mother's giving birth to a child, and effort is like a mother's rearing a child. The child must be nursed and nurtured in many ways. The profound scholars (*daru*) of old realized an infant's "difficulty in growth and difficulty in cultivation," and so they spared no effort in teaching the proper ways, whereas petty scholars in recent times tend to think that an infant in a natural way can "grow easily and be nurtured easily," thus ignoring postnatal guidance.[55] In other words, nature must be complemented by culture.

Gu insists that there is no *wu* (enlightenment) without *xiu* (cultivation): "There is no enlightenment which does not begin with cultivation.

Does the *Analects* not say that in study, [Confucius] starts from below and reaches what is up above? Starting from below is cultivation; reaching what is up above is enlightenment."[56] Cultivation is practice (*xing*): "Where does enlightenment begin? It begins with practice. Where does enlightenment end? It ends with practice."[57] Moreover, our nature can never be fully realized and understood without earnest study. Gu criticizes many of his contemporaries for seizing upon the *Doctrine of the Mean*'s idea of "apprehension without thought" (*busi er de*) and "hitting what is right without effort" (*bumian erh zhong*), forgetting that crucial to such attainment are the requisite acts of "choosing the good and firmly holding onto it," "extensive study, accurate inquiry, careful reflection, clear discrimination and earnest learning."[58] Unfortunately, many scholars "presumptuously rely on their cleverness, readily ignore the sages of old, rendering the Six Classics into footnotes, talking big in lofty terms, no longer having any inhibitions."[59] Gu's goal is to underscore the pointlessness of pursuing enlightenment and nature in the absence of cultivation and learning, that is, earnest effort.

Gao Panlong, following his senior colleague, attacks abstruse learning by pointing to the ultimate peril of the dissolution of the ethico-moral traditions of society as purposeful actions are deemed to be irrelevant and unnecessary:

> As a start, [scholars following Wang] swept away [knowledge gained from] seeing and hearing in order to illuminate the mind-heart. In the end, the mind-heart was pursued but learning was abandoned. As a result, the *Odes, Documents, Rites* and *Music* have been slighted, and concrete understanding has been ignored. As a start, [distinction between] good and evil was swept aside in order to [apprehend] the empty mind. In the end, vacuity was pursued but action was abandoned. As a result, integrity, loyalty and rightness have been slighted, and solid self-cultivation has been ignored.[60]

In Gao's view, to reassert the absolutely good *xing* is to reestablish a firm source of moral and intellectual values. The good *xing* in turn demands incessant solid efforts for its realization.

Gao Panlong enjoins scholars to solemnly seek knowledge of the fundamental substance, that is, the good human nature: "The beginning of learning and inquiry is knowing nature, followed in the middle by recovering nature, ending with the extension of nature to the utmost. . . . Nature is known through sincerity; nature is recovered through sincerity; nature is extended to the utmost through sincerity. . . . To learn is to learn about this; to meditate is to experience this."[61] By indenturing the realization of nature to sincerity, Gao urges us to turn within and seek authenticity in our true self. But this inward turn toward nature nullifies no external authority and negates no established way of acting: "Inwardly, one preserves an anxious sense of avoiding the tabooed. Outwardly, one abides by rules and norms. . . . The anxious sense of avoiding the tabooed is the spirit of nature's substance; rules and norms are the true organizing principles of nature's substance."[62] Although apprehending nature is the ultimate goal, it can only be achieved through exercising efforts in the world of binding observances: "Do not worry about not illuminating the fundamental substance. Worry only about efforts' not being meticulous."[63] Gao thus forges fundamental substance and effort as one inseparable whole: "Fundamental substance is taken as effort; effort is taken as fundamental substance. Being ignorant about fundamental substance is entirely due to inadequate effort; not pursuing efforts is all false fundamental substance."[64] The two key efforts in the maintenance of this crucial oneness are quiet-sitting and study, each effort consuming half a day. In practicing the first, one "concentrates profoundly and cultivates deeply" (*houzhu shenpei*) the essential, and so overcomes a besetting problem in cultivation, that is, "being short on spirit and shallow in the vital material force" (*shenduan qifou*).[65] With quiet-sitting, one focuses unerringly on the quest for the realization of one's nature: "To perceive in quietude the state before the arousal of pleasure, anger, sorrow and joy . . . is precisely to be tacitly aware of the mind-and-heart's substance when it is not settled in any specific place. This is the ready method of perceiving nature."[66]

But this quietistic effort of contemplation and meditation alone is not enough. It requires the complement of study which, in uprooting the "vulgar roots" of scholars long "immersed in vulgar practices," brings about the "harmonious coalescing of moral principles."[67] Small wonder that Gao links Mencius's teachings on nature with the endeavor of learning. According to Gao, the sagacious sage devoted his life to "solely talking about the one word of nature." But Mencius's nature is "most commonplace." It is not something abstract and undefinable; it defies no cultural and social circumscription. It has its natural "laws and measures." Consequently, it is pointless to talk about nature without proper learning. As Mencius puts it, just as a great crafstman will not alter the plumb line for the benefit of an inept carpenter, and Yi would not change the way of drawing the bow for the clumsy archer's sake, so too when he "discusses the Way and virtues, he praises Yao and Shun, and when military exploits are discussed, [he] praises [King] Tang and [King] Wu." The utmost extension of study and inquiry (*xuewen*) is the unwearying adherence to the established plumb line and the way of drawing the bow. To do so, Gao argues, is to realize human nature itself. In fact, he concludes,

"What Mencius calls human nature is what Confucius calls learning."[68] Therefore, learning must not be pedantic and bookish learning: "When scholars read books, they must reflect upon every sentence in terms of one's own self. . . . On the one hand, one ponders and seeks fundamental understanding. On the other, one practices what one learns. Only then is one actually studying."[69] As it became evident that many of his contemporaries succumbed to the self-indulgent and effortless quest for fundamental substance, Gao reminded them of Zhu Xi's call for "plumbing principles" (*qiongli*):

> Since Wang Yangming, seeing the flaws of vulgar learning [of his time], miscontrued Zhu Xi's [idea of] plumbing principles and established a partial view with particular emphasis, scholars have been saying that to study is to follow the external. The literate do not investigate deeply the classics and histories; the common folk listen only to hearsay. Writing about what is empty and vacuous, there is not one bit of solid learning. Management of the economy is not based on governance and techniques; [the so-called] actual cultivation does not have any solid basis.[70]

Apart from plumbing principles, one must also pursue "investigation of things" (*gewu*) to determine whether learning is "concrete" or "empty."[71] "The effort of investigation of things is no different from knowing the root. The goal is to apprehend the "highest good," as stated in the *Great Learning*. "To dwell in the highest good" is the basis of "illuminating the clear character" and "renovating the people." Through investigating things, one gets "to know the root" (*zhiben*) of abiding in the highest good, which begins with "self-cultivation."[72] In short, one must "do good" (*weishan*):

> To ceaselessly do good upon waking up with the cock's crow is my lifelong pursuit of nurturing virtue and cultivating my calling. But to do good must entail knowing good, so that one's action is distinguished and practice is scrutinized. What is knowing good? Goodness is *xing*. . . . Knowing it, its essential substance (*ti*) can be established; acting upon it, its practical function (*yong*) can be extended. . . . Recovering *xing* in this way and extending *xing* in this way can be thus described as a simple and easy [means] to apprehend heaven-and-earth's principle.[73]

The inquiry of nature means not the building of a private inner world free from disciplines and social bounds. It is the active viewing of the self in relation to the world. Gao's theorizing on human nature ends with his urgent call for practical realization of the goodness of human nature. His final aim is to galvanize individual moral responsibility and social activism stemming from our nature.

Liu Zongzhou's ideas of a moral will and vigilant solitariness, as both Tu Wei-ming and Tang Chün-i have shown, imbue transcendental ultimate goodness (*benti*) in humanity with an integral immanent experiential dimension (*gongfu*). In Tu's words: "Liu . . . interprets the 'ultimate good' as the basis for self-cultivation. . . . Moral action is possible because the ability to dwell in the ultimate good is inherent in our nature. It is our birthright, as moral agent, to manifest the ultimate good in our daily affairs."[74] According to T'ang Chün-i, Li Zongzhou's will, predisposed to and knowing goodness, finds existential fulfillment through the requisite moral practice of self-reverence (*jing*): "The practice of this self-reverence or self-respect to keep one's self-dignity is called *kung-fu*. What is realized through practice is the reality (*pen-t'i*), substance or nature (*hsing*). . . . Hence, Liu Tsung-chou talked about the 'identity of practice and substance' (*chi kung-fu chi pen-t'i*)."[75] Indeed, Liu declares, "Some claim that there is simultaneity of knowledge and action. So there is no need to pursue action outside of knowledge. [They] stress the fundamental substance but not practice. As a result, our Way has degenerated greatly."[76]

Fundamental substance, as Liu asserts, inheres in "daily utility and normal activity." If the former is regarded as some entity independent of the latter, one will then futilely "pursue the Way in the vacuous and nonexistent."[77] Fundamental substance is indefinable and ineffable, and so once one seeks to describe it, one has no choice but to speak of its expression as efforts. Liu explains that this mutuality of substance and function stems from the fact that substance is good and prescribes the good. Here, Liu again attacks the proposition that fundamental substance is beyond good and evil, which nullifies any deliberate and conscious act as the means toward realizing the end. How does one act when there is neither goodness to pursue nor evil to remove? In contrast, once fundamental humanity specifies the good and impels one to do good, efforts become meaningful and purposeful. Liu likens some of his contemporaries' preoccupation with an abstruse substance transcending good and evil to Jilu's (Confucius's disciple) speculation about spirits and life hereafter. Liu sees his own emphasis on efforts as an echo of Confucius's response to Jilu, namely, that knowing humanity and life takes precedence over the contemplation of spirits and death. Confucian learning "seeks the ultimate destination in ordinary human relations and quotidian utility, and absolutely refrains from any empty discussion of fundamental substance." "To exhaustively develop nature" (*jinxing*) is "to serve humanity" (*shiren*); the manifestation of fundamental substance is the realization, through effort, of what we innately know to be good.[78] To provide a blueprint for the development of ultimate personhood (*renji*) through constant moral practice, Liu wrote the *A Manual of Personhood* (Renpu), which Tu Wei-ming describes as a "strategy for learning to be human by putting 'vigilant solitariness' into practice as a daily ritual."[79]

Liu thus dismisses the idea of instantaneous realization of the ultimate good: "Individuals should exert efforts in study and inquiry. The sages' words should be repeatedly examined, repeatedly authenticated and doubted. Efforts must be concrete, experienced with our own bodies. Only in so doing can the actuality and truth of the sages' words be seen."[80] Even the ancient sages such as "Yao, Shun, Tang, Wen and Wu all did not have inborn knowledge (*shengzhi*)." Their "allotted talents" (*fen*) had to be cultivated through learning "before they could in fact be fully realized."[81] For "apart from things, there is no knowledge. If one wishes to seek knowledge outside of things, it will be like what Master Cheng [Yi] described as seeking one's image while turning over the mirror."[82] By the same token, Liu does not accord "following heaven-conferred virtuous nature" (*zun dexing*) priority over "following the path of study and inquiry" (*dao wenxue*). They "are not two kinds of knowledge. . . . Now, some wish to discard experiences and discuss virtuous nature. This is not virtuous nature."[83] Knowledge, to Liu Zongzhou, encompasses both moral and intellectual pursuits.

Chen Que, like his teacher, explores the experiential implications and consequences of the ontological assertion that the goodness of nature is the original substance of reality. He criticizes his contemporaries for their empty talk of *xing*: "Scholars today all discuss nature in their empty talk. Everyone claims that one knows nature. But the earnest effort to move toward goodness by rectifying flaws is nowhere to be seen. Where is the good nature that they proclaim?"[84] If the primordial nature is universally good, it must also be constantly nurtured and developed so that it is fully revealed: "There is no nature that is not good, but it can only be seen after it has been expanded to the utmost by exhausting the endowed capabilities."[85] That is the way taught by Mencius, as Chen remarks:

> Although nature is good, it cannot not be promoted. Therefore, Mencius teaches us to expand [nature] to the utmost; teaches us to act, to be patient, to preserve [nature] and to nurture [nature]; teaches us to be generously forgiving and to forcefully act on the good. . . . It is like the five grains. Although the seeds may be fine, if there is no planting and cultivation, their fineness cannot be seen.

Chen observes that while Mencius "inevitably talks about nature when talking about effort (*gongfu*), the Song Confucians first and foremost seek the original substance (*benti*). When Mencius talks about nature's substance, he refers to that which is concrete and tangibly reliable."[86]

Chen aims to overcome the ontological prejudice against effort in Song learning's contemplative tradition of pursuing original substance. The core of his argument is the recovery of the ordinary experience and action of our being, that is, our nature, before its reification as some sort of ultimate substance. Small wonder that Chen even takes issue with the *Great Learning*'s notion of "ending in the ultimate good" (*zhi yu zhishan*). In his *Disputation with the Great Learning* (Daxue bian), he casts doubt on the tenability of such ontological foreclosure since "learning can never be exhausted," for not only is there "further goodness within goodness," there is also "further ultimate goodness in ultimate goodness." Therefore, the pursuit of learning is a lifelong process, without an end. Since goodness cannot ever be grasped once and for all, the idea of "ending in the ultimate good" erroneously suggests that there is the possibility of an ontological precomprehension of the world. It is supercilious self-deception to think that "there is the day when one suddenly knows all and becomes completely at ease with the principles of things all-under-heaven."[87] Thus, Chen Que not only ascertains the mutuality of original substance and effort, he also asserts the historicity and dynamism of the process of the realization of our good nature.

In explicating the nexus between original substance and effort, Huang Daozhou first equates the original substance with one's own mind-heart and one's own body (*benshen*), thereby declaring the fact that the realm of human affairs is no longer just an object for one's philosophical comprehension but is also the site for one's action: "How does a superior person pursue learning? . . . The sages and the upright deliberate in terms of their own body. . . . [They] all use their own mind-heart to establish a goal on behalf of all-under-heaven."[88] This consecration of the self as the locale of action is propelled and acccomplished by taking reverential care (*jing*) of the obligation to cultivate oneself: "When the sages and the upright use their own body as the exemplar, they cultivate themselves with reverence. Only then will there be [the fulfillment of] the original substance and effort."[89]

According to Huang, the pursuit of moral self-cultivation with reverence not only means the concatenation of substance and effort; it also means the extension of the self's effort and its achievements to other people. Reverential self-cultivation certainly enables the superior person (*junzi*) to successfully pursue his "affairs and projects" and "learning and inquiry." But it also ineluctably involves the enterprise of "bringing peace to the people, to the multitude." This is the "original substance of the superior person" (*junzi benti*). In fact, Huang asks, "It is of course difficult to both cultivate oneself and bring peace to the multitude, and so there must be reverence. If it is not done for the sake of the multitude all-under-heaven, then what good is it for oneself?"[90]

Conceptions of *Xing* as an Integrated Whole

As the late Ming and early Qing scholars affirmed the goodness of human nature, seeing its realization in the phenomenal, experiential, and corporeal, they also increasingly conceived this nature as holistic. *Qizhi zhi xing* (material nature), one's existential being comprising the affective, conative, emotive, and sensory, no longer seemed the second and secondary nature, perennially submitting to the noumenally superior *yili zhi xing* (moral nature). It is well known that Cheng Yi, Zhu Xi, and Zhang Zai all embraced the view of a bipartite human nature. In terms of their anthropology, there is "heaven-and-earth nature" (*tiandi zhi xing*), or moral nature which, as the perfect manifestation of principle, is invariably good. It is what, according to them, the *Classic of Documents* calls the subtle "mind-heart of the Way" (*daoxin*). Then there is material nature, or what the *Documents* calls the "human mind-heart" (*renxin*), which is prone to error. Material nature can be bad because "material endowment" (*qibing*) from heaven varies in individuals. Some are given a pure, clear, and brilliant material force, while others receive an impure, turbid, and cloudy one. Although principle does not exist in the absence of material force, it is only in the realm of material force that evil arises. Moreover, principle and human nature are prior to material force. Thus the *li-qi* metaphysical world is animated by a sense of duality. As the manifestation of principle, the prior moral nature is always good. The posterior material nature, while good in the state of purity, is the repository of both good and evil.[91] To illustrate the interrelationship of principle and material force with regard to human nature, Zhu Xi often employs his favorite analogical imagery of the penetration of light. Moral nature, as principle, is analogized as the rays of the sun or moon. Shone on dewy ground (the metaphor for pure human material nature), the brilliance of the rays comes into full view. On the other hand, when they shine through the thatched roof of a hut (the analogy for one's impure material force), light will be blocked and diffused, unable to cover the entire floor of the hut.[92] In short, Zhu Xi states that material nature is the source of evil.

Now, many late Ming and early Qing thinkers appeared to privilege a more holistic vision of *xing*, stressing the essential oneness of moral and material natures. This holistic conception, as Qian Mu argues, was a clear expression of scholars' increasing concern with coming to grips with the concrete and tangible in life. In particular, Qian Mu points to the Donglin scholars Qian Yiben (1539–1610) and Sun Shenxing (1565–1636).[93] It is therefore useful here to briefly review these two scholars' views on nature and the effort to realize it. Qian Yiben shares with his Donglin colleagues, Gu Xiancheng and Gao Panlong, the principal conviction that human nature is good, inasmuch as the virtues of "humaneness, rightness, propriety and wisdom are immanent in humanity." He repeats Mencius in asserting the goodness of *xing*:

> Mencius uses the idea of native endowments (*cai*) to discuss human nature. Human beings are naturally able because they combine the powers of the three realms [of heaven, earth, and humanity] and are also the most intelligent among the myriad beings. There is no person who is without natural abilities. There is no natural ability that is not good. As substance, they are called intrinsic abilities (*caixing*); as function, they are called expressed abilities (*caiqing*). . . . There is no natural ability that cannot do good.[94]

However, Qian dwells not on intrinsic goodness as a static quality. He sees it as a dynamic process of development that requires constant, purposeful realization. His favorite illustrative metaphor is the planting, germinating, and growing of seeds. What Mencius calls the sense of "sympathy" is truly only a "beginning and not a root. It is like the five grains. Are they not all wonderful seeds? It can be said that human beings cannot live without these seeds. But although [people] may have the same seeds, those who do not know how to plant them can only regard them as dead grains of seeds."[95] "The four sprouts (*siduan*) are only the sprouts, and if their growth is not fully promoted, they will die right there in the soil."[96] Even the sages cannot "hit the mark without effort and achieve understanding without thinking." The "Way of heaven" (*tiandao*) is not separate from the "Way of humanity" (*rendao*),[97] nor can "the mind-heart of humanity" (*renxin*) be distinguished from "the mind-heart of the Way" (*daoxin*).[98] The word *sheng* (at birth) in the phrase "to know at birth" (*shengzhi*) is fundamental substance; the word *xue* (to learn) in the phrase "to know with learning" (*xuezhi*) is "everyone's effort. It cannot be claimed that since antiquity, there has been a sage who is complete in himself at birth, so that he does not have to learn gradually."[99]

Since efforts and learning are the realizations of natural abilities that define one's authentic nature, and since humanity is at one with heaven,

Qian refuses to accept the Song masters' view that natural abilities belong to the realm of material force (*qi*) and that there is a separate "material nature" (*qizhi zhi xing*):

> Gaozi does not know that there are native endowments and so in his discussion on human nature, nature is likened to straight willow, to moving torrents of water, or is seen as nothing more than the desire for food and sex, categorizing it as desires for things. Moreover, [he] removes from it humaneness and rightness, emptying it of and casting it outside of heaven's principle. [He] only knows that that which is born is nature and does not know that that which is realized is nature, thereby equating the way of humanity with that of animals. . . . When Mencius refutes him with words, [Mencius] does not move at all from the line of Confucius's argument that the realization of nature is the continuation of [innate] goodness. The Song Confucians slightly diverge [from both] and claim that native endowments are endowments [in the realm] of material force, and furthermore recognize that there is a separate material nature. Do they not know that they may have corrupted the idea that [everyone] can become a Yao or a Shun?

In other words, nature is good as a whole, not bifurcated into two unequal natures. Nonetheless, everyone imbued with good endowments of natural abilities has to exert concrete effort so as to complete nature. Qian concludes that Cheng Yi's and Zhang Zai's advocacy of material nature is at variance with Mencius's principle of goodness of nature.[100]

Similarly, at the heart of Sun Shenxing's position is the conviction in the goodness of human nature. Explaining the opening line of the *Mean*, "What heaven mandates for humanity is called human nature," Sun says. "There is no goodness that is not rewarded by heaven, no evil unpunished. There is no person who does not like goodness and loathes evil."[101] Because heaven imparts this concrete mandate, "our nature is solidly imbued with this goodness," and "our Way is certainly the actual realization of this goodness."[102] This fundamental truth is therefore no fixed and abstract dictum apprehendable through some sudden enlightenment. Rather, the Confucian way of understanding goodness, as opposed to the Chan Buddhist one, inexorably entails concrete study and effort:

> The Way of the Confucians does not begin with enlightenment. A superior person who daily learns, inquires and reflects critically on his deeds simultaneously is daily wary, circumspect

> and watchful while being alone. How could there be free time when he could quest for the realm of the ineffable non-mind? Therefore, to abandon learning, inquiry and critical reflection on deeds, and to pursue the alternate efforts of preserving equanimity and scrutinizing actions so as to nurturing equilibrium and harmony is to drift into Chan learning.[103]

Sun's overt stress on the experiential owes much to his accommodation of "material disposition" (*qizhi*) as integral to a holistic *xing*. In Mencius's theory of the innate goodness of nature, Sun points out, "the body, and its appearance and functions, are the heaven-endowed nature." But later Confucians, while adhering to the idea of inborn human goodness, create the dichotomy of moral and material natures. Their claim that the latter gives rise to evil because of the paucity and turbidity of "native endowments" (*cai*) essentially dilutes the notion of nature as good. They fail to fully acknowledge Mencius's statement that "the doing of evil is not the fault of natural capabilities." Instead, they contend that "inferior people with low intelligence could not change because of their native endowments." In so doing, they practically demolish Mencius's belief. They in effect are saying that "the theories that there are natures which are not good or can be made to be not good are right, while Mencius's discourse on goodness is wrong." Sun argues that if nature is good, then material disposition must also be good. He explains with the analogy of a barley seed:

> The tendency to grow is nature. When this tendency to grow quietly pervades, there is then material force. When this tendency to grow becomes manifest and produces shapes, there is then material disposition. How can one take a grain and divide it into two entities, saying that nature is good whereas material disposition is not good? It is a fact that material endowments vary. Some are born stupid, intelligent, pure or turbid, taking different paths. So how can it be said material dispositions are all good? Nonetheless, even the most stupid and the most turbid of people do know of filial piety to parents and respect for elders. This is the substance of continuing the goodness [of nature], whose existence does not depend on stupidity or turbidity. It can thus be known that material disposition is not without good.

Sun further posits that the distinction between "the mind of humanity" (*renxin*) of "matter and form" (*xingqi*), and "the mind of heaven" (*daoxin*) of moral principles (*yili*), is a false one. The latter inheres in the former;

they are one and inseparable.[104] Sun charges that Cheng Yi's theory of human nature, which "states that evil exists in nature, has caused no small harm."[105]

Although on the surface, Gu Xiancheng follows the classic Cheng-Zhu position in pitting principle against material force, he tends to disqualify material nature as nature at all: "[To say that] nature is principle is to say that material nature cannot be recognized as nature. [To say that] the mind-heart is principle is to say that the heart of blood and flesh cannot be recognized as the mind-heart."[106] While "there is the one primal material force, the controlling master is principle. . . . Although human nature cannot be detached from material force, one must know that it comprises that which does not degenerate into the realm of material force. Only then can the real appearance of human nature be seen." The realm of material force "abounds in confusion, being clear, turbid, pure and mixed, having myriad shapes and numerous looks." It is therefore impossible to precisely locate human nature therein.[107] In his *A Treatise in Corroborating Nature*, Gu also claims that "to speak of nature in terms of material disposition does not capture the original face of nature. . . . That which is not nature cannot fail to be mixed up with material nature."[108] Interestingly enough, then, Gu does seek to construct an integrated nature—not, however, by affirming materiality as nature but by excluding it, preserving only the primary moral nature.

Gao Panlong's position is more ambiguous. On the one hand, he follows Cheng-Zhu in identifying human nature with principle, which is ultimately "heaven's principle" (*tianli*). To him, this identification distinguishes the Confucian conception of human nature from the Buddhist one.[109] Material force is "in the midst of the corporeal forms" (*xingxia*), while principle is "above the corporeal forms" (*xingshang*).[110] On the other hand, Gao makes it clear that if one "wishes to understand principle, [one must first] understand material force." He proclaims that "what pervades heaven-and-earth is nothing but material force. What is material force in heaven becomes the mind-heart in humanity."[111] In fact, he equates material force ultimately with human nature. In his essay "Discourse on Material Force, the Mind-Heart and Human Nature" (Qi xin xing shuo), Gao proposes the oneness of the three entities: "To the sages, material force is the material force that nurtures the Way and morals; the mind-heart is the mind-heart that preserves humanity and rightness. Just as material force is human nature, so too the mind-and-heart is human nature."[112]

Not surprisingly, then, Gao develops a more sympathetic view of material nature as integral to human quiddity: "Material nature comes into being after the formation of shape. After one receives one's shape, heaven-and-earth's nature becomes material nature. It is not that outside of heaven-and-earth nature, there is yet another material nature. . . . Therefore, to say that they are two is incorrect."[113] It is only "after one knows material nature that human nature can be discussed." Gao likens human nature to water in a receptacle. The clarity or turbidity of the water is a result of whether the receptacle is clean. Clear or turbid water is nonetheless water. Gao concludes, "One may question that since nature is nature and material endowment is material endowment, they cannot be mixed up. This is again wrong. . . . The Way of heaven-and-earth is such that [the nature] of all beings is the same. Thus, human nature is material force and material force becomes [material] endowment."[114]

In the case of Liu Zongzhou, we find a clear rejection of the view that human nature is something abstrusely fundamental, supracognitive, preconative, and transsensory. To him, *xing* is not some transcendent faculty or reality; it is simply the natural human faculties: "Master Zhu describes *xing* as that which is before the issuance of feelings (*weifa*). This is a view that eschews concreteness and degenerates into the illusory. Human nature is the natural principle that comes with birth. It is omnipresent. For instance, that the mind is capable of thinking is the nature of the mind; that the ears can hear is the nature of the ears; that the eyes can see is the nature of the eyes."[115] Liu consequently objects to the division of human nature into moral and material natures: "Principle is the principle of material force, which is definitely not prior to and outside of material force. Knowing this, then it is known that the mind-heart of the Way is merely the original mind-heart of the mind-heart of humanity. Moral nature is the original material nature."[116]

Liu addresses the problems intrinsic to dualistic conceptions of human nature. First, if there is the coexistence of two natures, there is always the possibility that some scholars will pursue material nature at the expense of neglecting moral nature. We have then to accept the idea that, as a rule, some may do good and some may not. Second, when moral nature alone is affirmed, casting aside concrete matters, there is then the tendency to submit to the notion of nature as beyond good and evil. Third, in the case where material endowment and moral principle are both accepted and equally valued, opposing views on human nature will emerge—human nature as good versus human nature as not good. It is precisely because of these problematic and inconsistent conceptualizations that "the principle of innate goodness of nature has been overshadowed" in his days, according to Liu. To reaffirm the unalienable view of inborn human goodness, we have to develop the

> knowledge that human nature is but material nature, and that moral principle is regarded as nature because it is that which

> is naturally so in material endowment. The mind-heart is but humanity, and the Way is regarded as the mind-heart because it is that which is naturally so in humanity. The mind-heart of humanity and the mind-heart of the Way are but one mind-heart. Material endowment and moral principle are but one nature. Knowing that there is only one mind-heart and one nature, [we also know that] there is only one effort. There is no scrutinizing of deeds that lies outside of [the effort of] preserving quietude; there is no plumbing of principles lying outside of [the effort of] dwelling in sincerity. In the final analysis, effort and fundamental substance are one.[117]

In so defining human nature, Liu forges a holistic view of the essential human constitution in experiential and physical terms.

Given Liu's rather naturalistic conception of human nature and his stress on the experiential elements, it is not surprising that Liu even accommodates desires generously as part of authentic human nature. He repudiates Cheng-Zhu's pitting "heaven's principle" (*tianli*) against "human desires" (*renyu*), and their identifying the former as "the mind-heart of the Way" and the latter as "the mind-heart of humanity." The mind-heart of the Way simply refers to the Way of the mind-heart of humanity, that is, to the quiddity of humanity as it naturally is. It is not that apart from the human mind-heart, there is the transcendent higher mind-heart of the Way.[118] Liu avers that heaven's principles and human desires "move together but are manifested differently, and so to engage in desires could lead to the return to the original principle."[119] For desires are "that which [are] natural to life and its changes, and [are] beyond one's control." But Liu is quick to point out that "indulging in desires will result in flaws. At worst, [desires] become evil."[120] Similarly, emotions (*qing*) must not be simply seen as posterior manifestations of fundamental human nature; they are integrally nature in themselves. In the postscript of *The Essentials of Sagely Learning* (Shengxue zongyao), a 1634 work that presents a synopsis of the thoughts of Zhou Dunyi, Zhang Zai, Cheng Hao, Zhu Xi, and Wang Yangming, Liu argues that emotions are integral to the ontological substance of "vigilant solitariness" (*shendu*). To be vigilant in solitariness is the pursuit of "exhaustively developing nature." This solitariness embodies the sentiments of "joy, anger, sorrow and pleasure," which are really alternative names for "humaneness, rightness, propriety and wisdom." In nature, they are known as the "spring, summer, autumn and winter." In so doing, Liu promptly consigns emotions to the realm of nature. In terms of human nature, they are, as with the four cardinal virtues, manifestations of fundamental humanity. In terms of the nature of the physical world, they are the nature of things, such as the four seasons. Moreover, Liu does not see emotions as the posterior arousal of nature:

> Just as there is not a time when heaven does not have spring, summer, autumn and winter, so in human being, there is not a time when one does not have joy, anger, sorrow and pleasure. Thus, it can be known that, in the final analysis, it is incorrect to say that nature, while quiet and still without movement, is in a state of imminent arousal (*weifa*), and while responding to things empathetically, is in a state of arousal (*yifa*).

Thus, Liu confers on emotions a pre- or supraexperiential status. They are coimmanent with human nature. Nature and emotions "are not distinguished by priority and posteriority, or by internality and externality. [They are] holistically one body." Liu espouses such a conception of emotions so as to rectify the Song–Ming scholars' tendency to privilege the "equilibrium" (*zhong*) of nature in its state of imminent arousal. The result has been that scholars "degenerate into the sick pursuit of the vacuous and empty." Liu sees the neglect of emotions as a distortion of the teachings of the *Doctrine of the Mean*. By giving emotions first-order status, the "harmonization" (*he*) of sentiments no longer has to play second fiddle to the introspective pondering of the interior substance of nature. It is a fundamental and yet tangible, describable, and concrete effort in one's quest for vigilance in solitariness.[121] As Liu expands the human substance to include the experiential and affective, he broadens the existential site on which meaningful individual practical actions can be undertaken.

Liu's disciple, Chen Que, is also explicit in rejecting the rendering of *xing* into a bipartite phenomenon: "The Song Confucians perversely demarcate the nature of heaven-and-earth from material nature, claiming that material force, emotion and native endowment are not the original nature, since they all contain that which is not good. [They] separate out an independent original substance which is the good nature."[122] In an essay devoted to defending the physical and affective as integral parts of fundamental *xing*, "Disputations on Material Force, Emotion, and Native Endowment" (Qi qing cai bian), Chen counters, "There is one nature. In terms of its origin, it is called heaven's mandate. In terms of its extension, it is called material force, emotion and native endowment." Material force is "nature's becoming omnipresent"; emotion is "the outward expression of nature"; native endowment is "the functioning of nature." Specifically, they constitute our faculties: "The mind-heart has consciousness, and the ears and eyes have hearing and sight. That is material force.

That consciousness has intelligence, or that there is knowing through hearing and sight, is native endowment." In fact, only in these faculties can the goodness of *xing* be seen. They are nature's "good capabilities" (*liangneng*). As such, they "possess only the good and not the bad."[123]

Chen agrees that the "material endowment" (*qibing*) does vary among individuals. Such endowed materiality may be pure or turbid. But such variance cannot be used to distinguish the good from the bad. To him, both pure and turbid endowment is part of the good nature. Chen sees such endowment in terms of intelligence. Those blessed with pure material force may be clever, but they may be prone to taking shortcuts and be adventuresome. Those imbued with turbid material force may be dull, but they are often serious and prudent. In other words, the physical qualities and appearances of our being are the highest mode of being since they alone show the goodness of nature. It is therefore not surprising that Chen was against the Song Confucians' call for "extirpation of desires" (*jueyu*). Desires are natural and inevitable, intrinsic in biological needs such as "eating, drinking and the commerce between men and women," and in social pursuits such as "success in the government and wealth." They are desired by both the sages and ordinary folk, except that the sages do not abuse and indulge in them. Desire, as Chen interprets it, is "the breeding of intention in the mind-heart, and all the myriad good comes from them." While the Song Confucians pit the so-called heaven's principle (*tianli*) against human desire (*renyu*), Chen contends that "heaven's principle can precisely be seen in human desire."[124]

What, then, is the source of evil? Chen posits that "The difference between good and evil is a result of practice (*xi*). How can it have anything to do with nature? Regardless of whether the material force is pure or turbid, if it is practiced on the good, it is good, and if it is practiced on the bad, it is bad."[125] Chen's thinking on nature may thus be described as being (*benti*/original substance)-as-action (*gongfu*/effort). His ontology of a good nature ultimately has no criterion of discrimination between good and evil other than effort. Nature itself, being entirely good, is not divisible.

Huang Daozhou expresses a view that is close to Chen Que's with regard to the question of why people differ despite their commonly good nature. Huang's starting point, as with Chen's, is Confucius's statement that people's "nature is alike," and if "in the end, there are indeed those who are intelligent and those who are dull, it is all a matter of practice (*xi*). How can it be a matter of nature?"[126] Since evil comes not from nature but is the result of the failure to develop nature, Huang, like Chen, rejects the Song Confucians' consignment of evil to a secondary material nature. There is only one *xing*, and it is undeniably good. However, Huang parts ways with Chen when he claims that material disposition is not nature. Chen, as we have just seen, dismantles the Song dualism by elevating material nature to be on a par with moral nature. In fact, the goodness of *xing* is manifested in material nature. What Huang does is to relegate and isolate material disposition (*qizhi*) so that it is no longer a part of nature at all. He seems to adopt a strategy similar to Gu Xiancheng's, although he is explicit and direct in attacking the Song dualistic scheme, whereas Gu launches no such criticism. Huang faults Zhu Xi for including material disposition in his elucidation of *xing*, yielding an inconsistent "dual nature" (*erxing*): on the one hand, Zhu argues that "nature cannot be separated from material disposition"; on the other, he maintains that nature "is not mixed up with material disposition."[127] Huang rejects the former argument and praises the latter. He explains material disposition vis-à-vis nature as follows:

> Materiality can be pure or turbid, and disposition can be smart or dull. There is material disposition which has nothing whatsoever to do with the matter of nature. For instance, the bursting of heat is the nature of fire. Its brightness is its material force which, when directed at wood, will make it dim or bright, blue or red, dry or damp. It is disposition. How is it nature? The moistening spread of water is the nature of water. Its flow is its material force which, when directed toward soil, will make it light or heavy, fertile or muddy, sweet or bitter. It is disposition. How is it nature?[128]

Huang concludes that the ancient sages truly know what *xing* is, whereas the Song Confucians confuse material disposition with nature.[129]

It is no accident that Huang refuses to use the *Classic of Documents*'s notions of "mind-heart of humanity" (*renxin*) and "mind-heart of the Way" (*daoxin*) to respectively represent material nature and moral nature. To him, the classic's notions refer to two modes or ways (*dao*) of cultivation, and not two natures. Since the mind-heart of the Way is subtle, "the difficulty lies in constantly thinking about it and promoting it." There is thus the need "to nurture and preserve its subtlety so that it naturally gets to the point where it is profoundly magnificent on its own." On the other hand, the mind-heart of humanity, being prone to error, demands "steadfast cultivation to gradually reach enlightenment as a result of sincerity, when the danger of committing errors is squelched." These two modes of cultivation in no way refer to two diffferent "natures that produce principle or desire, good or evil."[130] Huang Daozhou's refusal to accept evil as rooted in nature stems from his conviction that practice and action ultimately define our being.

Metaphysics and the Ming–Qing Intellectual Transition

A generation of literati from the late sixteenth century on reformulated views of human nature. But this preoccupation with human nature was no disinterested and pedantic pursuit of metaphysical insight. Many saw the key to combating the futility of jejune and abstract introspection in the redefinition of just what constituted human nature. They sought to establish the ontological basis for individual moral and social activism. Hence, the perspective of fundamental reality would now focus on the vital manifestation of human action in the experiential world. Ultimate reality was ipso facto the reality of lived experience. The scholars underscored the fact that everything which in any sense partook in reality appeared within the individual. By affirming an individual's nature as the universal ultimate predicate, they established the unalienable presupposition and inexorable demand that every domain of reality—moral, emotive, cognitive, sensory—must involve direct individual action. Human nature was not some mysterious faculty that could, in a self-referential way, award itself the prize in every competition. It demanded verification in lived experiences: engagement with oneself through ceaseless self-cultivation, association of one's pursuits with other individuals in the web of social relationships, and confrontation with affairs of the state and the world. Individuals must actively desolitudinize themselves, as it were, and reenact ultimate reality in purposive actions. Thus, Qian Mu concluded that such philosophical endeavor, most notably exemplified by the Donglin scholars, was in actuality "solid learning" whose ultimate goal was "actual practice." He suggested that early Qing learning originated in this enterprise of solid learning with its practical import.[131] Indeed, the thinkers we examined thought of themselves as participating in the life of society, and of their philosophical cogitations as possessing a social context.

While it may be true that the early Qing intellectual world displayed some revulsion against the Song–Ming tradition of moral speculative philosophy, a tradition that came to be known generically as Song learning, it should also be noted that the formation of the so-called Qing learning, which became increasingly oriented toward the solid and concrete, such as the study of institutions, history, government, and classical texts, did involve some rather intense debates in the domain of metaphysics in the late sixteenth century, when there was the internal reformulation and reconception of human nature. The reconceived metaphysics of human nature might well have served as the meta-practical point of departure for Qing learning. As we shall see, Song learning in the early Qing, as represented by Li Guangdi, also evaded the allure of abstruse introspection and issued clarion calls for concrete practice and solid effort.[132] Therefore, no master story can be fully told about the dynamics of the Ming–Qing intellectual transition without acknowledging and understanding its metaphysical dimensions, in particular, the views on human nature.

TWO

The Life of a Scholar-Official

> Everyone who has the power to live according to his own choice . . . should set up for himself some object for the good life to aim at . . . by reference to which he will do all that he does, since not to have one's life organized in view of some end is a sign of great folly.
>
> —Aristotle, *Eudemian Ethics*

Li Guangdi was born on September 29, 1642, into a middling literati family of modest means in the province of Fujian. His father, Li Zhaoqing, was a *zhusheng* (a first-degree graduate) of the Ming civil service examinations. As a fervent upholder of the orthodox Confucian learning (*zhengxue*) promoted by the court, the elder Li made a point to teach in his household the proper rites, rituals, and moral prescriptions. Guangdi was a precocious child of considerable native intelligence. It was said that once, at the age of four, before receiving any formal instruction, he saw the two characters of *zhong* (loyalty) and *yi* (rightness) on the gate of a temple, and he proceeded to copy and write them out on the ground with a piece of charcoal. Guangdi began schooling at the age of five and quickly excelled in his studies. In his very first recitation, he surprised his tutor by missing not one word. When he was seven, he went to study at his maternal grandparents' house and learned from his grandfather the composition of poetry, which he supposedly mastered in one day. At that early age, Guangdi already comported himself in a mature fashion, behaving with the dignified deliberation and decorous gravity of an adult.[1] Such recording and celebration of the intellectual precocity of renowned scholars ubiquitously appears in many of the traditional Chinese biographical portrayals. Yet we need not readily discount it as the stuff of legend and mythmaking. Guangdi's prolific scholarly output throughout his life apparently bespeaks his endowed talents, which were duly complemented by his assiduity.

Although his family had been an established literati household with some means, its fortune declined precipitously in the waning years of the Ming dynasty when China was engulfed in turmoil. In the early years of the Qing, the new regime had yet to fully pacify and subjugate many parts of the central and southern coasts. Not only were these areas targets of attack by the Ming loyalists, but they also suffered from banditry. Guangdi's family in Fujian was not spared the ravages of his time. They fell victim to the lawlessness of the day. In fact, at the age of fourteen, in 1655, he and eleven members of his family were kidnapped by bandits and held for ransom. Freedom did not come until a year later, when one of his uncles orchestrated a successful rescue.[2]

This tumultuous episode in his early life seemed to have goaded him into diligent learning, for in its aftermath, he showed nothing but unrelenting commitment to hard work. By the age of sixteen, he was already an accomplished writer of prose. When he was eighteen, Guangdi declared his allegiance to Cheng-Zhu learning. His choice might have been influenced by his father's devotion to the Song masters' teachings. The elder Li, despite his poverty, spared no expenses when it came to purchasing the books he admired. Guangdi, in particular, immersed himself in the questions of *xing* (nature) and *li* (principle), selecting and copying thousands of passages and words from pertinent writings on these problems, which he would faithfully memorize and deeply ponder. Moreover, he pledged himself to living the life of a true follower of the moral way, taking care with his attire and watching his every word and every movement, hoping that his own living would meet the requirements of the learning of the Way (*daoxue*). In the same year that he confirmed his moral calling, he also got married.[3]

Two years later, in 1661, he attained his first examination degree, having also written an exegetical work on the *Four Books* and another one on the *Classic of Changes*. His studies also expanded in scope and range, as Guangdi developed interests in, and began to write about, sundry subjects such as divination, calendar, and music. In 1666, he obtained the second examination degree of *juren*. At the age of twenty-nine in 1670, he became a *jinshi* and was chosen as a bachelor in the Hanlin Academy. One of his assignments was to learn the Manchu language. That he was chosen for the language acquisition might have something to do with his burgeoning interests in phonetics and linguistics after reading Gu Yanwu's writings on these topics. Two years later, he was promoted to be a compiler in the Academy. In spring of the ensuing year (1673), he served concurrently as an examination official in the metropolitan examination. In summer, he secured a leave to return home to visit his family.[4]

Just as Guangdi's professional career as a scholar-official was moving smoothly in the right direction, larger political events beyond his control took an unexpected turn and threatened to thwart his progress. In 1673, the Rebellion of the Three Feudatories was about to erupt. The three regional satraps—Wu Sanguei in Yunnan and Gueizhou, Shang Kexi in Guangdong, and Geng Jingzhong in Fujian—had been enfeoffed by the Shunzhi emperor (1644–1661), largely because their assistance had been crucial to the Qing's efforts to stamp out the remnants of the anti-Qing movements and to counter the threat of the Ming loyalist forces. The causes of the outbreak of this rebellion, which was to last eight years, at one time engulfing almost the whole of South China, need not concern us here. Suffice it to say that when the Kangxi emperor moved to curb their power and divest them of their hereditary privileges and princedoms, instead of accepting the imperial fiat, the feudatories chose to rebel.[5]

When Guangdi returned home in 1673, it became quite evident to him that Geng Jingzhong, the feudatory who controlled Fujian, was harboring antidynastic designs. He in fact sent a letter to the newly arrived governor-general there, urging him to mobilize and reposition his troops to leave Fuzhou, the provincial capital city, the stronghold of Geng. The troops should instead be stationed at the strategically located town of Yanping, north of Fuzhou. In so doing, the imperial troops would not only discourage Geng's northward movement, but also stay out of reach of Geng's direct grasp, should Geng spring into insurrectionary action. The governor-general vacillated and never did make any decisive move to guard against the probable eventuality. Reportedly, he told Guangdi that he was prepared to live and die with the city, and die he did when Geng launched his rebellion in the following year (1674).[6]

Geng's goal was to rally the literati and the talents in the region to his cause. Upon hearing that Guangdi had returned home, he summoned him for an interview at the provincial capital city of Fuzhou. Guangdi and his family were well aware of the perils of this trip. They therefore hatched the plan that within three days of Guangdi's arrival in Fuzhou, the family would send a letter reporting severe illness on the part of Guangdi's father, so that he might immediately ask for permission to return home. The plan worked and he was able to leave and thus escape being drafted into Geng's service.[7]

Yet the urgent question remained for literati such as Guangdi: How should they handle Geng's insurrection in their home province, and what should they do to protect themselves? Guangdi and his good friend Chen Menglei (b. 1651, *jinshi* 1670),[8] a fellow Fujian native who had also returned home from his post in the Hanlin Academy, decided to collaborate in order to ensure their well-being during and after the rebellion. Since Chen's home was in Fuzhou, he had little choice but to enter the service of Geng. Moreover, Chen's parents were both in their seventies, and he did not want to endanger his family as a result of any demonstrated recalcitrance toward Geng. It should be noted that Chen later claimed that with the pretext of illness, he actually eschewed participation in Geng's regime. In any event, it was decided that Chen, being in Fuzhou, would be on Geng's side, while Guangdi would go with the dynasty. Chen would supply information on the rebels to Guangdi for transmission to the Qing court. With the two friends on opposite camps, regardless of whether it was the Manchus or Geng who would emerge victorious, one of them would be in a position to help the other eventually. Chen could speak in support of Guangdi in the event of Geng's triumph, and Guangdi would dispense the favor if the insurrection was squelched. In the meantime, Guangdi and his parents withdrew to the mountains of southern Fujian in order to take refuge from the uprising.[9] Even though he was in a sort of self-imposed exile, thrice he was approached by the emissary of Zheng Jing (d. 1681), the eldest son of the famous Ming loyalist, Zheng Chenggong (1624–1662), who had established a stronghold in Taiwan. Zheng Jing, now an ally of Geng, sought Guangdi's service and tried to convince him that the Ming dynasty should be revived, but he adamantly refused, threatening suicide if pressed further.[10]

In 1675, Guangdi sent a secret memorial to the Kangxi emperor, placed inside a wax ball and dispatched by a trusted retainer.[11] The memorial offered a tactical plan of attack on the rebels in the Fujian area. Unfortunately, it did not reach the emperor until months later, through a Fujian native who was then serving as a grand secretary in the *neige* (Grand Secretariat). Guangdi urged the court to seek control over three key strategic points, and the best way to pierce through to the heart of the defensive weakness of the rebels was to launch a quick strike on the Dingzhou prefecture which, according to Guangdi, was undergarrisoned. Upon receiving the memorial, the emperor commended Guangdi as a genuinely loyal official. He turned the document over to the Board of War and ordered the officials in charge of the campaigns to study the feasibility of the memorial's suggested stratagem. But the lapse of time had dated Guangdi's information and recommendations, which were therefore never implemented. In any case, Geng was soon to be subjugated. Toward the end of 1676, Geng surrendered. Although Guangdi did not play any direct role in the quelling of the rebellion in Fujian, he greatly impressed the Kangxi emperor with his loyalty and was rewarded with promotion to a readership in the Hanlin Academy.[12]

Ostensibly, Guangdi emerged from the crisis of rebellion not only unscathed but in fact rewarded with a career boost in the officialdom, acknowledged by the emperor himself to be a loyal official of the Qing court. But the imbroglio of his involvement and activities in this entire affair would afford the opportunities and occasions for some contemporary Confucians and later critics to impugn his character, specifically on the matter of friendship. A perpetual shadow of doubt would be cast over his behavior toward his friend Chen Menglei, which some alleged to be less than honorable. As it happened, after Geng Jingzhong's rebellion had crumbled, Chen, who had been in the loser's camp, appealed to Guangdi, who was now in Fuzhou, for help. According to Chen's account, Guangdi would inform the emperor that the "wax ball memorial" had been coauthored by the two of them, and that Chen had also intended to help the Qing subdue the rebels. The fact that Chen's name was not included in the memorial was deliberate, a way to guarantee his safety. Their concern was that if the memorial was discovered by the rebels, Chen would be in great jeopardy, since he was in rebel territory. In 1677, the two friends were about to depart for the capital, but news came that Guangdi's father had passed away, and so Guangdi had to return home to observe a period of mourning.[13]

In the absence of Guangdi, Chen went to Beijing in 1678 and found himself accused by former rebels that he had indeed joined the renegade government. He returned to Fujian in an effort to gather evidence and proof of his innocence, but to no avail. In 1680, he was formally charged with treason as an aide to Geng's turncoat court. In despite of his proclamation of innocence, together with Geng Jingzhong and his cohorts, he was sentenced to death. Yet two years later, when Geng and others were executed, Chen received a reprieve. His death sentence was commuted to enslavement and exile to Manchuria, where Chen stayed until 1698.[14] This lifesaving reduction in punishment probably owed much to Guangdi's intercession in the form of a private memorial to the emperor pleading for leniency. Guangdi's petition stated clearly that his friend, owing to the old age of his parents, could not flee from Fuzhou, and was therefore forced to remain with the rebels' camp. Guangdi further argued that when Chen was held by the rebels, he refrained from service with the excuse of illness. Chen's intent, Guangdi asserted, was to work to overthrow the insurgency.[15] Guangdi's intervention might have saved his life, but Chen never did forgive Guangdi for failing to come fully to his aid by, for instance, pronouncing the coauthorship of the "wax ball memorial." In exile, Chen publicized his severance of friendship with his old friend, accusing him of perfidy. In 1705, this lifelong grudge surfaced again when Chen attempted once more to publicly redress his case by memorializing his side of the story to the emperor. Chen by now had been fully rehabilitated and was serving in the court as the secretary and teacher of the third son of the emperor. But the officials in charge did not transmit this memorial to the throne and Chen's plan did not come to fruition.[16]

It is difficult to ascertain what precisely occurred. Much of this episode of supposed betrayal of friendship is based on the various accusatory essays and the 1705 memorial that Chen penned.[17] A version of Guangdi's side of the story can be found in the *Rongcun pulu hekao* (An Investigation into the Events Recorded in Guangdi's *Biographical Annals* and *Recorded Sayings*), compiled by one of his grandsons, Li Qingfu, whose objectivity can of course be questioned.[18] What is clear, however, from the narratives of the two sides is that when the circumstances of the day dictated their parting of ways, Guangdi and Chen did pledge to help each other in the future. It was also possible that Chen might have supplied some information to Guangdi. But by the time Guangdi wrote the "wax ball memorial," the two had been separated for almost a year, with Chen in Fuzhou, the stronghold of the rebels, and Guangdi in the hilly area of the Quanzhou region. It was most unlikely that Chen could have been a coauthor in any substantive fashion at all. Moreover, apart from Chen's words, there is no evidence that Guangdi had agreed to say that both of them wrote the memorial. On the other hand, it is a fact that Guangdi did intercede on Chen's behalf and implored the emperor for clemency. He did ultimately fulfill his part of the bargain. It does not seem fair to castigate him for breach of his friend's faith. Given what we can determine from available sources, the foul hint of ignoble act that would haunt and follow Guangdi for the rest of his life should be attributed to the personal jealousy and animosity engendered by court politics. As we shall see, his political enemies' effort to discredit Guangdi probably contributed much to perpetuating the charge of Guangdi's treachery and unscrupulous pursuit of personal advancement at the expense of a friend.

In 1677, in the wake of the suppression of Geng's rebellion, as we recall, Guangdi secured a promotion but suffered the loss of his father. He thereupon returned home to observe mourning, but the situation in the Fujian province and the surrounding areas was far from peaceful. Zheng Jing and his "white-head army," so called because the soldiers wrapped their heads in white turbans, continued to harass the region. In 1678, a branch of the rebel forces actually threatened Guangdi's home district, Anxi. As an official in mourning at home, Guangdi helped organized the defense by conscripting soldiers and setting up garrisons. He issued warnings to the various nearby village communities that under no circumstance should they supply any provisions to the rebels. Otherwise they would be regarded as bandits themselves and face prompt punitive attacks. He also encouraged defection and surrender by granting amnesties. Having relieved his own district from rebel threat, he further instructed and dispatched his various relatives to provide guidance to the Qing forces in pursuit of the rebels in the area surrounding the city of Quanzhou in southern Fujian. He also raised and arranged provisions and victuals for the government troops. With the various members of the Li family serving as effective pathfinders for the imperial troops, using little known routes, the Qing contingents arrived expeditiously at Quanzhou, quickly driving the rebels back to Taiwan and pacifying southern Fujian. The Manchu general in charge of the expeditionary force memorialized the throne and commended Guangdi's contributions to the successful campaign. Later that year, as a reward, Guangdi was made a subchancellor of the Grand Secretariat. In 1680, after the mourning period for his deceased father had been completed, he and his mother went to Beijing, where he assumed his new position.[19]

By this time, the Rebellion of the Three Feudatories was already in its final stages. The forces of two feudatories had been vanquished. The remaining one was gasping its last breaths. At the beginning of 1681, the emperor assembled the court officials to deliberate on the situation in the south, including Taiwan, which was under Zheng Jing's control. Guangdi expressed the view that the Qing forces should move to recover the island now. Thus, the Kangxi emperor, upon the advice of Guangdi and some of his officials, decided to launch a campaign against Taiwan, particularly since news also came that Zheng Jing had died early in the year. But there was no consensus among the officials. Some doubted the wisdom of a campaign against Taiwan. In face of divided opinions, the emperor sought counsel from some of his trusted officials. Guangdi, in the middle of the year, was consulted by the emperor. On this occasion, he strongly advanced the idea of using force on Taiwan, saying in rather prophetic terms that the Zheng family, having been antidynastic bandits for some sixty years, had exhausted its fortune and that its imminent destruction was sealed. To undertake the task of the final subjugation of Taiwan, Guangdi recommended the appointment of Shi Lang (1621–1696).[20] Shi had been a supporter of the Zheng family, but defected to the Qing in 1646. Versed in naval tactics and familiar with the Zheng forces, he would indeed be the appropriate person to lead the expedition. In fact, already in 1668, Shi had submitted a plan to retake Taiwan but it was not acted upon. It would be a task that Shi finally accomplished in 1683.[21]

Guangdi not only recommended Shi's initial appointment, but also supported his strategies, several times convincing the emperor not to cast doubt on the soundness of Shi's plans and designs.[22] In June 1682, Guangdi requested leave to take his mother back home to Fujian because she had been having difficulty acclimating to the weather and foods of the north. At first, the emperor was reluctant to let one of his trusted officials go, but he was persuaded by the argument presented by some of Guangdi's friends that Shi Lang, based in Fujian and poised to attack Taiwan, would benefit from the informal participation of Guangdi on the scene. Therefore, back home, Guangdi continued to be in an indirect way involved in the Taiwan campaign and with Shi Lang who, on one occasion, actually divulged in detail his strategy to Guangdi.[23]

Guangdi remained at home for four years, during which time he immersed himself in scholarship and writing, having already completed a pivotal work the year before he returned home, the *Zun Zhu yaozhi* (Principal Purpose of Honoring Zhu [Xi]), a homage and declaration of his allegiance to the Cheng-Zhu school of Confucian teachings. He built a study for himself, calling it the "Banian Village House of Study" (Rongcun shuwu), so named because of the several sizable Banian trees that shaded the premises and the surrounding area. Thus he also came to be known as Mr. Rongcun in the community of literati. Moreover, as a leader of his lineage, he reorganized the ancestral rituals, a project which prompted him to write a good deal on rites and music, as we shall see.[24]

In 1686, he returned to the court and was received by the emperor in several audiences, during which he discussed the classics and state policies, particularly with regard to the question of Taiwan. Since the pacification of Taiwan in 1683–1684, the court had yet to make a decision about what to do with the island. Guangdi was at first of the opinion that no direct permanent administration and military presence need be established. Owing to its geographic isolation and the lack of knowledge of the territory on the part of the Qing, direct rule would be both expensive and dangerous. Lives of the mainland soldiers and officials might be at risk, or at least they would suffer hardship, if they were sent across the strait and stationed there. It would be economically profitable and strategically prudent to simply accept tributes and land rents from the natives or even the Dutch in Taiwan. But as the Kangxi emperor favored the posting of garrisons and erection of administrative apparati, Guangdi changed his view and offered his ideas on the incorporation of Taiwan into the larger bureaucratic fold of China.[25] Trusted by the emperor as a loyal and able official, Guangdi enjoyed yet another promotion that same year when he returned to the capital. He was made chancellor of the Hanlin Academy with a concurrent position in the Board of Rites. In addition, he was appointed as one of the officials responsible for the emperor's education, participating in both of the formal tutorial programs for the ruler: the *jingyan* (the Lecture on the Classics) and *rijiang* (the Daily Tutoring).[26]

His rapid rise up the ladder of officialdom elicited jealousy from some of his colleagues. In the years subsequent to the suppression of the Rebellion of the Three Feudatories, court politics was much intertwined with factionalism that pitted the "northern party" led by Mingju (1635–1708) against the "southern party" headed by Xu Qianxue (1631–1694), who had earlier been allied with the former. Both were powerful officials. Mingju gained great political power and prominence during the rebellion years, when he gained the confidence of the emperor, who consequently relied much on his views and leadership.[27] Xu was an erudite scholar in charge of the compilation of the dynastic *History of Ming* (Ming shih) and was successively appointed to a series of high-ranking positions in the 1680s, such as subchancellorship in 1685, vice presidency of the Board of Rites in 1686, presidency of the Censorate in 1687, and presidency of the Board of Punishments in 1688.[28] Many officials attached themselves to one or the other clique. The extent to which Guangdi was embroiled in this confused heap of intrigue is not clear, although he was generally regarded as one associated with the Mingju group. In any case, in 1687, he asked for leave, having been in court only a year following the four-year hiatus in Fujian.

His *Biographical Annals* refers to his wish to avoid the fractious court life and being the target of jealousy. One of the jealous officials was none other than Xu Qianxue, the leader of the southern party.[29] Xu and Guangdi obtained the *jinshi* degree in the same year, but Xu earned the high distinction of being the *tanhua* (the third highest ranked metropolitan graduate). They had similar career paths, serving in the Hanlin Academy, the Grand Secretariat, and the Board of Rites. But Guangdi's promotion was more rapid; for instance, he assumed the subchancellorship of the Grand Secretariat in 1680, a position which Xu gained five years later. Moreover, Guangdi seemed much closer to the center of power by virtue of his appointment as a lecturer and tutor to the emperor. In particular, Xu coveted the chancellorship of the Hanlin Academy, which Guangdi now occupied. Xu, envious of Guangdi and eager to undermine his reputation, had much to do with encouraging Chen Menglei to air his grievances against Guangdi for his alleged betrayal of friendship. By the way, Chen was a *tongnian* (graduate in the same year) of both Guangdi and Xu. It is reasonable to assume that the whole incident of the "wax ball memorial" could not have escalated to the point it did had Xu not played an active role in fueling the flames in an effort to besmirch Guangdi's character.[30]

Against this background, it made sense that in 1687 Guangdi again asked for permission to return home. He talked, without naming names, about one incident, which clinched the decision for him. There was a certain administration commissioner (*buzheng shi*) with a bad reputation. Nonetheless, an official of power and authority asked Guangdi to recommend this corrupt commissioner to the court. Guangdi refused, but regretted having to face the potential political fallout. He therefore memorialized the court, asking for retirement from office in order to care for his aging mother. The court refused, only granting him a leave of one year and urging him to return as soon as he could, since his position at the Hanlin Academy would not be replaced. This imperial decision did not please Xu Qianxue at all, for the chancellorship would remain Guangdi's even though he would be on leave.[31] Xu would continue his treachery against Guangdi.

Before Guangdi was to return home in 1687, out of courtesy, he bade farewell to his colleagues, including Xu. He expressed to Xu his wish that he really preferred retirement in order to take care of his mother. But the court only permitted a year's leave and so he was at a loss as to what he should do. Xu told him that he could always ask for retirement later. Xu also promised that should he decide to ask for permission to retire, Xu would offer help, and he asked Guangdi to first send the memorial to him to ensure the language was appropriate when it came time for the submission of the request. Needless to say, Xu did not offer his assistance out of the goodness of his heart. Rather, Xu's plan was to discredit Guangdi while he was gone, by spreading the rumor that the latter no longer wanted to serve the court and was more interested in building power and prominence in his locality. When and if Guangdi did made the proposal to retire, Xu could then use that as incontrovertible evidence of Guangdi's intent to desert his official duties.

As it happened, Guangdi, after returning home, did decide to ask for retirement. But to play it safe, he composed two memorials, one asking for retirement and another simply requesting extension of his leave. He entrusted one of his brothers, who was going to be in the capital for the metropolitan examination, to carry the two memorials to Beijing. He was to consult with Xu, who had promised Guangdi help in presenting his case. When Guangdi's brother arrived, Xu was visibly most pleased, gloating over the imminent success of his conspiracy. Xu immediately suggested to the brother that the request for retirement be submitted. He also recommended the revision of some words. The brother was suspicious and left, using the excuse that he had to help his travel companion get settled. When he and his companion met fellow Fujianese officials, they found out from them that Xu and his minions had been blackening

Guangdi's name, saying that he took constant leaves not because of his concern for his family but because he saw himself as too important and elevated to serve the emperor; he was actually building power at his local base and biding his time. Sooner or later, he would ask for retirement. If Guangdi had submitted the request for retirement, it would have lent much credence to the ugly rumors about him. Fortunately for Guangdi, his brother, having discovered Xu's plot and recognizing the gravity of the situation, concealed himself, stayed out of reach of Xu, and promptly submitted to the commissioner of the Transmission Office (*tongzheng shi*) the request for extending his leave on grounds of his mother's ill health. Xu, not knowing that such request had been submitted, at one meeting in the court, advertised that Guangdi was to retire, just as he had been predicting. The commissioner, who was present, surprised him by announcing that there was no plea for retirement from Guangdi but rather that it was a request for extension of leave. Xu was totally taken aback and was reportedly livid.[32]

The following year (1688), because of the death of the empress, Guangdi rushed to return to Beijing to observe mourning. Xu Qianxue again attempted to sabotage him. On his way from Anxi to Fuzhou, Guangdi received two letters from Xu assuring him that he need not hurry back. He also wrote the governor of Fujian, asking him to delay Guangdi. The goal was to eventually reprimand him for tardiness in front of the emperor. But this Fujian official was friendly to Guangdi and duly warned him of Xu's machination. Failing this ploy, Xu seized on yet another opportunity to castigate Guangdi. It so happened that in 1687, before Guangdi returned home, he had had an audience with the emperor and highly recommended an official who unfortunately turned out not to be quite as competent in scholarship as Guangdi had suggested. Under pressure from Xu and his faction, the official was convicted of dereliction. Guangdi, as the referee of the fallen official, was thus drawn into trouble. He was accused by Xu and others for colluding with the disgraced, since the convicted had praised Guangdi's ability and touted that he could serve well as the governor-general of Fujian. After all, Guangdi did want to be back in his home province and had asked for leave. Such mutual recommendation smacked of collusion on the part of the two officials for their respective private gains.

But once again, Xu's plan was foiled. After the various officials had interrogated Guangdi, the emperor was satisfied that Guangdi's recommendation of the convicted official was an exception, a one-time lapse in judgment. The emperor proceeded to remind Guangdi's accusers of his contributions to the plan for the pacification of Taiwan. He therefore simply censured Guangdi without inflicting any further punishment. However, he made a point to admonish Guangdi to plan no future leaves and to focus on his job in the capital as the chancellor of the Hanlin Academy.[33] Thus, the Kangxi emperor spared Guangdi any official penalty and he appeared to emerge from this episode unharmed. But the fact was that the entire incident did shake royal confidence in him. Apparently, Guangdi himself realized that his enemies' relentless assault on his motives and character had weakened his standing in the eyes of the monarch.[34] As we shall see, this mitigation of the emperor's trust in Guangdi would result in yet another circumstance, as with the case of the "wax ball memorial," which would contribute to the long-lasting detriment of Guangdi's reputation. It should be mentioned here that Xu himself soon ran into trouble. First, it was revealed that he took bribes. Then one of his sons was found to have obtained his *jinshi* by fraud. Consequently, in 1690, he had to retire from the capital to return home. A year later, he was stripped of his official rank and honors because of continued acts of malfeasance and oppression of the people in his hometown.[35]

In 1689, Guangdi was made a commissioner of the Transmission Office, and a few months later, in early 1690, he became the junior vice president of the Board of War. These positions were of a lower rank than the chancellorship of the Hanlin Academy. In other words, Guangdi was demoted, albeit only slightly, from rank 2B to 3A. The cause of his demotion is difficult to ascertain. It might well be related to the domination of the court at the time by Yu Chenglong (1638–1700).[36] Guangdi does tell us that when Yu was the governor of Zhili, he rose to great prominence in the court, so much so that many ingratiating officials flocked to him. Guangdi and several others, however, while being respectful to Yu, did not become his cohorts. Moreover, Guangdi was particularly opposed to Yu's policy of using the sale of ranks as a principal means of raising revenue. Reportedly, Yu rather sardonically said to the emperor that his policy was well received by most, except those who pursued "the learning of the Way" (*daoxue*), referring to punctilious scholars such as Guangdi who, obdurately tied to their pedantic understanding of the Confucian Way, adopted the posture of the vigilant cock.[37] Yu's influence might therefore have contributed to the reassignment of Guangdi to positions of lower ranks.

Guangdi wrote a letter to his brothers after he had been made a commissioner of the office of transmission. In a rather melancholy tone, he informed them that since being transferred, work and responsibility had been light and simple. But the jealous ones had also retreated somewhat. Then he waxed dolefully philosophic, lamenting that one's future career and the will of heaven were hard to divine. He admonished his brothers that they must remain vigilant and prudent, be fearful of all violations, and be content with their humble station. This letter amply captured and reflected the weariness with which Guangdi was understandably saddled, after all those recent baleful events that could easily have wrecked his life.[38]

This jeremiad, however, was by no means a declaration of Guangdi's cynicism. He remained committed to his sense of integrity and responsibility. In 1691, the censor, Lu Longqi (1630–1693), who had gained his position the previous year largely because of Guangdi's recommendation, memorialized the court, vehemently protesting the use of the sale of government positions as the major avenue through which funds were raised to finance the military campaign in Mongolia. He was particularly incensed by the new practice that those who contributed more than the officially set amount would have priority in appointment, overtaking other legitimate potential appointees. Lu's memorial was rejected, but he persisted and submitted another memorial, which employed even stronger invective, thereby bringing upon himself the wrath of the officials and the court. He was accused of recklessly questioning official policies. Since his action amounted to wanton obstruction of the smooth conduct of the military campaign, Lu was condemned to exile. Since Guangdi was Lu's referee, he was implicated and drawn into the incident. Guangdi pleaded his friend's case in front of the emperor. Instead of distancing himself from the accused, he courageously defended his friend: "When Lu fails to understand what is correct in handling affairs, I will surely point that out. But if his words prove the innocence and integrity of his own self, then I dare not have anything different to say."[39] Lu gained the imperial pardon as a result.[40]

It would not be the last time that Guangdi stepped forward to defend a fellow scholar in distress. It is appropriate here to jump ahead in our chronologically ordered narrative to mention briefly the famous case of literary inquisition of 1711. In that year, Dai Mingshi (1653–1713) was accused of using, in a letter he wrote, the tabooed southern Ming reign-titles, which in the eyes of the Qing court, amounted to subversion of the Manchu dynasty's authority. This letter was included in a collection of essays which Dai entitled *Nanshan ji ou chao* (Occasional Jottings from the Southern Mountains), to which several scholars contributed prefaces, including the well-known ancient prose writer, Fang Bao (1668–1749). For Fang's involvement, the Board of Punishments recommended in 1713 that Fang, together with Dai and the others, be given the capital punishment.[41] It is reported that, thanks to Guangdi's praise of Fang's unsurpassed ability among his contemporaries in composing prose in the ancient style, the emperor decided on leniency. Fang was consequently imprisoned for a short while and then ordered to serve in the Imperial Study (Nan shufang) after his release; he was later transferred to the Imperial Studio in the emperor's country villa.[42] According to Fang's own description, when Guangdi made a point to extol his scholarly virtues, those who were present feared for his life, for after all, he was commending one charged with treason. Thus Fang gratefully remarked that Guangdi's intention could never be understood by the sycophantic.[43]

In 1694, Guangdi's mother passed away and so he immediately asked for the usual leave of three years to observe proper mourning. The Kangxi emperor rejected his request. Guangdi, who then held the concurrent posts of junior vice president of the Board of War and director of education of Zhili, was told that educational affairs were of the utmost importance and therefore the court could ill afford his absence. He was instructed to expediently avoid elaborate funerary observances and to mourn his mother's death while in office. The precise reasons for this imperial denial cannot be established for certain, but most likely, stemmed from the emperor's reprimand of Guangdi in 1688, after Guangdi had faced relentless assault on his motives in seeking leaves to return home. As suggested earlier, Guangdi's action did result in the mitigation of the emperor's trust in his loyalty. As we recall, even though Guangdi escaped direct punishment, the emperor ordered that he abandon further thoughts about taking leaves. Faced with this imperial rebuff and heartbroken by his mother's death, Guangdi sent a memorial to suggest an alternative plan. He begged for a nine-month leave instead. The censors promptly pounced on him. They memorialized the throne, decrying the aberrant request, notwithstanding the fact that Guangdi's move was precipitated in the first place by the emperor's refusal to grant him the normal three-year absence. Nonetheless, the censors focused on Guangdi's protocol-defying proposal of a nine-month leave and painted him as one who violated the rites and neglected his filial duties. The emperor, confronted with such protests issued in the name of Confucian rites and sense of obligation, thus allowed Guangdi the three-year mourning leave. But still, he would not be allowed to go home and would have to observe mourning in the capital.[44]

This episode again left an indelible black mark on Guangdi's name. In the case of the "wax ball memorial," he had been impugned for betraying a friend. Now, he was lambasted for doing violence to the sentiment and virtue of filiality, placing his official duty before his filial obligation. His reputation suffered considerably, even though his predicament was induced by the decree from above. In a court meeting held in response to the protests, the ruler chided one of the memorialists for implying that the throne did not know the proper mourning convention by lodging his complaint. Of course the throne knew, but the Kangxi emperor explained that he had his reasons for denying Guangdi's routine request for mourning leave.[45] As has been surmised, his decision in all probability had much to do with his weakened confidence in Guangdi's loyalty, hence his reluctance to let him return home. In any event, Guangdi, as a self-touted Cheng-Zhu partisan and known in court as a follower of the learning of the Way, would have to endure his contemporaries' second-guessing of his intentions and suffer their doubts about his moral integrity. In the eyes of some, he was a hypocrite, failing to do what he preached. Moreover, he suffered great mental and physical anguish because of his inability to return home to properly mourn his mother's death. His son wrote that Guangdi was afflicted with chronic stomachache due to sorrow and stress.[46] Perhaps to demonstrate his allegiance to the teachings of the *daoxue* masters, or perhaps to reinforce psychologically his convictions in the moral learning of the Way, during the period of mourning, he compiled and edited the writings of Zhu Xi and the Cheng brothers. His *Biographical Annals* also remark that by 1696, many of Guangdi's enemies and detractors had either been purged, been demoted, or were dead, thus affording him, the one who survived, a certain poetic justice.[47]

Toward the end of 1696, mourning was completed and Guangdi resumed his official positions. Indeed, with his foes gone, Guangdi's official career once again enjoyed a steady rise. In 1697, apart from holding his continuing position as director of education of Zhili, he was made the vice president of the Board of Works. Early in 1699, he became the governor of Zhili, concurrently occupying the presidency of the Board of Civil Service. In 1705, he was given the illustrious and important position of Grand Secretary, which he held for thirteen years until his death in 1718.[48]

During these two decades of service, Guangdi distinguished himself with various administrative and bureaucratic accomplishments, which will be examined in chapter six. It should be noted here that in the capacity as the Grand Secretary, Guangdi also played very active and pivotal roles in upholding and promoting what Wm. Theodore de Bary calls the "Mandarin orthodoxy" of Confucianism, the ideological and ethico-moral foundation of the Ming and Qing civil bureaucratic system.[49] In fact, de Bary credits Guangdi as the "most important figure in the formulation of the official orthodoxy of the Ch'ing."[50] He was, in the last twenty years of his life, a foremost official spokesperson for Cheng-Zhu Confucianism, the orthodoxy championed by the Kangxi emperor, responsible for heading the editing and compiling of the Cheng-Zhu canon. Under imperial aegis and with the editorial supervision of Guangdi, the *Complete Works of Master Zhu* (Zhuzi quanshu) in sixty-six fascicles was completed in 1714. Known particularly as an expert in the

Classic of Changes, Guangdi was given the task of annotating the classic, yielding the *Zhouyi zhezhong* (Balanced Annotations of the Classic of Changes) which was included in the *Siku quanshu* (Complete Works of the Four Literary Treasuries). Moreover, he was responsible for producing the synoptic text of *Xingli jingyi* (Essential Ideas of Nature and Principle), meant to be the encapsulation of the quintessential teachings and ideas of the Cheng-Zhu school.[51] Guangdi also authored many other writings on the classics and the like, in which he propounded his own coherent philosophy in the Cheng-Zhu vein.

Apart from some setbacks at different points in his life, Guangdi appeared on the whole to be a skillful navigator in the stormy seas of court politics. In the last years of his life, he regained the confidence of the Kangxi emperor and became a trusted imperial advisor. The emperor consulted with him, for instance, on the paramount issue of choosing his heir apparent. In 1708, one month after he had relieved Yinreng (1674–1725),[52] hitherto the designated heir, of his position, he asked Guangdi for his views on educating his potential successor.[53] The following year, when Yinreng's position was restored by the emperor, it was Guangdi who was chosen to write the imperial confirmation, and the prince was sent to him for instruction.[54] In 1712, when the emperor once again decided to strip Yinreng of his title, he summoned Guangdi to a private audience for advice.[55] Despite Guangdi's involvement in this major affair, which saw the various princes vying for power by forming cliques, with apparent adroitness, he succeeded in avoiding the power struggle and offending any of the competing imperial sons. When the Yongzheng emperor (r. 1723–1734) ascended the throne in 1723, he bestowed posthumously on him the title of Grand Preceptor of Heir Apparent, thereby acknowledging his educational role in the imperial household. Ten years later, Guangdi was inducted into the Temple of Eminent Statesmen.[56]

In 1715, Guangdi finally got his leave, which the emperor had for a long while been reluctant to grant. However, retirement was not to be; he was only given a two-year leave. Before departing, he was received warmly in Rehe by the emperor, who gave him a votive tablet with his own calligraphy and some poems as farewell gifts. Back home in Fujian, he reorganized the lineage rules, renovated his studio, and continued his writing. A year after he had returned to the capital to resume his position, he died after a brief illness, on June 26, 1718.[57] The Kangxi emperor, himself also an old man now, must have felt a sense of loss of his long-time official. In his commemorative edict, he said, "Only I knew him most thoroughly, and only he knew me the deepest."[58]

Judging from what Guangdi did in his life, he was by and large a capable scholar-official who dedicated himself to his responsibilities, within the confines and limits imposed by the throne. Throughout his career, he patronized and recommended many of his colleagues, saving some in distress from punishment and degradation by interceding on their behalf, such as in the cases of Lu Longqi and Fang Bao. Yet, he never managed to outlive the doubts cast on his character as a result of the case of the "wax ball memorial" and his petition for the nine-month mourning leave. He became a convenient target of the moralists with ulterior political motives. One of the reasons, clearly pointed out by Fang Bao, could be that Guangdi consciously sought to eschew factional affiliation. In his effort to stay aloof from sectarian strife, he lived a relatively secluded life, although he did not refrain from recommending and defending his friends if need be. But he did not open his house to entertaining and accommodating guests, and therefore did not actively build his own network of patronage and personal relations. Thus, it was easy for those jealous of his success to spread ruinous rumors about him.[59]

Among the assessments of Guangdi, the most damning was perhaps the one by the illustrated scholar, Quan Zuwang (1705–1755),[60] whose popularity in the later Qing means that his statements would be given weight, thereby contributing to the confirmation of Guangdi's questionable deeds in life. In other words, Quan's negative evaluation molded to a great extent the remembering of Guangdi who, as a historical personage, would thenceforth appear in the historical limelight with shadows cast on him. Quan's haughty disdain of Guangdi might have stemmed from Quan's identification with the Lu-Wang school. He might therefore not have been readily inclined to be charitable to an official promoter of the Cheng-Zhu orthodoxy such as Guangdi. Instead, he seized upon his alleged faults and flaws. A testimonial to Quan's partisanship in his estimation of Guangdi was his reference to Guangdi's criticism of the Ming scholar, Chen Xianzhang (1428–1500), who was regarded as affiliated with the Lu-Wang school. Quan claimed that Guangdi had no right to criticize the Ming scholar since Chen, in both scholarly and personal terms, was a person of greater accomplishments than Guangdi himself. Quan then went on to demolish Guangdi as a person and a scholar. To him, it would be a completely ignorant view to claim that Guangdi succeeded in continuing and promoting the received wisdom of Zhu Xi's teachings. Guangdi was accomplished only in the study of music, calendar, mathematics, and phonetics. The rest of his learning, according to Quan, was not worth mention. With respect to Guangdi as a person, Quan essentially defined his life in terms of the three putative transgressions at three stages of his life. When he was young, he betrayed his friend. In middle age, he did violence to his filial sentiment. In old age, he received into his family an illegitimate son by a mistress.[61] As pointed out above, the first two accusations were quite baseless, for these supposed moral-ethical infringements were very much the by-products of political jealousy and factional partisanship. Regarding the third, there appears to be no substantive historical evidence, save Quan's reference. Therefore, Quan seemed quite unfair in portraying Guangdi, the person, in such generalized terms and in such a deprecating light. As for Quan's estimation of Guangdi as a worthless scholar and thinker, the following chapters will speak volumes as its refutation.

THREE

General Theory

Metaphysics and Metapraxis

I do not think that the world or the sciences would have suggested to me any philosophical problems. What have suggested philosophical problems to me are things which other philosophers have said about the world or the sciences.

—G. E. Moore, *Principia Ethica*

When one looks at the development of Confucianism as a system of thought and learning, one may well recall Whitehead's proclamation that the entire Western philosophical tradition was "a series of footnotes to Plato." On the surface a radical statement, it may simply be construed as a rather sensible articulation of the understanding that ideas are continuous, that every system of learning, however novel in its intent, expression, and construction, must honor its conceptual debts to its predecessors. To examine any one thinker or philosophy of any one time is to in some inexorable way sense the cumulative effect of the entire intellectual tradition of a culture. Just as one considers the Western philosophical tradition to have stemmed from Plato, so too one can reasonably ascribe the same seminal role and significance to Confucius as the very fountainhead of the Chinese Confucian tradition. Such ascription would have elicited a hearty endorsement from a Cheng Yi or a Zhu Xi, who in turn became the acknowledged wellsprings from which supposedly gushed the authentic classical teachings of Confucius. To be sure, Cheng-Zhu learning in time met its challenges with the rise and consolidation of Lu-Wang learning. Nonetheless, however much Lu Xiangshan and Wang

Yangming might be at odds with Zhu Xi, and no matter how fierce the contestations might be between the two camps to represent orthodox Confucianism, much of Ming and Qing thought in late imperial times tapped the reservoir of usable principles and formulas propounded by Cheng-Zhu and Lu-Wang.[1]

It is, therefore, not unreasonable to suggest that most Ming and Qing thinkers were willing captives of the Cheng-Zhu and Lu-Wang metaphysical and philosophical past,[2] until the maturation of *kaozheng xue* (textual evidential learning) in the eighteenth century enabled scholars to carve out the narrowly restricted tradition of textual exegesis and pare it into a clear philological and evidentiary orientation in learning.[3] The question and the act of acknowledging debts of appropriation, of placing oneself within the continuity of an intellectual tradition, and correspondingly, of refuting false doctrines, became more acute when the early Qing court, especially beginning with the Kangxi reign, began to actively promote Cheng-Zhu learning as the orthodoxy. It was of paramount importance for scholars such as Li Guangdi, who proclaimed their devotion to such learning, to reinvigorate and reinvent the sense of its relevancy. Their first and foremost goal was to demonstrate their ancestral piety to Cheng-Zhu learning and argue why Zhu Xi was their ultimate hero and sage, the true mouthpiece of the ancient sages. In order to understand the development and content of Li Guangdi's thought, we must logically start with the very foundation and basics, namely, his affirmation of Zhu Xi's doctrines, or to put it another way, his writing of footnotes to the master's master narrative.

The Metaphysics of Principle (*Li*) and Material Force (*Qi*), and the Mediation of Nature (*Xing*)

A most helpful point of entry into Li Guangdi's thought can be located in a direct homage he paid to Zhu Xi, an essay he wrote in 1681, the "Zun-Zhu yaozhi" (Principal Purpose of Honoring Zhu [Xi]), when he was forty years old.[4] It is important, however, to note that while this work shows Guangdi's allegiance to Zhu Xi's *li*-based metaphysics and its various philosophical manifestations, and delimits the general perimeters within which Guangdi's own thought operates, Guangdi is no slavish follower of the master. On the one hand, in our effort to delineate the outline and ascertain the contents of Guangdi's philosophy, it is most helpful to employ his tributary essay to Zhu as the point of departure. For in writing this essay, Guangdi himself pinpointed the core issues and ideas that a devotee of the Cheng-Zhu persuasion should pursue, and in the process, created a usable past for himself. In an explicit fashion, he inherited and claimed the philosophical issues and positions that mattered the most to him. On the other hand, Guangdi had his own philosophical present. He reformulated Zhu's ideas, investing in them new meanings and emphases. In order to duly appreciate his innovation and rescue him from the condescension of faithful and uncritical partisanship, our inquiry into Guangdi's thought begins with his reaffirmation of the main elements of Zhu's philosophy in the 1681 essay, but continues with an examination of his other complementary writings, in which we find the construction of a general theory that is his own, the retention of the general Cheng-Zhu contours notwithstanding.

At the very outset of the 1681 essay, Guangdi renews Zhu's views on *li* (principle) and *qi* (material force), and asserts their fundamental soundness. His defense of Zhu means outright refutation of the most direct and dangerous criticisms against the master. In particular, Guangdi rejects the questioning of the *li-qi* ontology by Luo Qinshun (1465–1547). As a self-proclaimed Cheng-Zhu follower, Luo is nonetheless well known for his challenge to Chang Yi's and Zhu Xi's metaphysics. Luo criticized them for their apparent inability to resolve satisfactorily and convincingly the dualism of *li* and *qi*. Their systems, laden with tension between these two categories, fail to "finally achieve unity" (*ding yu yi*), as Luo complains:

> "Principle is one; its particularizations are diverse," comes from a statement made by Master Cheng in his discussion of the "Western Inscription" (Ximing). These words are extremely simple, and yet when they are extended to the principles of the universe, there is nothing that is not comprehended. . . . If one discusses the nature on the basis of this statement, there will naturally be no need to postulate a dichotomy between the endowment of heaven and the physical being—this is unmistakably clear. Yet Yichuan [that is, Cheng Yi] did use such terms. He also thought that capacity (*cai*) came from *qi*. Could it be that when he spoke of the diversity of particularizations he was referring only to *qi*? Master Zhu, in responding to a disciple's question concerning *li* and *qi*, praised these words of Yichuan's, though he finally came to regard *li* and *qi* as two things. This is precisely what I mean by suggesting that I doubt he finally achieved unity.[5]

Luo traces Zhu's dualistic conception to Zhou Dunyi's discourse on the Great Ultimate (*taiji*) in his "Explanation of the Diagram of the Great Ultimate" (Taiji tushuo). In this essay, Zhou avers, "When the reality of the

Infinite and the essence of yin, yang, and the Five Agents come into mysterious union, integration ensues." Luo takes issue with the metaphysical picture portrayed here:

> I can only be skeptical when it comes to . . . [this] statement. . . . Things must be two before they can be said to come into union. Are the Great Ultimate, and yin and yang really two things? If they are really two things, where was each prior to their integration? Throughout his life Master Zhu regarded *li* and *qi* as two things, and this was the source of his idea.[6]

To rectify this inconsistency, he instead argues that *qi* is the whole of reality; *li* is merely the "name" (*designation*) to describe the phenomenal and physical workings of *qi* that constitute the universe:

> That which penetrates heaven and earth, and connects past and present is nothing other than material force (*qi*), which is unitary. This material force, while originally one, revolves through endless cycles of movement and tranquillity, going and coming, opening and closing, rising and falling. . . . It produces the warm, the cool, the cold and the hot of the four seasons; the birth, the growth, the assembling and storing of all living things; the constant moral relations of the people's daily life; and the victory, defeat, gain and loss in human affairs. And amid all of this prolific variety and phenomenal diversity there is a detailed order and an elaborate coherence that cannot ultimately be disturbed, and which is so even without our knowing why it is so. This is what is called principle. Principle is not a separate entity which depends on material force in order to exist or which "attaches to material force in order to operate."[7]

Li Guangdi castigates Luo for "failing to understand principle." Luo not only falls outside the pale of Cheng-Zhu learning, but he comes close to being squarely within Wang Yangming's camp:

> Mr. Luo regards his learning as the essence of the Song masters, different from that of Yaojiang [that is, Wang Yangming]. But if he fails to understand principle in the case of Master Zhu, can the rest of his learning be accepted? And if he is mistaken about Lianqi's [that is, Zhou Dunyi's] Non-Ultimate (*wuji*), how good can the rest of his learning be? Although pursuing the Song masters' learning, [he] first misses Zhou's and then [he] misses Zhu's. That is even worse than Yaojiang![8]

According to Guangdi, Luo falsely claims that because Zhu Xi places principle before material force, he necessarily separates the two, not knowing that in Zhu's grand scheme of things, they are in fact one. Indeed, as Guangdi reiterates, Zhu's conception of principle and material force has two premises. First, "Principle is prior and material force is posterior." Second, "Principle is material force (*li ji qi*) and material force is principle (*qi ji li*)." Guangdi explains the interrelationship between these two metaphysical entities:

> What is material force? [It is] yin and yang, moving and resting, brightness and darkness, going and coming, rising and falling, pure and turbid, and melting and congealing, which pervade heaven and earth, variably manifesting the mandate that has been bestowed. . . . It is constantly so since antiquity and is no different today. That there is no difference is constancy. Where there is constancy, there is that which must be so (*dangran*). That which must be so is that which is naturally so (*ziran*). That which is naturally so is that which is consequently so (*suoyiran*). . . . Confucius calls it the Way and the Great Ultimate. Master Cheng and Master Zhu call it principle. In discussing the Way and its implements (*qi*), Master Cheng says that the Way is on top and its implements are down below. But yet implements are the Way, and the Way is implements. In discussing principle and material force, Master Zhu says that principle is prior while material force is posterior. But yet principle is material force and material force is principle.[9]

In other words, principle is the ultimate pattern and configuration of the dialectics and changes of material force in its multifarious particularizations. Principle, or the Way, is prior to material force and implements, even though the former is also the latter, as Guangdi reminds us. But this reminder is neither explanatorily cogent nor analytically rigorous. The sense of antinomy lingers in spite of Guangdi's attempted refutation, and it is precisely this sort of apparent antinomy that has goaded Luo Qinshun into interrogating Cheng-Zhu metaphysics and searching for resolution and unity. It can be fairly said that Guangdi's polemical edge here is conspicuously blunted by his failure to offer any logically rigorous argument to reconcile the simultaneous oneness and separateness of principle and material force. His unsparing refutation of Luo in the tributary essay of 1681 amounts to little more than an utterance of a shibboleth of the Cheng-Zhu school.

As Guangdi himself later recalled and admitted, it was not until the age of fifty-one that he finally realized exactly why Luo and others who cast doubts on Zhu's metaphysics were wrong, even though all along, he had felt that something was amiss in their skepticism:

> There is first principle and then there comes material force. In the Ming, even the most learned Confucians did not understand this principle. Cai Xuzhai [that is, Cai Qing, d. 1555] claims that the two material forces of heaven and earth mingle to form one mass. Principle is the order [of such mingling]. Luo Zheng'an [that is, Luo Qinshun] claims that where material force activates changes, there is principle. For instance, as regards spring's changing into summer and summer's changing into autumn, from antiquity to the present, there has not been one bit of error. This is precisely principle. When I first read such statements, I only felt that they were disquieting, but I did not know where they went wrong. But upon reading Xue Wenqing's [that is, Xue Xuan, 1389–1464] "A Record of Learning" (Dushu lu), I came across [the statement that] nature (*xing*) is where material force is at its best. I rather appreciated such a statement, but did not quite fully understand it. It was only when I was fifty-one years old that I suddenly realized that the problems with these three ideas rested on the failure to distinguish the sequential ordering of principle and material force. There is first principle and then there is material force. It is not that today, there is principle and then tomorrow, there is material force. Look at the case of the Way, which is above the corporeal, and that of implements, which are in the midst of the corporeal. They are not demarcated and separated into two truncated parts. It is just that in terms of hierarchy, the Way ultimately belongs to that which is above, and implements belong to that which is below. In terms of sequential order, principle is ultimately prior, and material force is posterior. Principle can generate material force, but material force cannot generate principle.[10]

Guangdi asks us to test the tenability of this abstract metaphysical theory by looking at our own emotional and bodily experiences:

> A person's joyful enjoyment and violent outburst are material force, but there is never any sudden joyful enjoyment in an unmoved state of joylessness; nor is there a matter of sudden violent outburst in an indifferent state of angerlessness. Why

> is there joy? It is because there is the principle of humaneness (*ren*). Why is there anger? It is because there is the principle of rightness (*yi*). If joy is expressed in a state of equilibrium (*zhong*) in due degree with the mediation of humaneness, then joy has its principle. If anger is expressed in a state of equilibrium in due degree with the mediation of rightness, then anger has its principle. As the antecedent of that which is before manifestation (*weifa*), principle is complete and strong in a state of equilibrium. Therefore when it is manifested (*yifa*), there is naturally pattern and organization. Understanding this, we then know that although throughout heaven and earth, material force changes, moves and intermingles, there are times when it cannot control itself. But there is this one nature (*xing*) which does not change through the ages.[11]

The reference here to the locus classicus of the *Zhongyong* (Doctrine of the Mean) is clear. That which is before manifestation is surely prior to that which is manifested. To Guangdi, people like Luo Qinshun and Cai Qing only focus on "the harmony (*he*) that results from proper manifestation in due degree, but lose sight of the equilibrium (*zhong*) in the state of pre-manifestation." It is perfectly reasonable to say that "material force moves as a mass without confusion and that the lack of confusion is principle." But still, "there is at the very bottom something which cannot be confused," namely, principle. Similarly, one may correctly maintain that "material force flows and moves ceaselessly, and that where there are such changes, there is principle." But "at the very bottom, there is something whereby (*suoyi*) changes occur." This very something is principle, or nature.[12] Principle/nature thus appears as a sort of transcendental category that determines experience a priori. The welter of experience stems from this constant principle/nature.

To make sense of the duality of principle and material force, Guangdi often resorts to an exploration of nature (*xing*). In fact, the locus of his philosophy is human nature, precisely because the abstractness of metaphysical reasoning can only achieve clarity and be existentially meaningful if concrete lived experiences are involved. To be sure, Guangdi vigorously upholds the notions of principle and material force as the foremost metaphysical categories for explaining the truth about reality, and regards the priority of principle to be an unquestionable truism. But he also seeks to make them readily intelligible and relevant by often explicating them in the context of human acts and virtues. The importance of nature in Guangdi's philosophical system merits an independent examination in the next chapter. Suffice it here to note that he makes it a habit to illustrate the *li-qi* continuum in relation to human experience and action. For instance, he contends that

> principle and material force can certainly never be separated into two truncated parts. But how can there be no order of which comes first and which comes last? For instance, there is the principle of *ren* (humaneness) which, upon empathetically responding to things, yields the material force of warmth and peace. There is the principle of *yi* (rightness) which, upon empathetically responding to things, yields the material force of determination to act.[13]

Principle and material force are indissolubly united in the organic personality and emotion of the living person. But the former is the very essence that causes things to be as they are; it is the self-same nature from which normative rules are derived, conducting humanity toward virtuous and proper act and feeling.

Interestingly, when Guangdi finally came to grips with the meaning and import of principle and material force at the age of fifty-one in 1692, as he told us, he also completed the *Notes from Early Summer* (Chuxia lu),[14] which is a compilation of his musings on the contents of some of the classics, like *Mencius* and the *Doctrine of the Mean*, and his elucidation of some of the cardinal Confucian concepts, such as the Great Ultimate (*taiji*), heaven-and-earth (*tiandi*), and the mind-heart (*xin*). Guangdi's self-proclaimed enlightenment at age fifty-one finds documentary and textual expression in the detailed expositions on these two metaphysical entities that lard many parts of his 1692 *Notes*. In this work of two fascicles, Guangdi routinely discusses principle and material force in conjunction with nature. In fact, not once does he belabor these metaphysical entities in the absence of nature. Whatever the splendor and validity of the *li-qi* architectonic scheme, only in the province of nature and humanity can we develop a sense of our knowing ourselves, a sense in which we act as participants in, and indeed as authors of, the reality that Zhu has described in cool, objective terms. Having accepted and echoed the master's thesis, he then, with some audacity, modifies and adds to it. The following is a typical example of how Guangdi expands the meaning of principle and material force by dint of emphasizing the relevance of nature. Here, in particular, he is affirming the priority of principle:

> Although there is no order of priority and posteriority with regard to principle and material force, what is called the nature of heaven and earth is pure and most good. It is of

> course above and beyond the superficiality of shapes and material force. Nature is the root of the production of things. Material force is the completion of the production of things. Judging from this, how can there be no high and low as regards the Way and implements? . . . There are intermingling and distinction between heaven and earth, but their nature has not changed since antiquity. Regardless of whether it is intermingling or distinction, there is first and there is second. Judging from this, how can there be no order of priority and posteriority as regards principle and material force?[15]

To put it tersely, "material force is born out of nature, and so it is the function (*yong*) of nature." It is in this sense that we can say that "they are one but also two; two but also one."[16] In other words, their oneness can only be established not in terms of substantive identification, but inextricable interdependence. Guangdi is prompted to discriminate between the two because, as far as he is concerned, since Han times, scholars have erroneously identified nature as "material endowment" (*qizhi*). It is thanks to Cheng Yi that the correct view—nature is principle—has been reasserted, but misunderstanding of the truth still prevails in his own time:

> Since the Han, scholars regarded material endowment as nature. Therefore Master Cheng established this view: nature is principle. When speaking of the equilibrium of material force, there is the immutable principle throughout the ages, which is called nature. Material force cannot be regarded as nature. Even today, although people can talk about principle, they cannot avoid saying that material force is principle. Therefore, it is appropriate that we reestablish this view: principle is nature. Speaking of the equilibrium of material force, there is the immutable nature throughout the ages, which is principle. Material force cannot be regarded as principle.[17]

While it is certainly true that Guangdi did not veer from Zhu's thesis that *li* was the basis of all reality, yet in honing and refining his arguments over the years to explain Zhu and to defend him against challenges from skeptical critics, Guangdi also brought the significance of nature and humanity to bear on the master's metaphysical *li-qi* scheme, seeking to infuse the immediacy and vibrancy of life in the pondering of the ultimate principles of reality. Indeed, in Guangdi's 1681 essay, "The Main Purposes of Honoring Zhu," having first defended *li-qi* as the foundation of Zhu Xi's teachings, he next identifies the understanding of *xin-xing* (the mind-heart and nature) as the second main purpose in the pursuit of the master's learning. His main goal here is to reaffirm the Cheng-Zhu thesis that "nature is principle," thereby also rejecting Wang Yangming's idea that "the mind-heart is principle."

Beginning with the *li-qi* premise, Guangdi proclaims, "Speaking mainly in terms of heaven, there are principle and material force. Speaking mainly in terms of humanity, there is nature and the mind-heart. However, whether in terms of heaven or humanity, the two are one. When they are one, they do not separate. When they are two, they do not mix (*buza*)." In short, there is this alignment of separate entities: nature-*qua*-principle is distinct from the mind-heart-*qua*-material force. If they are one, it is because the latter is incorporated into and subsumed under the former in a profound state; they become one as "the things of Heaven, [which are] without sound and smell,"as described in the *Classic of Odes*.[18] Neither Confucius nor Mencius suggests the mutual identity of the mind-heart (identified with material force) and nature (identified with principle), although they do talk about their unity (*he*): "Confucius's idea that humaneness (*ren*) is humanity (*ren*) refers to the unity of the mind-heart and nature. Mencius's idea that a humane person is the mind-heart refers to the unity of the mind-heart and nature." However, to the extent that "there are people who are not humane, and that there is the mind-heart which is not humane, the mind-heart and nature can be in disunity." Moreover, according to Guangdi's gloss, Confucius does not use the term "humanity" to refer to people with their innate nature, but rather to the "Way of establishing humanity." Mencius's mind-heart, on the other hand, is the "sprouts" (*duan*) of our virtues and not the whole of nature itself. Further evidence of the separateness of the mind-heart and nature can be found in this well-known statement from *Classic of Documents*: "The human mind-heart (*renxin*) is prone to error; the mind-heart of the Way (*daoxin*) is subtle." If the mind-heart is human nature itself, which is good, then how can the human mind-heart ever be prone to error?[19]

The duality of the human mind-heart and the mind-heart of the Way, depicted in the *Mean*, is a perfect illustration of both the intrication and demarcation of principle/nature and material force/emotion. In his *Notes from Early Summer*, Guangdi devotes much effort to explicating the interrelation of these two "mind-hearts":

> Speaking in terms of the human mind-heart, if there is no pleasure, anger, sorrow and joy, then humaneness, rightness, propriety and wisdom cannot be realized and seen. Therefore, the *Doctrine of the Mean*, in talking about the Way of nature, focuses on the question of the manifestation and pre-manifestation of these four [virtues/emotions]. When Mencius and

> Han Yu talk about nature and emotion, [they refer to their relationship] as the interaction between the outer and the inner. This is what is called their inseparability. Nonetheless, even though humaneness can be issued as pleasure, it cannot be said that pleasure is humaneness; even though rightness can be issued as anger, it cannot be said that anger is rightness. Emotion is emotion; nature is nature. Therefore, the sages talk both about the mind-heart of the Way and the human mind-heart.[20]

If it is absolutely correct to say that the manifestation or realization of nature's inner goodness is unquestionably dependent on the outer workings of the human mind-heart, it is nevertheless a mistake to see them as one and the same. Guangdi in fact ratchets the issue of metaphysical anthropology up one notch farther: nature/principle, being the universal essential substance, is distinct from material force. He uses Mencius as his authority:

> As far as elaborating the purport of the human mind-heart and the mind-heart of the Way is concerned, no one has done it better than Mencius. What he calls the mind-heart of humaneness and rightness is the original mind-heart (*benxin*) or the good mind-heart (*liangxin*), which is the mind-heart of the Way. Thinking is the faculty of the mind-heart, and thinking is the way to the Way. What he calls taste with regard to the mouth, smell with regard to the nose, sound with regard to the ears, and color with regard to the eyes, are what is called the human mind-heart. . . . The faculties of the ears and eyes are the human mind-heart, but they are not what is called the original mind-heart. Therefore it does not have the great substance (*dati*).[21]

Our innate ability to do good and be virtuous, to be *ren* and *yi*, is the great substance. It is the universal, knowing consciousness and reality as it is. No other real world need be supposed behind or above this mind-heart, this Way. On the other hand, the human mind-heart is an individuated mind-heart, with particular thought and experience.

In a separate entry entitled "The Human Mind-Heart" (Renxin), Guangdi offers another definition of the human mind-heart:

> The person itself is the shape, while the Way is the nature. The mind-heart resides in between shape and nature. To the extent that shape and nature are in intriguing harmony (*miaohe*), the mind-heart is the master. Therefore there is the mind-heart of

> the Way and the human mind-heart. Nature is the root of the production of things. Since it moves upward from the mind-heart and ultimately reaches the virtue of the mandate of heaven, it is called the mind-heart of the Way. Shape is the actual traces of the production of things. Since it moves downward from the mind-heart and manifests itself as the senses of hearing, seeing, tasting, smelling and of the four limbs, it is called the human mind-heart. There are not two mind-hearts.[22]

Even though in the state of harmony (*he*), the two mind-hearts are really one, they are and ought to be separated after all, both functionally and substantively. Functionally speaking, one reaches upward toward heaven's virtues while the other moves downward and manifests itself as our psychosomatic attributes. Substantively speaking, the human mind-heart belongs to the domain of material force, as Guangdi argues: "That the human mind-heart is distinct as such and described as being prone to error is due to the fact the functionality of shape and material force can readily degenerate into evil, thereby losing the ultimate essence of the mind-heart."[23]

Here Guangdi engages the inevitable question of why and how humanity, endowed with a universally and innately good nature, identified with principle, nonetheless runs afoul of its true nature:

> It may be asked that if nature is good, then why is there evil when [nature] is attached to material force? [I will] say that that which is above the corporeal is called the Way, and that which is in the midst of the corporeal is implements. The nature that is profound and replete within the Way is the talents (*cai*) that are manifested in the utility of implements. Since nature is good, there is nothing in talents that is not good. But whereas there is only one nature, talents are selectively endowed. . . . Being uneven, lacking in some and having an excess of others, there emerges a situation in which some lean to one side and some are in a state of equilibrium. Furthermore, nature is shapeless whereas material force has its traces. Once there are traces, there is the difference between that which is refined and coarse, mellow and harsh.[24]

Guangdi's answer to the problem of reconciling a good nature with evil human deeds follows Zhu Xi's; it is to consign the origin and development of evil to material force. Guangdi likens nature to the five colors or the five palates which are perfectly good in themselves. But with the inevitable mixing of colors in painting and the blending of flavors in cooking, good and bad become distinguishable; colors may be uneven, or flavors may be unbalanced.[25]

In his "Principal Purpose of Honoring Zhu," Guangdi also clearly maintains that the mind-heart belongs to our material endowment (*qizhi*), quite distinct from our nature which, as heaven's mandate (*tianming*) in humanity, is innately and inexorably good. In three separate sections with the title of "Material Endowment," Guangdi expounds Zhu Xi's philosophical anthropology on the question of human evil, the gist of which is that the mind-heart and material endowment are the source of evil:

> There is nothing in nature that is not good. But as far as the mind-heart is concerned, there is excess, insufficiency, confusion, and lack of order. Hence the germination of good and evil. There is nothing in heaven's mandate that is not good. But as far as material force is concerned, there is excess, insufficiency, confusion and lack of order.[26]

On the other hand, nature, and principle for that matter, are "complete" (*quan*) in themselves; they are ultimate reality in "equilibrium" (*zhong*), always "correct" (*zheng*):

> If heaven's Five Agents all lean to their respective one side (*pian*), leading to the myriad things' death, or if the five natures [that is, humaneness, rightness, propriety, wisdom, and trustworthiness] all lean to their respective one side, leading to the degeneration of all affairs, it has nothing to do with what principle and nature naturally are. It has to do material force's leaning to one side. Principle is complete, not leaning to one side. Only equilibrium characterizes it. Therefore, any discussion of the Way values equilibrium.[27]

Material force's leaning to one side in no way detracts from the fact that nature is innately good and fully bestowed on humanity, even though it does conceal true nature:

> Humanity comes into being endowed with the equilibrium of heaven and earth. Even if it leans to one side in the most extreme degree, its principle is never incompletely bestowed; its nature is never ever not complete. But material force's leaning to one side does becloud it. As it becomes concealed, it cannot realize itself. It may in time be stimulated and respond; it may learn to gain understanding; or it may achieve awareness with suffering. Only then can the tiny and

> illusive beginnings [of the goodness of humanity] be seen and obtained. But the main point is that all [of humanity] possesses in its origin [goodness].[28]

To bring the distinction between the mind-heart of the Way and the human mind-heart (and that between *li* and *qi*) into sharp relief, Guangdi asks us to look at the opposition between human desires (*renyu*) and heaven's principle (*tianli*). This opposition is a cornerstone of the Cheng-Zhu teachings. He reminds us that "only the human mind-heart has desires and so it is prone to error." On the other hand, "the Way is principle, and since principle's origin is heaven, which is soundless and odorless, it is subtle."[29] Guangdi does not say that desires in themselves are necessarily bad or evil, but the existence of desires provides the occasion and opportunity for the rise of evil. In particular, he refers to those basic psychosomatic needs that we all must have and satisfy: "As for human desires, those desires of the ears, eyes, mouth and nose and the four limbs cannot fail to exist. They are not evil. But when their excesses are followed, there is evil. Therefore, it is said that [they are] prone to error."[30] Moreover, Guangdi states clearly that "the desires that do justice to all-under-heaven do not constitute evil." Only those that are exclusively focused on oneself, in other words, private desires, are the source of the problem. Hence Confucius's admonition that propriety-norms (*li*) must be employed to restrain the self.[31]

From Zhu Xi's principle-based metaphysics, Guangdi constructed a philosophical anthropology of nature, with an attending phenomenology of evil: one's nature comes into being as the good fundamental substance, but its becoming, as a result of material force's intervention, can be an opaque process that can only be illumined and clarified by existential encounter with the external world. In the addendum of the "Principal Purpose of Honoring Zhu," Guangdi concludes by summoning again all those key terms he uses throughout the essay to elucidate and characterize principle. Principle is "that which must be so" (*dangran*), "that which is naturally so" (*ziran*), and "that which is consequently so" (*suoyiran*). "Not leaning to one side," it is in a state of "equilibrium." "Not mixed up with [material force] (*buza*)," it is "good" (*shan*). He also reaffirms the priority of principle over material force. Because there is first the "nurturing" (*airan*) principle, there is as a result the nurturing material force that is responsible for the "germination of things" (*shengwu*). The "majestic" (*suran*) material force, which "completes things" (*chengwu*), comes from the majestic principle. Principle in itself is good and in a state of equilibrium. Just as the flesh of the millet is tasty and a fine silk garment warms the body, so overeating millet harms the body and putting on too many garments causes discomfort. Millet and garment, Guangdi's analogies for principle and nature, are good in themselves, but the way they are used, or what they generate, constitutes the source of problems.[32]

If Guangdi's aim in writing the essay was explicitly to promote Zhu Xi's fundamental metaphysical assumptions, it was also to demote Wang Yangming's philosophy, which had become pervasive in the intellectual world of the literati. To assert that principle and nature are good and prior is ultimately to attack Wang's most pernicious thesis, namely, that nature is "beyond good and evil," a thesis that stems from the refusal and failure to distinguish between the mind-heart and nature. Guangdi disparages Wang for wrongly identifying nature with the "original mind-heart" (*benxin*). In so doing, Wang ignores the differences between the mind-heart of the Way and the human mind-heart:

> [Wang] Yaojiang's teaching claims that the mind-heart is naturally humane, the mind-heart is naturally right, and the mind-heart naturally feels sympathy, shame, humility and right and wrong. That which goes wrong is not the original mind-heart. Therefore, he claims that the mind-heart is nature. His words resemble [the sages'] but his ideas do not. For has it not been said that the mind-heart of humaneness and rightness is the mind-heart of the Way and that if there is error, it is the flow of the human mind-heart? The distinction between the mind-heart and nature is thus clear.

Since Wang's philosophy is essentially a theory of the ultimacy and primacy of the "substance of the mind-heart" (*xin zhi ti*), and since, according to Guangdi's understanding, the mind-heart is the site of consciousness (*jue*), Wang ends up "regarding the Way as consciousness." Once the Way is seen as consciousness, it is identified with "vacuity" (*wu*); once vacuity is taken as the principal (*zong*), the Way is no more. This, in short, is the crux of the genetics of Wang's proposition that "the substance of the mind-heart is beyond good and evil."[33]

In *Notes from Early Summer*, Guangdi reiterates the basic difference between Lu Xiangshan and Zhu Xi, and attributes Wang Yangming's deleterious notion of the mind-heart's being beyond good and evil to his failure to discriminate between the posterior mind-heart and the prior nature:

> The teachings of Xiangshan do also talk about goals, reverence, discursive clarity and practice. But what can be said to be the difference [between him] and Master Zhu rests simply on the distinction between the mind-heart and nature. Xiangshan

> claims that the mind-heart is principle and so when he discusses [Zhou Dunyi's] *A Discourse on the Diagram of the Great Ultimate* (Taiji tushuo), he claims that yin and yang belong to the realm that is above the corporeal. . . . The more recent learning of Yaojiang has the same root, so throughout [Wang Yangming's] life, when it comes to the two words of "mind-heart" and "principle," [he] always mixes them up as one. In his letter of reply to Gu Dongyuan, [he] cites the *Classic of Documents,* beginning with the words, "The mind-heart of the Way," and cuts out the preceding statement, ["The Mind-heart of humanity is prone to error"]. Therefore, late in his life, he develops the idea that the mind-heart is beyond good and evil.[34]

Guangdi declares that many of the critics of Lu-Wang learning of his day often only focus myopically on its symptomatic problems: "leaning toward honoring the virtuous nature (*dexing*) and lacking knowledge and inquiry (*xuewen*)," or "emphasis on making the will sincere (*chengyi*) and neglecting the investigation of things (*gewu*)." It behooves them to pinpoint the ur-problem, which rests not in the experiential and existential domain of "teaching and learning" (*jiangxue*), "steadfast observation" (*qishou*), and "knowledge and action" (*zhixing*), but which stems from the ur-domain of "the mind-heart and nature."[35] In short, the fundamental flaw of Wang's learning is that it wrongly identifies what ultimate reality is.

From Metaphysics to Metapraxis: The Genetics of Virtues

Such are the a priori metaphysical truths taught by Li Guangdi. But how do these philosophical figments necessarily relate to and reflect upon the external world, that is, the world in which human lives are actually lived? What are the de facto existential truths, or norms, that stem from the incorporeal ultimate reality? How do we, as human agents, act out and come to terms with the endowments we are born into and born with? In the metaphysical universe of principle, nature, and material force, there are human necessities and the utilities of the social world. Behind metaphysics are vision and claims of such necessities and utilities, namely, cultural norms and moral ethics. In other words, a sort of deontology must follow ontology. Hoyt Cleveland Tillman has aptly reminded us that the Confucian tradition comprises three interrelated and yet distinct levels of discourse: speculation on ultimate reality and first principles, definition of values and culture, and advocacy of statecraft and governance.[36] To the extent that there is such intrication in the

Confucian enterprise, writing about its metaphysics begs writing about its values and norms that are the putative organic outgrowths.

In fact, it may be argued, as Tillman does, that Confucians were, in the final analysis, most concerned with this level of discourse, that is, values and norms. If they staked their metaphysical claims with gusto, it was because such iterations lent the necessary credence to what they considered as proper moral work, ethical practice, and discursive thinking. *Theoria* of *logos* is never sufficient in and of itself; it must be embedded in and embodied by *praxis*, the emulation and living out of an ideal mode of behavior. As Judith Berling puts it, philosophy must always be "embodied" from the Confucian perspective of philosophizing about truths. Since truths had already been ascertained by the ancient sages, and the fundamental moral basis for human institutions and acts had already been prescribed by them, abstract speculation about the ultimate nature became secondary to the primary project of learning about, acting out, and transmitting those very known verities.[37] In brief, as Philip J. Ivanhoe points out, moral self-cultivation, the motivation and act of doing and becoming good, was persistently one of the most dominant issues in Confucian ethical thinking, overshadowing the theoretical concern with defining what was good and moral, a concern that has consumed ethical ruminations in the West.[38]

Thus, in honoring Zhu Xi's metaphysics, Li Guangdi also paid homage to the master's moral and ethical edification tout court. In "Principal Purpose of Honoring Zhu," Guangdi ascertains not only truths about the universe but also specifies the proper development, manifestation, experience, and realization of such truths. The telling conjunction in this work is the linkage of speculation about ultimate truth and engagement in lifelong moral and investigational quest. In other words, principle and nature are not general abstract descriptions, but lived conditions, positive guidance to and constraint on quotidian activity. They are, in the social world, values, virtues, and norms and their cultivation. Ultimate truths mean engagement with moral self-cultivation and abnegation of meretricious entanglement. They demand, in the words of Lee Yearley, a "practical theory," complementing the "primary" and "secondary" theories of cosmology, metaphysics, and the realities of nature. Practical theory aims at providing guides to the full actualization of our potentialities as human beings, and is therefore concerned by and large with what we generally describe as ethics.[39] In short, systematic speculation and assertion of truths ultimately demand a mode of living that involves the interlacement of domains: moral virtues, intellectual activity, and ethical practice.

Guangdi addresses the domain of moral virtues in a section entitled "Wisdom, Humaneness, and Courage" (Zhirenyong). Although Guangdi does not here explain clearly why these three virtues are singled out and discussed as a cluster, the *Doctrine of the Mean*, which referred to them as "universally binding virtues" (*dade*), must have been the source of his thinking on virtues.[40] It is therefore not surprising that explanation and elaboration of these three virtues can be found in Guangdi's works on this classic. In one of his later compositions, the *Chapters and Verses of the Doctrine of the Mean* (Zhongyong zhangduan), written in 1716, two years before his death, he wrote, "As for the main bonds of nature, there are but wisdom and humaneness. As for the effort of learning, there are but knowing and acting. Courage is that which enhances these [virtues]."[41] In yet another work on the *Mean*, *Further Discussions on the Doctrine of the Mean* (Zhongyong yulun), completed in 1710, Guangdi makes a point to explain why courage is included to form a triumvirate of cardinal virtues:

> It is a universal fact that wisdom and humaneness are nature's virtues. But courage belongs to the realm of material force. Why is it called a virtue? The three virtues are rooted in sincerity. Humaneness is the preservation of sincerity. Wisdom is the comprehension of sincerity. Courage is the serious extension of sincerity. . . . Where are humaneness, rightness, propriety, wisdom and trustworthiness if there is no courage? . . . Sincerity is solid [virtue] and courage is its fructification.[42]

Thus, Guangdi sees courage as the experiential pullulation of the virtues that stem from our nature, that is, humaneness and wisdom. Lee Yearley's taxonomy of virtues is useful here. According to his scheme, humaneness and wisdom are "virtues of inclination or motivation," whereas courage is a "preservative" virtue that protects "inclinational virtues by resisting desires that impede their actualization. Inclinational virtues, in turn, often produce the goals for which preservative virtues strive." Guangdi's "courage," in his own elucidation, seems to perform precisely a preservative function.[43]

In "Principal Purpose of Honoring Zhu," Guangdi proffers an exposition on the genetics of virtues. He declares that the moral virtues of wisdom (*zhi*), humaneness (*ren*), and courage (*yong*), and their obverse, vices and flaws, stem either from material force's leaning to one side or maintaining equilibrium. Just as the workings of material force, with the dialectical interaction of yin and yang, yield the pure and the turbid, the crooked and the straight, the thick and the thin, and the incomplete and the complete, so too in humanity, imbued with those traits, there are those who are bright and dull, good and shameful, strong and weak, and perverted and wholesome. Those who are bright have the virtue of wisdom; those who are good are humane; those who are strong possess courage.[44] Guangdi quotes the famous passage from the fifth chapter of "The Great Treatise" (Dazhuan) in the *Classic of Changes* to illustrate his idea that the Way begets virtues and reveals itself to each individual according to the development of one's own nature:

> The Way is that which lets the dark [yin] and the light [yang] appear now and again. That which continues this is good; that which completes this is nature. The humane person discerns it and calls it humaneness; the wise person discerns it and calls it wisdom. But the ordinary folk use it day after day and are unaware of it, for the way of the superior person is rare.[45]

The good that continues the Way, with its completion, becomes nature. But the intervention of material force means that the good in nature is seldom discerned and grasped. Hence the rarity of humaneness and wisdom associated with a superior person.

In his *Notes from Early Summer*, Guangdi discusses human virtues more systematically in a section entitled "Humaneness and Wisdom" (Ren zhi). He makes it clear that while the origin of virtues are guaranteed in nature, they are realized and operate in the realm of material force, associated variously with yin or yang; their development in the domain of material force depends on ceaseless cultivation.[46] By and large, following Zhu Xi, Guangdi affirms the primacy of the fundamental virtue of humaneness as the "virtue of the mind-heart" (*xinde*), which encompasses the virtues of rightness, propriety, and wisdom.[47] After all, Confucius has admonished us to "cultivate the Way with humaneness." But Guangdi asks us to view the "virtues of nature" (*xing zhi de*) on two levels. Notice here the divergence from Zhu Xi's terminology, that is, the pegging of virtues onto nature as opposed to the mind-heart. Speaking on the ontological level of heaven, "humaneness-above" (*shangren*) indeed embodies all cardinal virtues.[48] It is the "real substance" (*shiti*) of the Great Ultimate, so much so that "the dichotomy of yin and yang is not adequate as a description of it."[49] However, speaking on the experiential level of everyday living, "humaneness-below" (*xiaren*) comes before rightness and propriety but is preceded by wisdom.[50] Guangdi explains the relative importance of humaneness and wisdom:

> There is the humaneness that comes after wisdom and there is that which precedes wisdom. That which comes after wisdom is the function of humaneness. That which precedes wisdom is the substance of humaneness. . . . Substance is that which is the authentic self in a state of inchoate profundity, before its manifestation. How can wisdom come before it? When it is

> revealed in function, then wisdom precedes humaneness. Wisdom is nothing but the manifestation and revelation of the roots of humaneness.[51]

If there is an ontology of virtues based on the holism of humaneness, there is also the human existential design to realize them in the province of everyday living. This design of realizing virtues in action has an inexorable epistemological foundation. Innate virtues are only truly virtuous to the extent that they are implemented, and their implementation depends first on our awareness of their goodness and the need to put them into action. Thus, Guangdi ties his conception of virtues and their experiential realization to Zhu Xi's call for "developing knowledge to the utmost" (*zhizhi*). This quest for knowledge is the sine qua non for virtuous action:

> Although the substance of knowing may not yet have the traces of earnest action, it is that which seriously scrutinizes [action], and so it is the foundation of action. . . . Therefore, speaking in terms of the realm of material endowment of humanity, there must be first the knowledge of the three grades (*sanpin*) [of human nature] and then the realization of the three grades. Speaking of learning, there must first be the yearning for learning before there is earnest effort; there must first be the illumination of goodness before there is the making of the self sincere.[52]

Guangdi exposes the inadequacy of simply viewing virtues as components of nature. He takes a logical step farther and insists on seeking knowledge of them as the basic way to practice them: "The sages taught us to nurture the mind-heart so as to extend knowledge to the utmost, and to extend knowledge to the utmost so as to act appropriately on things."[53] With regard to the pursuit and realization of virtues, Guangdi puts great store on the idea of "enlightenment resulting from sincerity" (*chengming*), an idea from the *Doctrine of the Mean*, from which he quotes these words: "Enlightenment resulting from sincerity is to be ascribed to nature; sincerity resulting from enlightenment is to be ascribed to learning."[54] Guangdi proceeds to argue that, in fact, "to speak of wisdom, humaneness and courage is to speak of enlightenment resulting from sincerity." He glosses the notion of "enlightenment resulting from sincerity" by using Zhang Zai's words:[55] "By 'sincerity resulting from enlightenment' (*mingcheng*) is meant the development of one's nature fully through the plumbing of principle to the utmost; by 'enlightenment resulting from sincerity' (*chengming*) is meant the plumbing of principle through the development of one's nature to the utmost."[56] In short, virtues mean at once the quest for knowledge of principle and extension of our nature in an exhaustive manner. Ideal human virtues may be abstracted from the ultimate reality of heaven or the Great Ultimate, but in the final analysis, virtues are simultaneously the cause and the result of the human existential endeavor to realize the potentiality of nature, which entails knowing and acting, spurred on and guided by an earnest sense of sincerity:

> The learning of the sages is simply knowledge and action. The basis of knowing and acting is establishing the will (*lizhi*) and holding onto respect (*qijing*). Yet establishing the will and holding onto respect are based on sincerity. . . . Without sincerity, the will cannot be the will, respect cannot be respect, and knowledge and action are flawed. . . . That is what is called enlightenment resulting from sincerity.[57]

By resorting to the idea of *chengming*, Guangdi first conflates virtues with nature and establishes an innate condition of humanity. But such metaphysical pronouncement may easily degenerate into a sort of moralistic truism that merely invokes nostalgic distance between the ideal and the quotidian. Therefore, he also strives to show that this "organic" relation has to be nurtured and cultivated through learning, knowing, and acting, all animated by the spirit of sincerity. Ontological understanding must thus be a result of earnest existential engagement, undergirded by proper epistemological apprehension, and indeed appropriation, of the interaction between knowing and acting.

Metapraxis: A Program of Moral Self-Cultivation

Small wonder that following a discussion on virtues, in the "Principal Purpose of Honoring Zhu," Guangdi outlines a cultivational and investigational program, which in effect amounts to a praxis, or more precisely, a metapraxis, for developing our virtues and fulfilling our nature. By praxis is meant disciplines and activities, including knowledge-seeking and theorizing, which consciously seek to guide, animate, and facilitate proper living. It is contrasted with *theoria*, whose end is knowing for its own sake. The former actively pursues the "ought," prescribing the *value* of living well; the latter passively ponders the "is," describing the *fact* of reality.[58] But the "ought" and value are culture-specific. Each philosophical or religious tradition develops its own logic, rationality, and justification of praxis. Therefore, in the context of particular traditions, Thomas

Kasulis suggests the use of the term and concept of metapraxis. If metaphysics refers to the theorizing of that which lies beyond and behind natural things and powers, metapraxis points to the establishment of philosophical positions and arguments concerning the nature of a specific praxis. Metapraxis is a philosophical endeavor in that it is reflective and critical; it proposes and justifies the ends and means of action, devising competing answers to the questions of why we act, on what we act, and how we act.[59]

Guangdi discusses in particular three cultivational dicta that we may regard as metapraxis in "Principal Purpose of Honoring Zhu:" "knowing and acting" (*zhixing*), "establishing the will" (*lizhi*), and "emphasizing reverence" (*zhujing*). Not surprisingly, in his discourse on the first dictum, namely, the intimate interrelation between knowledge and action, Guangdi summons Zhu Xi's classic epistemological premise that knowing precedes acting. Zhu's stance, according to Guangdi, is not based on a conception that knowing is more difficult than acting. In fact, Zhu argues quite the opposite: "It is not that knowing is difficult; it is that acting is difficult."[60] Nevertheless, one simply cannot act if one does not know what to act out and act upon. Hence the priority of learning. Zhu expresses what the various ancient classics have already clearly stated. For instance, the proper order of things is illustrated in this admonition of the *Analects*: "Extensively study all learning and be circumscribed by the rules of propriety." The *Great Learning* teaches that in the grand enterprise of moral self-cultivation, the investigation of things comes before the extension of knowledge to the utmost, and making the thoughts sincere is followed by rectification of the mind-heart. The *Classic of Changes* proclaims that it is with *qian*'s knowledge of the "great beginning" that *kun* "produces and complete things." Thus, Guangdi concludes:

> The virtues of human nature are roused into action with wisdom, and are born with humaneness; [they] flourish through rituals, and end in rightness. On the other hand, the learning of a morally sovereign person starts with wisdom, is preserved in humaneness, reaches rituals, and is completed in rightness. The order of knowing and acting, and the principle of nature and fate cannot be changed.[61]

In short, the wisdom that comes from knowledge is the point of departure of the flourishing and realization of nature's virtues.

This promotion of Zhu's view also serves as the prelude to Guangdi's attack on Wang Yangming's metapraxis. To be fair to Wang, Guangdi actually misrepresents and distorts his ideas. Most notably, Guangdi completely ignores Wang's sequence-nullifying tenet of the oneness of knowing and acting. Instead, Guangdi imposes sequentiality in Wang's idea where there is none, in effect putting words in Wang's mouth: "Mr. Wang of Yaojiang said, 'Action is prior; knowledge is posterior.' He only chose to see what the sages said about the will and reverence, both of which come before learning, inquiry, reflection and discrimination." In any event, given his own partial understanding of Wang's philosophy, Guangdi claims that Wang had only one-sided understanding of the sages' teachings. Consequently, Wang developed a philosophy that privileged a sort of transcendent understanding, or knowledge, that appealed directly to the exercise, or action, of the will (*zhi*) and reverence (*jing*). On the surface, this philosophy may be seen as a simple, wrong-headed affirmation of the priority of action, but Guangdi further implies that the rapacity of such thinking lies in the fact that it results in completely bypassing the action-knowledge continuum. He quotes the following array of Wang's statements as proof of his flawed teaching:

> The energy that is left after action may be used to learn about words. . . . The superior person, without moral gravity (*zhong*), will not command veneration (*wei*) and cannot hold on to knowledge.[62] . . . Honoring the moral nature (*zun dexing*) [comes before] following the way of inquiry and learning (*dao wenxue*). . . . The way of learning and inquiry is nothing but striving to emancipate the mind-heart (*fangxin*). . . . The nurturing of virtue (*hanyang*) rests with reverence; the enhancement of learning (*jinxue*) rests with knowledge.

According to Guangdi, the effort of commanding veneration "belongs to the realm of the will," while honoring the moral nature, emancipating the mind-heart, and nurturing nature all "belong to the realm of reverence." This sole concentration on the will and reverence in effect negates the requisite knowledge-action praxis. Consequently, what Wang preaches cannot possibly be "the words of the sages"; it in fact violates "the virtue of nature and the principle of heaven-and-earth."[63]

Guangdi attributes Wang's obscurantism to his fundamental belief in the "extension of spontaneous moral knowing to the utmost" (*zhi liangzhi*). This belief in itself "does no harm to all-under-heaven," because it commendably urges "the singular pursuit of experiencing and realizing the virtuous dispositions of our body, mind-heart, nature and sentiment." The problem is the question of the source of spontaneous moral knowing, and Wang had the wrong answer. To Guangdi, Wang's ontology is premised on the conception that "the mind-heart is principle." Therefore, any effort to exhaust our innate knowing of the good perforce means the fulfillment of the mind-heart. Herein lies the fatal flaw of Wang's teachings. As Guangdi once again reminds us, the mind-heart may indeed be "intriguingly mysterious" (*miao*), but it is not the "solid reality" (*shi*) of principle. The mystique of the mind-heart lies in its "vacuity" (*xu*), the ultimate of which is "emptiness" (*wu*). It is small wonder that Wang arrived at the conclusion that "the root of the mind-heart is beyond good and evil." So caught was Wang in the power of this transcendent mind-heart that he troubled no longer to devote time and effort to study, as Guangdi accuses:

> Since he claims that the mind-heart is naturally humane and righteous, and naturally sympathetic, shame-conscious, humble, and aware of right and wrong, writing about the words of Confucius and Mencius is not the main goal. Therefore, [he] leaves books and histories behind, neglects writings and words, and sweeps reading, recitation and what is seen and heard aside, thinking that they are not the mind-heart, and not the Way.[64]

Against Wang's statements, Guangdi unleashes a torrent of counterstatements which, to him, correctly represent the views of the sages:

> Books, histories, writings and words are nothing but the Way. Reading, recitation, and what is seen and heard are nothing but the mind-heart. The ancients did not talk about perceiving principle but about broad learning; [they] did not talk about seeking the Way but about the investigation of things. There is broad learning before there is earnest resolution; there is studious inquiry before there is intimate reflection of one's self; it is only after the classics have been studied that there is critical discrimination of our will; it is after paying respect to one's own occupation that there is gregarious communal link with the like-minded; there is broad study before establishing relationship with teachers; there is discussion on learning before one knows how to choose friends; knowing individual categories comes before the comprehension of the universals; there is control of the musical instruments before there is harmonious melody; there is broad adherence to the rules of rhymes before there is harmonious poetry; there is knowledge of the miscellaneous ritual garbs before rituals can be secured. There is no choosing between the inner and outer, and there is no abandonment of either the root or the branches. . . . As for plumbing principles and seeking the Way, how can there be the choosing of one over the other?[65]

In essence, Guangdi charges Wang with claiming ultimate knowledge by a direct act of metaphysical intuition or clairvoyance with the extension of spontaneous moral knowing, but since this claim is derived from Wang's fundamental ontological misapprehension—the assertion that the mind-heart is principle—it is a vacuous argument premised on the celebration of ultimate emptiness. To Guangdi, we cannot, unaided by and in the absence of knowledge, intuit, understand, or grasp the Way. Understanding is a process that begins with the acquisition of data, that is, learning. The formation of society and culture is a result of our possessing knowledge gained by an orderly and sequenced method of acquiring information. Whether it is the discovery of our selves, the creation of relations with friends and teachers, the playing of music, the composing of poetry, or the practice of rituals, knowledge is the point of departure. Such an epistemology begins with the sheer "phenomenology" of human experience and activity, or as Guangdi puts it, the "outer" and the "branches," the study and learning about which enable our ever-deepening apprehension of the world, of our self, and eventually of the Way.

Insofar as Guangdi embraces the irreducibility of phenomena, he rejects Wang's use of the analogy of human learning as the growing of a tree. Wang argues that just as the branches should be pruned as a tree begins to grow, so too should a person rid oneself of the miscellaneous unruly preoccupations when one begins the process of learning. Putting his own spins on the analogy, Guangdi counters that to mess with the branches is to harm the root. The prospering of the branches means the strength of the root. In any event, regardless of the botanical metaphor, Confucius has made it very clear that "the abundance of what is seen and heard" (*duowen duojian*) is a merit. For the master says, and Guangdi quotes, "I am fond of antiquity, and earnest in seeking knowledge of it." It is curious that Guangdi does not quote the immediately preceding statement, "I am not one who was born in the possession of knowledge,"[66] which could have been used, at least polemically, to cast doubt on Wang Yangming's notion of spontaneous knowing of the good. He does, however, make a point to summon Confucius's injunction that "there is one thread that runs through" his doctrines, thereby reminding us that the diversity and breadth of learning must be subsumed under and realized in our virtuous nature. It is in this sense and in this manner that the "outer and inner," the "root and branches," and "the plumbing of principles and the seeking of the Way" are ultimately one.

Elsewhere, in a piece entitled *Recorded Notes on the Classics* (Jingshu biji),[67] Guangdi expands on the sense of unity inherent in the apparent duality of knowing-acting. His own interpretation of the relationship between knowing and acting would obviate the need for Wang Yang-ming's alternative theory of uniting knowing and acting in the process of extending spontaneous moral knowing:

> The theory of extending spontaneous moral knowing to the utmost claims that in making the will sincere and in being vigilant while alone, knowledge therein is extended to the utmost. I don't think that it is correct. People's endowments are different and their efforts vary. Although everyone is imbued with the sense of right and wrong, there are few who can respond to their thoughts and become readily conscious [of right and wrong]. Even if they are vaguely conscious, they may not develop an intimate conception and a profound awareness, and so in the final analysis, the sense of shame cannot flourish and be transformed into courageous and resolute action. Therefore, there must be the plumbing of principles, the extension of thinking, and the clear expositions of ideas to open up understanding, constantly encouraging oneself so that daily, one cannot help ceaselessly acting out what one knows. What Cheng and Zhu call plumbing principles does not refer to the pursuit of things and affairs while forgetting the principle of the self and mind-heart. . . . It also does not refer to the fact of knowing today and acting out [the knowledge] tomorrow. The more is known, the more earnest is the action; the more studious the action, the more is knowledge extended. This is the enterprise of simultaneous enhancement. How can there be a choice between the two?[68]

In other words, initial knowing, followed inexorably by genuine moral acting in accordance with our nature, is knowledge *per caussas*—knowing why, and not merely knowing that, or knowing how. This authentic (*zhen*) knowledge and the resulting studious (*li*) action are simultaneously and mutually enhanced. As Guangdi points out, "what Master Zhu calls knowing and acting are not separated and divided into two." But Guangdi also cautions that "the two cannot be confused as one," thereby maintaining Zhu's supposedly efficacious scheme of cultivating knowledge and compelling action.[69] Knowing and acting are experientially and existentially one in that they are linked by the one thread of moral nature, as Confucius had taught, but they are procedurally and structurally demarcated.

Consequently, knowing-acting, as both duality and oneness, is not simply recording, classifying, or deducing from external data; it is the internal capacity to learn, to want to learn, and to bring virtues to fruition. The internal aspects of the metapraxis of "knowing-acting" find expression in the two metaphysical dicta of "establishing the will" and "emphasizing reverence," which Guangdi expounds in his "Principal Purpose of Honoring Zhu." Establishing the will "is the general summation of knowing-acting," for it is with the established will that learning is pursued, and with learning, there is the extension of knowledge which enables us to act appropriately in accordance with the Way. Such reverential acting in tune with the Way in turn means that the will is truly established. As Guangdi contends, "In willing the self toward the Way, the will is thereby established. With deep knowledge, virtues have their basis; with the completing of action, humaneness has its support; with the transformative knowing-acting, one truly finds relaxation in the arts."[70] Thus, this holding firm of the will is a crucial step in a purposive tendency that canalizes the self toward the particular sequence and pattern of behavior, that is, knowing-acting with its admirable moral transformative consequences. The importance of the will is attested by Confucius's own famous description of his moral progression in life. Guangdi, paraphrasing the *Analects*, reminds us that "the sageliness of Confucius began with the will to learn, after which came standing firm, having no doubts, knowing the mandate of heaven, his ears' openness to the reception of truth," and finally, "following his heart's desires without transgressing what is right."[71]

Establishing the will is a sort of substantialist armature in conjunction with the other cultivational requirements. Guangdi uses the analogy of the cultivation of plants to illustrate the process of effecting moral development. Establishing the will is likened to sowing seeds, exercising reverence to watering and banking up the roots, and extension of knowledge and studious action to careful examination and diligent tending:

> If one learns without first appealing to the will, it is like not having the seeds. If after the will is established and one does not work on acquiring knowledge, it is like the spouts' being afflicted with defects. They may likely grow in a disorderly manner. If one has the knowledge but does not act, it is like the inability to remove what is causing harm to the sprouts. If reverence is not exercised from beginning to end, it is like not adding water and not banking up the roots. The result is that the sprouts may die or be unhealthy.[72]

In short, to establish the will is first and foremost to constitute a proper psychological state for knowing-acting, a mental disposition toward knowing and doing good. In a work entitled *Detailed Recordings of the Analects* (Lunyu zhaji), Guangdi remarks: "Learning begins with the establishment of the will, followed by knowing-acting. One who has his will set on the Way acts in the direction of the Way and sees the Way as the destination. His thoughts are forever with [the Way], never leaving it."[73] But to urge the establishment of the will is also to make central the relation between internal discipline and external compliance with the requirements for self-cultivation. It is to repair the Cheng-Zhu web of cultivational practices and beliefs which Wang has rent asunder with his direct appeal to the mind-heart. Such repair begins with having the correct will, as Confucius has told us. Guangdi thus proclaims that the *Analects*'s chapter of "At fifteen, I established the will to learn" is more than Confucius's description of his own moral progress; it is "in actuality the pattern of method for scholars throughout the ages."[74]

To completely restore the damaged web, apart from revivifying knowing-acting and reinvigorating the disposition toward the good, there is also the need for the renewal of the exercise of reverence, the third metapractical dictum expounded in "Principal Purpose of Honoring Zhu." Using Zhu Xi's words, Guangdi shows the relation among knowing, acting, and reverence: "Knowing is the beginning of learning; acting is the end of learning; emphasizing reverence is the way by which learning becomes the beginning and end." In terms of the *Great Learning*, the investigation of things and the extension of knowledge is knowing. While making the will sincere and rectifying the mind-heart belong to the domain of action, they are also matters of reverence. In what way is acting differentiated from reverence? The latter, according to Guangdi's definition, refers to a special concentration of one's entire being on the endeavor of cultivating and realizing moral good, which suffuses and pervades our countenance (*rongmao*), awe-inspiring posture (*weiyi*), speech (*cise*), and inner thought and will (*xinzhi*).

This reverential focusing, manifested in action, engenders the movement toward the good, correction of faults, curtailment of selfish desires, and punishment of anger. To the extent that the success of the enterprises of making the will sincere and rectifying the mind-heart is determined and governed by the exercise of reverence, it is "omnipresent and the master of knowing and acting."[75] This reverential attention "unites the inner and outer, connects both movement and quiescence,"[76] providing both the beginning and end to knowing-acting. To put it another way, if knowing-acting, *in media res*, can ever be initiated and concluded, it is thanks to the unwearying concentration and single-minded focus generated by the abiding sense of reverence for knowing and doing good.

This ideal concordant structure of moral cultivation, with a beginning, middle, and end, is revealed in the organization of the *Doctrine of the Mean*, Guangdi posits. The classic's first chapter, in counseling us to "be cautious and apprehensive at all times, and being vigilant in solitude," actually urges us to cultivate reverence. The final chapter, in talking about "examining the inner being and thereby achieving reverence," clearly refers to reverence in relation to critical moral introspection. In the middle part, the classic speaks of the vicissitudes and caprice of the effort to follow the Way—"the talented go beyond it, and the stupid fail to come up to it." It deals with "the pursuit of the virtues of wisdom, humaneness and courage," and "the determination to choose good and to hold on to it."[77] Thus, the *Mean* is an exemplar of moral cultivation as a journey, with reverence as both the point of departure and destination, and along the way, there is the ceaseless flux of knowing-acting.

In his *Notes from Early Summer*, as we have seen, Guangdi elucidates the *Mean*'s notion of "enlightenment resulting from sincerity" (*chengming*) in order to show how virtues may be realized with sincerity. In that text, Guangdi talks about sincerity and reverence in the same breath, essentially equating them with each other: "The sages talked both about sincerity and reverence. With sincerity, the mind-heart becomes concrete reality and sees things; with reverence, the mind-heart becomes vacuous and is devoid of crookedness. The two matters are of one mind."[78] To the extent that sincerity refers to the outer and the corporeal, and reverence pertains to the inner and the incorporeal, in modern epistemological terms, the former may be construed as *objectivity* and the latter as *subjectivity*. Reverence, Guangdi states, "directly reaches the inner and fully embodies principle in the mind-heart." On the other hand, sincerity, which Guangdi equates with rightness (*yi*), "defines the outer and follows the principles in things."[79]

Although the fundamental initiative in Guangdi's oeuvre is not an epistemological one, insofar as he addresses the problem of knowing-acting via-à-vis the metapraxis of reverence and sincerity, he hints at an epistemology premised on a balance of subjectivity and objectivity. Reverence is the pursuit of truth in terms of the subjectivity of a human subject acting in a qualitative way. It speaks with reference to the subjective situation of the agent who knows and acts. Sincerity, in contrast, shapes and conceives reality as objectivity. It defines truth with respect to the nature of the external world and to the proper use of the principles of things. Yet, their simultaneous presence breeds no discord but finds resolution in their ultimate organic conjunction in the highest goal of moral cultivation. If knowing-acting is a subjective, introspective activity of self-cultivation, it is also deeply committed to the rational inquiry of, and commerce with, the objective world and its norms. In short, the crux of

Guangdi's metapraxis is the inseparability of logos and praxis, the collapsing of the objective and subjective. This is how Guangdi sums up the nexus among knowing, acting, the will, and reverence:

> Broad learning, investigative inquiry, careful thinking and understanding distinctions are all matters of the extension of knowledge to the utmost. Punishing anger, curbing selfish desires, moving toward the good and correcting flaws are all matters of studious acting. The will is there at all times. To establish the will is to plant the roots. To emphasize reverence is to bank up the roots. They are matters of extensive knowledge and studious action. With prudent scrutiny, they destroy the harmful insects and weeds. The establishment of the will is the basis; the emphasis on reverence is the crux.[80]

At work in this welter of interrelations is the "evaluating mind," to use Donald Munro's description, the exhaustive seeking out of the ethical and moral qualities of nature, so that we discriminate what is right and wrong, and undertake appropriate actions accordingly and obligingly.[81] Never is there the sense that knowing is for knowing's sake. Guangdi says nothing to imply that knowing truth and falsity in a disembodied manner is knowledge per se. Rather, knowing is a polysemic and multilayered concept: the persistent inclination to inquire into what can be known and to earnestly act out what is known.

Such is the general philosophy of Li Guangdi. Despite its polyphonic nature, dubbing the voices of metaphysics (principle and material force) into the calls of metapraxis (knowing-acting, establishing the will, emphasizing reverence), the central motif is not obscured. It remains, in its essentials, a theory of moral cultivation founded on a metaphysical conception of humanity's nature as driven on by its own inner purpose, that is, principle, and on a meta-practical program that demands humanity's self-fulfillment. Echoes of Cheng-Zhu can be heard loud and clear, as Guangdi intended it to be. Yet he did broach new ideas and offer new insights. He does not deserve deprecation as a mere epigone of the Cheng-Zhu school bent on hagiographic celebration and not philosophic innovation.

The fact is that Guangdi is far from an unimaginative custodian of Cheng-Zhu creed, as we have already suggested and shown to a certain degree. If we accept that ideas are historically anchored, playing their appropriate role in the ebb and flow of historical circumstances, it is reasonable to expect that Guangdi would reformulate Cheng-Zhu ideas as instruments of adaptation and adjustment in a new age. We have already reconstructed the intellectual climate of the Ming–Qing transition, a climate that viewed with askance abstract metaphysical speculation. Wang Yangming and his followers' idea of the fundamental substance (the mind-heart, the innate knowledge of the good) as beyond good and evil in particular elicited the wrath of many literati, who blamed it for generating the moral anomie that afflicted late Ming society and state. Philosophical inquiry must be relocated from the Lu-Wang camp to the Cheng-Zhu one, so many urged. Fundamental nature must be asserted to be good, so others argued. The self once more must be the site on which social, political, and cultural meaning is constructed. The philosophic dysfunction of infirm ethics and empty introspection must be displaced by thinking that stresses the practicality of being and living.

Guangdi's innovation emerged from this intellectual background. He honored Zhu Xi, to be sure, and proclaimed his allegiance. But Zhu was honored not necessarily as a *man* of a specific time, but a *text* from whose architectonic structure arguments might be isolated, lifted, and modified for philosophic purposes appropriate to Guangdi's own historically contingent needs. To be sure, Guangdi's innovations are not defined in terms of fundamental restatements of Cheng-Zhu philosophical premises, but in terms of his strenuous attempts to develop new emphases. Significantly, for instance, in his discussion of the metapractical initiatives by way of honoring Zhu, he left out the notion of "plumbing principles" (*qiongli*), near and dear to the master, mentioning it only in passing but not as an independent category. It is indeed strange that in a piece dedicated to Zhu Xi, such a central meta-practical precept in the Zhuian scheme is left out. The reason for this omission can only be conjectured, but a plausible explanation may be offered. In our exploration of Guangdi's metaphysics, we have already seen how he increasingly talked about the ultimate reality of principle with reference to nature (*xing*). Indeed, upon the general theory of principle-material force, Guangdi erected a new ontology, one premised on nature. To examine this ontology is to describe the parameters of a meta-practical program that induces more immediate ways of appropriating and realizing the potentialities of a person, removing the metaphysical distance between the self and principle.

FOUR

THE ONTOLOGY OF *XING* (NATURE) AND ITS META-PRACTICAL IMPORT

> Whatever touches or enters into a sustained relationship with human life immediately assumes the character of a condition of human existence. This is why men, no matter what they do, are always conditioned beings. Whatever enters the human world of its own accord or is drawn into it by human effort becomes part of the human condition. The impact of the world's reality is felt and received as a conditioning force . . . because human existence is a conditioned existence, it would be impossible without things, and things would be a heap of unrelated articles, a *non-world*, if they were not the conditioners of human existence.
>
> —Hannah Arendt, *The Human Condition*

A major theme in the Confucian discourse in the late Ming and early Qing was, as we have argued, the impetus to rethink the question of nature (*xing*). A generation of scholars, beginning with the Donglin participants, reasserted the goodness of *xing* as a certainty of faith, a *creencia*. They categorically repudiated the idea of fundamental human substance as beyond good and evil. As adumbrated earlier, the importance and centrality of *xing* in Li Guangdi's philosophical cogitation is unmistakable. Thus, while his general theory displays a Cheng-Zhu outline, his deliberate appropriation of Cheng-Zhu metaphysics was neither mimetic nor slavish. In fact, it was transformative and critical: he employed Cheng-Zhu resources to reconceptualize the nature of *xing*. Far from writing sectarian apologias, Guangdi brought to the traditional idea of *xing* a certain amount of interpretive violence, not to destroy it of course, but rather to lay bare the original meaning and spirit. Instead of seeing *xing* as the individual instantiation of *li*, the principle of being, he sought to reveal human nature as *the* underlying phenomenal reality, the ontological locus of life as it was lived by individuals. Once *xing* was properly identified as the very principle of reality, it could then be enlisted in the cause of articulating a fully interactive conception of metaphysics and metapraxis: nature is action, to the extent that the latter is the inexorable condition of the fulfillment of the former.

In this chapter, we examine specifically Guangdi's ontology of *xing* by recalling the items on the philosophic agenda that emerged in the late Ming: the preoccupation with the question of *xing*, the mutuality of substance (metaphysics) and function (metapraxis/praxis), and a holistic conception of *xing*. We show that Guangdi's views were developed in an intellectual climate that also nurtured a host of seventeenth-century scholars, although Guangdi perhaps was the most systematic and went the furthest in universalizing *xing* as the ontological center of reality. In addition, in order to throw Guangdi's thought on *xing* into sharp relief, we specifically interlard his ponderings with those of another latter-day Cheng-Zhu follower in the early Qing, Lu Shiyi (1611–1672).[1] Such an analytic and narrative arrangement serves two goals. First, it reestablishes the epochal intellectual context in which Guangdi's ruminations on *xing* ought to be situated. Second, by juxtaposing Shiyi and Guangdi, both acknowledged devotees of Cheng-Zhu learning, we portray the historically contingent parameters of an early Qing school that drew inspiration from and paid homage to the supposedly universal ideas first taught by the Song masters. Both Guangdi and Shiyi, as will be shown, succumbed not to nostalgic rehashing of the Song teachers' philosophy but creatively renewed it by giving it new appearances and emphases. Early Qing Cheng-Zhu Confucianism was a timely response to the predominant intellectual concerns of seventeenth-century China.

The Ontological Primacy of the Heaven-endowed Human Nature (*xing*)

As a student of Cheng-Zhu learning, Lu Shiyi, like Li Guangdi, basically subscribed to the ontology of principle and material force. As regards the relative ontological status of principle and material force, the former was prior, the latter posterior: "Master Zhu says that principle is prior to material force. . . . Suppose that which is light rises and becomes heaven, and we call it material force. Still, there must first be the principle of the rising of the light, and then there is [the phenomenon of] the light rising to become Heaven. . . . Without this principle, there is no such material force." However, Shiyi also makes it very clear that it is important to remember that, after all, "the two entities of principle and material force are originally indivisible."[2] In a letter to a friend, Shiyi belabors this metaphysical inseparability with reference to *xing*:

> Those who exist in the midst of heaven-and-earth are nothing but material force. But in talking about the fact of their being naturally so (*suoyiran*), it is nothing but principle. In heaven, principle and material force are the mandate of heaven. In humanity, they are humanity's nature. Nature and mandate are spoken of in terms of both principle and material force. . . . To speak both of principle and material force is to pursue the Way in its entirety. . . . If one desires to know nature and heaven, then one cannot not perceive them in their entirety. . . . That which is not embodied in nature is that which is not endowed by heaven.[3]

Shiyi thus reconciles the duality of the *li-qi* scheme by a process of anthropologization—the reality of principle and material force is instrumentalized as we come to know that humanity's nature is really after all the crux of the matter; the metaphysics of principle and material force instrumentally culminates in the fulfillment of *xing*.

Shiyi's interest in expressing the wholeness of ultimate reality in terms of *xing* is revealed in his elucidation of the Great Ultimate. The Great Ultimate, he posits, is the origin of heaven-and-earth, which is pervaded by the coeval principle: "This Great Ultimate is nothing but principle. . . . [It is] nothing but the one formless principle. It is the root-cause of the creation of heaven-and-earth."[4] Shiyi describes this as "the one Great Ultimate that is united in one body" (*tongti de yitaiji*), which is "the great virtues of great transformation." But there is also the "Great Ultimate that is immanent in individual things" (*wuwu zhi taiji*), wherein "principle and material force mysteriously unite to form a profound whole that is seamless. Whence comes the production of humanity and the myriad things." This is the "separate flow of the individual virtues."[5] In terms of the former, we may understand Zhu Xi's assertion that "there is first principle, then there is material force." In terms of the latter, Zhu's contention that "principle is in the midst of material force" also becomes comprehensible.[6] In other words, to Shiyi, the priority of principle can be explained only with reference to the incorporeal state before the Great Ultimate becomes individuated in things. Otherwise, principle and material form a seamless web of coexistence. In any case, the main import of the Great Ultimate is that "when it is seen from the immediate vantage point of one's self, it is nothing but the one word of *xing.*" Therefore, "everyone is innately endowed with the original substance of a sage. Everyone is united in the virtues of heaven-and-earth."[7] The dualism of *li-qi,* in the last analysis, finds resolution in the heaven-endowed goodness of *xing.*

In Shiyi's *Selected Notes of Reflections and Disputations* (Sibianlu jiyao), which he began compiling in 1637 and which was not completed and published until some two decades later (in 1661), he devotes three fascicles to "the Way of humanity" (*rendao*), wherein he presents the phenomenology of the goodness of human nature. At the very outset, drawing inspiration from the *Doctrine of the Mean,* Shiyi proclaims that "to extend to the utmost the Way of humanity is to be in accord with the Way of heaven," and "to follow the [heaven-endowed] *xing* is to extend to the utmost the Way of humanity." Thus, "humanity and heaven are not two."[8] Human nature, being one with heaven, is inexorably good:

> The sages established their teachings so that individuals could on their own change their evil ways and could on their own attain the Mean, standing still therein. . . . If human nature is not fundamentally good, how could [individuals] on their own change their evil ways and on their own attain the Mean, standing still therein? It is that the root of human nature is goodness possessed by all individuals.[9]

In Shiyi's attack on Wang Yangming's infamous four-sentence teaching, he goes right to the target: Wang's fundamental teaching is wrong because it consists of an "improper principal argument," that is, "viewing *xing* as beyond good and evil."[10] Small wonder that just six years before his death, in 1666, Shiyi penned the essay, "A Diagrammatic Discourse on the Goodness of Nature" (Xingshan tushuo). We shall return to this tract with a detailed examination of Shiyi's conception of *xing* in terms of its materiality. Suffice it here to note that Lu distinguishes human beings as the most exalted among all beings precisely because of the all-encompassing goodness of human nature. While all things and beings have their nature, only humanity's nature is imbued with a unique, abiding goodness.[11]

As with Lu Shiyi, in his systematic renewal of the Cheng-Zhu philosophy, Guangdi partook of the prevailing late Ming and early Qing preoccupation with the assertion of *xing* as innately and unalienably good. While he no doubt shared this epochal concern with many of his contemporaries, no less significant was his insistence that *xing,* not *li* (principle), was the ontological center and origin. Although Lu Shiyi did seek to reconcile *li* and *qi* in *xing,* he did not quite supplant *li* with *xing* as the ontological locus.

Guangdi did. In our earlier examination of Guangdi's general theory, it has been already suggested that he makes a habit of explicating the Cheng-Zhu metaphysical scheme of principle and material force with reference to humanity, its nature, experience, and action. In fact, he goes further. He recasts this scheme and declares the ontological primacy of *xing* over *li*: "*Xing* is the master, while *li* is its flow. *Ming* (destiny) is the source. Scholars follow the flow to reach the source. Therefore, it is said, 'To plumb principle is to extend heaven-conferred nature so as to reach destiny.' To reach destiny is to extend nature to the utmost."[12] Again: "What is called *li* is heaven-endowed human nature, which operates in and pervades things and affairs."[13] *Xing* is the "all-conclusive name" for *li*.[14] Thus, in contradistinction to the famous Cheng-Zhu dictum that "principle is one, but the manifestations are varied" (*liyi fenshu*), Guangdi maintains that "the diverse varieties of the myriad things are ultimately nothing but the completion of their immanent nature."[15] He illustrates this "immanent nature" by using the analogy of the growth and nature of grain:

> The germination of the seeds of grain is not nature itself. That which enables germination and is immutable throughout the ages is nature. Nature itself has no shape. But barley is always barley and wheat is always wheat. If not for their nature, why is that they never change? Because there is nature, there are multifarious things. If there were no such unchanging and yet non-stagnant entity, how could there have been the multifarious things? Therefore, it can be said that nature establishes the beings all-under-Heaven.[16]

Xing is the intrinsic force that gives particular specific patterns of life and growth to different species and categories of beings, plants or human beings, animate or inanimate.

Guangdi posits that there are three categories of *xing* in the universe. First is the seminal and all-pervading "nature of Heaven-and-Earth" (*tiandi zhi xing*), which he equates with the Great Ultimate (*taiji*): "Soundless and odorless, it is the overlord and fundamental bonds."[17] Stemming from this ultimate nature are both "human nature" (*renxing*) and "nature of things" (*wuxing*), both imbued with "goodness mandated by Heaven."[18] But only humanity receives the full endowment of goodness from heaven. Herein lies the difference between human beings and things: "Leaning to one side (*pian*) or straightness (*zheng*) is that which differentiates human beings from things. . . . Centrality (*zhong*) is exclusively human."[19]

Summoning the authority of Mencius, Guangdi asserts that humanity is the most privileged by heaven in that it replicates heaven's comprehensive goodness:

> Mencius, in the final analysis, claims that the innate goodness of human nature is different from that of things. Things may be brilliant in one respect but are dim in all other respects. The lack of likeness with heaven-and-earth means failing to measure up to goodness. Failing to measure up to goodness does not refer to the absence of just one beginning [of goodness]. [It refers] to failing to measure up to the origin of the most pure and good, the complete acquisition of heaven-and-earth's nature.[20]

In the most grandiose of terms, Guangdi describes his beatific conception of the oneness of all, in the image of heaven:

> The great intent of heaven is to create humanity. . . . Since heaven wants to create humanity, it cannot do otherwise but produce the world as the ground for [human activity]. It also must create things to accompany [humanity]. Although humanity amounts to millions and billions, none does not have the likeness of heaven. Therefore it can recognize the mind of heaven and embark on the Way of heaven. In extending to the utmost humanity's nature, the nature of things is extended to the utmost, indeed resembling heaven.[21]

In other words, the universal nature of heaven-and-earth finds full manifestation in humanity. Indeed, "Heaven and humanity have one nature."[22] Guangdi most often uses the word *xing* to mean specifically human nature, the manifestation of heaven.

The central reference point of Guangdi's thought is located exactly in the ontological primacy of *xing*. To begin with, Guangdi's hagiographic adoration of the paramount contribution of Cheng Yi and Zhu Xi is based on his conception of the duo's endeavor and accomplishment in "illuminating nature" (*mingxing*). It was because of such effort that Cheng and Zhu succeeded in "continuing the succession from Confucius and Mencius."[23] They, together with Zhou Dunyi and Zhang Zai, "continued the interrupted learning" (*ji juexue*) on the heaven-endowed human nature first propounded by the ancient sages.[24] The meaning of *xing*, after Confucius, Mencius, and Dong Zhongshu, had been distorted by Buddhism and Daoism, which "took material disposition (*qizhi*) as nature, and took the enlightened illuminated mind (*xin zhi lingming*) as nature." It was not until the appearance of Cheng and Zhu that the truth of human nature was once again thoroughly explicated.[25] Guangdi ascertains that "the learning of the sages" (*shengxue*), transmitted from Confucius to Mencius, is profound precisely because of its illumination of *xing*. This sagely learning was lost after Mencius because subsequent scholars had lost sight of the importance of the illumination of human nature.[26]

The transmission of the Way (*daotong*) is in essence the transmission of the meaning of *xing*, as Guangdi argues in an essay on the Song *daoxue* masters. He claims that there is a shared coherent vision in the four most important Song Confucian texts, namely, Zhou Dunyi's "Taiji tushuo" (Discourse on the Diagram of the Great Ultimate), Zhang Zai's "Ximing" (Western Inscription), Cheng Hao's "Dingxing shu" (Book on Securing Nature), and Cheng Yi's "Haoxue lun" (Discourse on the Favorite Learning [of Master Yen]). Guangdi explains that Zhou Dunyi's diagram depicts the "vitalistic creation of human beings and things," originating in the Great Ultimate. In the immediate human world, one "extends one's nature and becomes filial" because this nature is bequeathed by the parents. In the cosmic scheme of things, humanity and human nature are the progeny of "the vitalistic production of heaven-and-earth" by the Great Ultimate. Therefore, in essence, "humanity is at one with heaven-and-earth's nature." Zhang Zai's "Western Inscription" is an elaboration of this crucial idea propounded in Zhou's diagram. Since *qian* and *kun* are our "universal parents," the source of our nature, Zhang takes pains to elucidate the efforts of "plumbing principle and exhausting our nature so as to reach [heaven's] mandate." These efforts of "securing" one's *xing* means the pursuit of "impartiality, fairness, humaneness and rightness, emphasizing equanimity." Cheng Hao in turn explicates the question of an individual's "securing *xing*." In the midst of activity and effort, there must be the pervading sense of equanimity (*jing*), enabling one to be fully in accord with the profoundly just heaven-and-earth. In short, heaven-endowed nature can be secured by mastering equanimity, as Cheng Hao assures us.

Then comes Cheng Yi's grand summation of the previous three masters' messages. He spells out "the sequence and order" for securing *xing*: recognizing the goodness of human nature derived from heaven, securing this nature through mastering equanimity, enlightening the mind-heart, and ending with "diligent action" (*lixing*). Guangdi injects his own conclusion: "With the pinpointing of the two words of 'diligent action,' the way [of securing *xing*] becomes complete. The four works are coherent, complete with beginning and end." According to Guangdi's reading, a continuum from cognition to action inheres in the "learning of the sages," as admirably expounded in the four important pieces of writings by the Song masters: Zhou Dunyi establishes the universal truth of the oneness of human nature and the nature of the Great Ultimate and heaven-and-earth; Zhang Zai initiates the idea of extending this nature; Cheng Hao proposes the securing of this nature by emphasizing equanimity; Cheng Yi advocates conscientious, assiduous endeavor to complete the fulfillment of nature.[27]

Thus, for Lu Shiyi and Li Guangdi, the innately good *xing* came to be the assumed central reference point in philosophical cogitation. As the metaphysical dualism of principle and material force was increasingly subsumed under the monistic anthropologism of humanity's nature, reality was correspondingly reduced to human agency. *Xing*, as the ontological center of gravity of an anthropocentric universe, perforce extended to and in effect culminated in action. The invocation of the primacy of *xing* implied a metapractical teleology: the engagement with ultimate reality was the working out of *xing*'s potentialities.

The Metapraxis of *Xing*: Nature as the Ground for Practice and Action

It is not surprising that both Shiyi's and Guangdi's ontologies of the absolutely good *xing* move on the experiential fulcrum of practice and action. Indeed, they, like many late Ming and early Qing thinkers, sought to arrest the tendency toward the recondite. They deliberately combated the perceived twin-evils of latter-day Wang Yangming learning: the first, moral-ethical anomie prompted by the idea of "beyond good and evil"; the second, vacuous introspection engendered by the faith in a pure void and luminous original substance capable of sudden self-enlightenment. Any talk of the fundamental substance (*benti*) was meaningful only if it was not estranged from experiential efforts (*gongfu*).

Lu Shiyi had no use for the prevalent late Ming idea that practice was spontaneously realized with the manifestation of fundamental substance. He castigated scholars for "rashly talking about Heaven, regarding idle indolence as naturalness, taking emptiness as loftiness." For him, fundamental substance and practice exist in constant dialectic interaction: "To know *xing* is to know fundamental substance; to extend *xing* to the utmost is to extend practice to the utmost. Fundamental substance is heaven's lavish endowment to humanity. Practice is humanity's response to heaven."[28] Since what engages the intellectual energy of Shiyi is not any abstract description of universal reality, but the prescription of ways of educational, moral, and ethical cultivation, the metapraxis of *jujing qiongli* (dwelling in reverence and plumbing principles) assumes special significance in his writings: "The four words of *jujing qiongli* constitute the primary efforts of scholars' emulation of the sages. From the high to the low, from the beginning to the end, there are only these four words."[29] What is plumbing principles? As Lu explains, it is not an unworldly inner quest for ultimate reality remote from the worldly domain of action; rather, it demands seeking out principle "in the things in the world":

> The pursuit of plumbing principle is "the investigation [of things] and the extension [of knowledge]" (*gezhi*). Principle is within myself but it is sought in the things in the world. Why? . . . This is called the unity of "substance" (*ti*) and "function" (*yong*). . . . Scholars whose purpose is plumbing principle must observe everything, seek improvement every day and practice all the time, steadily working and steadily making progress, until the ultimate is reached, thereby becoming enlightened and sagely. . . . But it is not the indulgent search for the profound in the abstract. Indulgently searching for the profound in the abstract means the absence of focus, so much so that when a matter is at hand, there is no effort to scrutinize it, and when the matter is disposed of [in such manner], there is indolence.[30]

Plumbing principles is the incessant individual effort to study the external world. It is the investigation of things to arrive at moral and ethical knowledge, beginning with our very own self and *xing*, and extending it to the larger community:

> In the investigation of things, one must begin investigation in the near and dear, that is, body, mind-heart, nature and destiny, then in the Three Bonds and Five Relationships, and then daily practicality like drinking and eating. The rest of the myriad affairs and things will, in the process, be naturally apprehended. One must not first seek understanding in a blade of grass or a tree.[31]

What is dwelling in reverence (*jujing*), the complement to plumbing principles?

> Dwelling in reverence is purifying the will (*yi*). The beginning of purifying the will is to be honest. . . . With the progress of efforts, there will be the issuance of the real mind-heart. . . . As efforts progress further, there will the completion of prudence. . . . As there is even greater progress of efforts, there will be anxious wariness. Regardless of whether there is good to be followed or evil to be destroyed, one naturally acts astutely. This is the completion of sincerity (*cheng*), the completion of reverence (*jing*).[32]

If plumbing principles is action, dwelling in reverence is the motivation to act: "*jujing* is the root and origin, while *qiongli* is the site of progress."[33] Reverence, as the impulse impelling one to act correctly, encapsulates the essence of the entire moral enterprise of self-cultivation: "Broadly speaking, the effort of self-cultivation has the five concerns of countenance, speech, seeing, hearing and thinking; specifically speaking, it is only sincerity."[34] Shiyi in fact claims that to be reverent is to be reverent to heaven (*jingtian*). To seek reverence without respect for heaven is to lapse into a sort of mental torpidity and indolence. As he explains, the idea of heaven figures prominently in the sages' words, that is, the "Four Books and the Five Classics." Because the ancients properly honored the idea of heaven, they were "naturally sincere without deliberately working toward sincerity." In contrast, "most people nowadays do not know the word heaven, and speak only of sincerity. Many scholars' minds are confused and lazy. How can they be jolted into awakening?" In other words, to be reverent is to abide by some sort of normative ultimate—heaven/principle: "Heaven is principle. I say, 'Principle is heaven.' Only in knowing this can the effort of being sincere be developed to the utmost."[35] Shiyi also equates heaven with the watchfulness of the Lord-on-High (*shangdi*). A moral person invariably has the omnipresent sense of awe or anxiety vis-à-vis heaven (*weitian*), for if one "is not in awe of heaven's mandate, there is no restraining fear, and there is no hope of ever entering the Way."[36] Shiyi urges people to focus their mind-heart on the Lord-on-High. In so doing, they will "naturally feel their bones tremble in fear and will thus not be careless and slothful about even one thing or thought."[37]

What Shiyi aims to do here is to dispel the Lu-Wang myth of the internal meditative core of cultivation. Dwelling in reverence cannot be so radically subjectified that we only directly appeal to the mind-heart, and ignore heaven and principle, the normative order of the human community. Authentic reverence is the awareness that one's mind-heart is mediated and measured by heaven and principle: "What cannot be accepted by the mind-heart cannot be accepted by heaven. Only what can be accepted by heaven can be accepted by the mind-heart. This is how heaven and humanity become one principle (*tianren yili*)."[38] The gravity of dwelling in reverence can only be underscored by a moral activism that is essentially engaged with others, expressed in the reverence for heaven and principle. Therefore, the zealousness of dwelling in reverence allows no room for quiescence (*jing*): "Quiescence is not compatible with reverence," since "within the word quiescence can be easily hidden the appearance of Chan," whereas "the word 'reverence' is solidly concrete, an unbreakable principle."[39] Reverence is a Confucian virtue which must resist perversion by the Chan Buddhist penchant for inaction.

Wang Yangming, according to Shiyi, simplistically boils the acts of plumbing principles, together with *gewu* (investigation of things) and *zhizhi* (extending knowledge to the utmost), down to one, namely, that of "manifesting the clear character" (*ming mingde*). Wang does so through the broad enveloping idea of "extension of the innate knowledge of the good" (*zhi liangzhi*). In the process, the variegated efforts embodied in Zhu Xi's notions of plumbing principles, investigating things, and extending knowledge are reduced to one all-encompassing act:

> Although this idea of extension of the innate knowledge of the good is direct and to the point, it is ultimately not all-encompassing. It is not as solid and reliable as plumbing principle. If asked why, I would reply that there are matters in the world that could be naturally understood without deliberation. They are the mind-heart, nature, the Way and virtues. There are those which could only be understood with study . They are names, things, measures and institutions. . . . How can the innate knowledge of the good be solely relied upon? Therefore, the two words of *qiongli* can encompass *zhi liangzhi*, but the three words of *zhi liangzhi* cannot encompass *qiongli*.[40]

Wang's innate knowledge of the good may be adequate with respect to intuitive moral introspection, but it completely ignores the wider world at large. Wang's repudiation of the Cheng-Zhu idea of investigating things stems from his misunderstanding of its purpose, confusing it with the Chan Buddhist method of contemplation:

> Yangming told us that when he was young, he and his friend practiced Master Zhu's pursuit of investigation of things by together investigating the bamboo in front of the pavilion. They thought so hard and deeply that they became ill, eventually failing in the task of investigation. [Wang] therefore lamented that we could in no way emulate the sage [who had successfully investigated things in that manner], and that the investigation of things could not be realized. I would say that the method [as described by Wang] is that of the Chan school which contemplates bamboo steamers [as a means toward enlightenment]. It is surely not Master Zhu's advocacy. It was Wang Yangming's own error. Why should he blame Master Zhu?[41]

In advancing the metapraxis of plumbing principles and dwelling in reverence, Shiyi affirms a trajectory away from the putative Lu-Wang thesis of the ultimate disclosure of authentic being in the self. To cultivate the self is to comport oneself with a view to acknowledging the demands of heaven and principle, and in the process, realize that everything "is woven by the one thread of the innately good nature" (*yiguan xingshan*).[42] This one thread means the unity of knowledge and action: "Reverence is that by which the roots [of cultivation] are established. But without the investigation of things, the Way cannot be illuminated. Without earnest action, the Way cannot be activated. . . . Nothing amounts to action without knowledge; nothing can be called knowledge without action."[43] As with dwelling in reverence, plumbing principles also unites knowing and acting: "The endeavor of plumbing principle is not merely knowing it, but is the acting out of it," and when knowing and acting are both fully developed at once, our nature is simultaneously fully realized.[44]

By orchestrating the various metapractical theories of plumbing principles, dwelling in reverence, and uniting knowing and acting, Shiyi voiced his central message: the fulfillment of our innately good nature in action. Little wonder that he likened learning in his own time to the rapacious "pure talk" (*qingtan*) of the Jin period (280–316) that did violence to the teachings of Confucius: "In recent times, many scholars study in the same manner that the Jin people practiced pure talk. It is harmful to action. Not one word in the Confucian school does not teach one to work on the concrete. The *Analects* says, 'The superior person is slow in words but diligent in action.' . . . It also says, 'A superior person is shameful that his words exceed his actions.' All [these statements] caution people to be wary of words' exceeding actuality." Sadly in Shiyi's own days, "it has become a decadent vogue in the world to value one another's talk and speech. Thoughts and purposes are lost. Even if the words of the sages are uttered, they are futile words; they are pure talk."[45] Shiyi reminded his contemporaries that the peace and rule of the antiquity of the Three Dynasties owed much to action and practice, while the disorder that beset the late Ming was attributed to the empty polemics that consumed the energy of scholars: "In the Three Dynasties, rulers acted as rulers, fathers acted as fathers. Each pursued diligent actions, each was engaged in practical actions. In the schools, the classics are studied and recited, the rites and music are practiced. [Nowadays], scholars . . . follow shadows and chase after sounds, wasting time and losing sight of actual matters. . . . On whom could the world rely?"[46] Shiyi thus urged his fellow scholars to engage the complexities of the external world, to take up practical learning of all stripes:

> What today's scholars should be studying is not confined to the Six Classics. For instance, astronomy, geography, water transportation, military strategies and the like are all inti-

> mately related to utility. They cannot not be studied. Vulgar Confucians do not know the learning of internal sagehood and external rulership, and futilely discourse on nature and destiny, offering no aid to the world, therefore inviting derision for being impractical and inept.[47]

In fact, Shiyi drew up a three-stage master curriculum for the complete education of a scholar from ages five to thirty-five, seeking not only to mold a studious person of moral integrity, but also one with practical knowledge of governance. He prescribed the requisite categories of writings for each of the three ten-year curricula (ages five to fifteen, ages fifteen to twenty-five, and ages twenty to thirty-five). Apart from assigning the classics, commentaries on the classics, poetry, history, and the like, for every stage of intellectual cultivation there were readings on economy, institutions, laws, military affairs, agriculture, and so forth. His aim was that "students will become scholars embodying both substance and function," since in Shiyi's days, such students were sorely absent. He lamented that all he saw was the "wasting of the world's energy in writing examination essays. . . . Who would be a true scholar? How can the country reap the benefits of scholarship?"[48]

Thus, within the framework of Cheng-Zhu learning, from the ontological premise of the goodness of *xing*, Shiyi strove to clear a way through the profuse tangle of recondite metaphysical speculations of the late Ming, and pointed straight to action and practicality. Similarly, to Li Guangdi, the ontological reality of the absolutely good human nature seeks existential revelation in the human community. The *daotong*, the transmission of the Confucian Way, enlivened by the illumination of the innately good human nature, is nothing but the expression of fundamental moral ethics in the human social world: virtues of *ren* (humaneness), *yi* (rightness), *li* (propriety), *zhi* (wisdom), and *xin* (trustworthiness). The greatest contribution of Cheng-Zhu, Guangdi touts, is their explicit definition of nature as these virtues. In so doing, they revivified and continued the *daotong* by bypassing centuries of Buddhist-Daoist aberrations.[49] Following and expounding the Way transmitted by Cheng-Zhu, Guangdi declares that the innately good human nature is the key to transforming state and society:

> Therefore, when the idea of innate goodness of human nature is comprehended, it can be seen that people all-under-heaven have this innately good nature. While caring for one's elder relations, one cares for the other elderly; while nurturing one's young relations, one nurtures the young of others. With such nourishing and teaching, there are joy, pleasure, harmony and generosity.[50]

Again: "Seeing that human nature is innately good, oneself and others become one. Morally influencing one another, humanity is complete."[51] According to Guangdi, this sort of moral power originates in the four pristine qualities of the nature of heaven-and-earth, namely, *yuan* (origin), *heng* (success), *li* (furthering), and *zhen* (perseverance). In human nature, they become respectively, humaneness, righteousness, propriety, and wisdom, the so-called *siduan* (the four sprouts).[52] Of the four, humaneness, or *ren*, is paramount, being derived from the grand beginning of *yuan*. It embodies the other "sprouts." In the human world, the most eloquent expression of *ren* is the virtue of *xiao* (filial piety), which is the "basis of virtues" (*de zhi ben*).[53] In fact, filiality is the "basis of humaneness" (*ren zhi ben*), even though "humaneness is the basis of the Five Constants" (*wuchang zhi ben*).[54] In other words, nothing is more basic and significant than the virtue that is actualized in the most intimate and primal of human activities, namely, filiality. "To care for parents and follow elder brothers" is the concrete outer manifestation of the inner nature of humaneness, rightness, propriety, and wisdom:

> Nature resides inside, the Way outside. The principle of nature is apparently abstract and difficult to see, and so its concreteness is pointed out so that it can be followed. . . . Humaneness, rightness, propriety and wisdom are heaven-decreed nature; to care for parents and follow elder brothers is the Way of following nature.[55]

Here, Guangdi first explains the abstract nature as the concrete Way. He then conflates the ontological with the experiential by using the words of the opening verse of the *Doctrine of the Mean*: to follow the Way of nature as decreed by heaven. In so doing, he harks back to the classical Confucian polarity of the conditions bestowed by heaven and the control exercised by human actions, revealed prominently in both the *Mean* and the appendixes of the *Book of Changes*. While heaven decrees nature and the tendencies to realize this nature, it is human beings' incessant task to fully exhaust its potentialities.[56]

Because Guangdi is interested in revealing how heaven-and-earth's qualities are transposed into ethico-moral virtues as they are brought to bear on the human community, he finds the Cheng-Zhu tenet that *li* is prior to all as one susceptible to abstract philosophizing. While Guangdi, as we have seen, affirms *li* as the absolute truth, the notion of *li* in itself intimates no immediate connection with the human world: "Not knowing that principle is human nature, [many] seek the transcendent abstruse principle, falling short in pursuing quotidian practicality. Drowned in the deluge of principle, one is ignorant of the fountainhead."[57] The metaphysical category of principle creates a vacant space between that which is ultimate and ordinary human life. The notion of the primacy of *xing*, in contrast, directly establishes linkage between ultimate reality and humanity, while preserving the imperative of *li*. The world and human actions, as lived by oneself, need no longer be directly accounted for by the transcendental ideality of *li*.

Guangdi's conception of the doctrine of *gewu zhizhi* (investigating things and extending knowledge) is also filtered through the ontological spectrum of the primacy of *xing*: "[The pursuit of] humaneness, rightness, propriety and wisdom is *gewu zhizhi*. It is illuminating goodness and knowing human nature (*mingshan zhixing*)."[58] Thus, the foremost object of investigation is one's *xing* and its manifest virtues. To "investigate things" is to realize that "self-cultivation" is the "root":

> In investigating all affairs and things, it is invariably to thoroughly understand [their] root, branches, beginning and end. This is precisely the comprehensive accomplishment of investigation of things. The *Great Learning* is afraid that people may have doubts about the word "completion" in the phrase "completion of knowledge" (*zhizhi*), thinking that there is "completion" only when all the things in the world are exhaustively [investigated]. Therefore [the *Great Learning*] also says that all must regard self-cultivation as the root, and that there is never a case when the important becomes insignificant, or when the insignificant becomes important. This is called "knowing the root" (*zhiben*). This is called "completion of knowledge."[59]

Guangdi forges a specific focus for *gewu zhizhi*, to wit, "knowing the root," and the root is the self and self-cultivation. One must know that "the state and the world are the branches; the self is the root."[60] Knowledge of this fact entails responsible and studious actions on the part of individuals: "Knowing that the world and the state regard the self as the root, it is then known that the self and the mind cannot be indulgent, derelict and selfish."[61] One must develop to the utmost the root, one's nature, the vessel of goodness imparted by heaven: "*Xing* is just goodness. Knowing that . . . this root can be developed to the utmost in one's self, there is what is regarded as 'knowing nature and illuminating goodness.' There is what is regarded as 'knowing the root.'"[62] The investigation of things simmers down to knowing, and in turn, cultivating, one's *xing*.

Cultivating one's *xing* encompasses the family, state, and world. From the realm of *xing*, one moves to the contiguous world of social relationships (*renlun*):

> Father and son, brothers, ruler and subjects, friends and husband and wife are the social relationships. Humaneness, rightness, propriety, intelligence and trustworthiness are human nature. In terms of their fundamental unity, humaneness pervades the Five Relationships; rightness, propriety, wisdom and trustworthiness also pervade the Five Relationships. In terms of their separate functions, the closeness between father and son is based on humaneness; the right relation between ruler and subjects is based on rightness; the hierarchy of the old and young is based on propriety; the difference between husband and wife is based on wisdom; the trust between friends is based on trustworthiness.[63]

Human nature finds manifestation in human relationships, and human relationships are governed by human nature. In other words, human beings, although endowed by heaven with the innately good nature, are conditioned beings. Without things and affairs of the social world, life is impossible. The Way is nothing but the social web of relationships: "The Way is social relationships. The ruler and subjects constitute the ultimate of the Way. The Way cannot be followed without the establishment of one's self. Moreover, without serving the ruler and following the Way, one cannot establish one's self and serve one's parents."[64] Interestingly, then, Guangdi's celebration of the ontologically profound *xing* is very much tempered by *xing*'s finitude, in the sense that it is defined and conditioned by the publicness, as it were, of its manifestation and fulfillment in the social world, the only proper venue for authentic disclosure of the goodness of *xing*.

To the extent that the disclosure and opening of *xing* can only be achieved by everyday practices, the modus operandi of Guangdi's philosophy is the construction of the way of individual actions. If fulfilling *xing* means a full and complete grasp of our existence, learning related to the everyday must take precedence over learning of the sublime and ultimate. Hence his promotion of that part of Cheng-Zhu learning that encourages quotidian study and living, the practical cultivation of a responsible and productive social being. This was the practical spirit that guided Guangdi when he compiled, under imperial aegis, the *Complete Works of Master Zhu* (Zhuzi daquan) and the *Essential Ideas of [the Cheng-Zhu School of] Nature and Principle* (Xingli jingyi), both of which, in the words of Wing-tsit Chan, emphasized the so-called simple and straightforward "small learning," "elementary learning," and "great learning," as opposed to the abstract metaphysical speculation in "doctrines on nature, destiny, moral virtues, heaven and earth, *yinyang* and *gueishen*."[65]

There is a certain irony here that Guangdi's quest for the practical did not quite eschew, but in fact began with, metaphysical pondering, although, to be sure, his goal was to provide the fundamental explanations for practical action in the quotidian world.

Guangdi's conception of the primacy of *xing* takes on added significance in light of Yü Ying-shih's thesis of the rise of the Confucian "intellectualism" in the late Ming and early Qing. This "intellectualism" saw the overshadowing of the pursuit of "honoring the virtuous nature" (*zun dexing*) by "the pursuit of the way of inquiry and learning" (*dao wenxue*); the inward turn and focus on one's essential being was subsumed under the realm of outward engagement with knowledge of the everyday.[66] In effect, in arguing for the elevation of *xing*, Guangdi takes up these traditional dual and, oftentimes agonistic, paths of cultivation, synthesizing and externalizing them in such a way that the stress on the very internal ground of reality, our *xing*, nonetheless requires and demands confrontation with the everydayness of the social world. When Guangdi looks at the passage in the *Doctrine of the Mean* where the phrases *zun dexing* and *dao wenxue* appear, he sees not a dichotomy but a synthesis. He in fact rejects Zhu Xi's reading that the former is associated with the "ever-flowing" (*yangyang*) "substance" (*ti*) of the Way, while the latter is related to the "all-complete" (*youyou*) "function" (*yong*) of the Way. Rather, "any talk of *dao wenxue* must involve *zun dexing*. . . . This is the mutual reinforcement of the root and the branches, the complementary nurturing of the inner and outer. It is the complete picture of the sages' learning."[67] On the one hand, the Lu-Wang followers "dare not acknowledge that much in the outer world is virtuous nature." As result, they lose sight of the inexorable publicness and sociality of *xing*. On the other hand, some scholars, when reading the *Mean*'s phrases of "extending breadth and greatness to the utmost" (*zhi guangda*) and "raising to the greatest height and brilliance" (*ji gaoming*) readily associate them with *dao wenxue*; they ignore *xing*'s demand for painstaking and broad learning.[68] To be sure, our innately good *xing* is a sort of foreknowledge and inborn capability (*yizhi yineng*), but their actual realization depends on painstaking inquiry and learning in the midst of ordinary living. Guangdi analogizes our inborn "blood and breath" with our virtuous nature. While we may be resolved in nurturing our inborn qualities, such as in the case of honoring our virtuous nature, we also have no choice but to seek nourishment in the proper food and medicine, which is in essence the pursuit of the way of inquiry and learning.[69]

Guangdi's notion of *xing* as the progenitor of human activity, far from engendering a self consumed by itself, produces one that is preoccupied by relations with the outside world; productive comportment with things and affairs is the only means to know *xing*. Guangdi's theory of human nature, mediated by Qing "intellectualism," demands a praxis of learning and action: "Learning involves knowledge and action, rooted in *xing*'s wisdom and humaneness."[70] Knowledge is derived from wisdom, displayed in the serious learner as "broad learning, critical inquiry, careful thinking and seeing distinctions clearly." Action, on the other hand, stems from humaneness, demonstrated in people as "curtailing anger, curbing desires, moving toward good and rectifying mistakes."[71] *Xing* affords the natural wherewithal for effective learning and appropriate action. Yet a method, sequence, or order of knowledge and action must be followed: "The learning of the sages is nothing but knowledge and action. The roots of knowledge and action are establishing the will and maintaining reverence."[72] Establishing the will means constant development of the "tendency" toward the Way and humanity.[73] Reverence means "an empty mind without depravity."[74] If one can continue to "establish the goal and dwell in reverence," one can "realize [these pursuits] in human nature."[75] A teleological metapraxis emerges: establishing the will, dwelling in reverence, gaining knowledge, and undertaking action—all realized and completed in human nature. In the previous chapter, we pointed to the metapraxis that inheres in Guangdi's general ontological and metaphysical theory. Here, we see more specifically how such metapractical impulses are at once generated by and fulfilled in the flourishing of our *xing*.

Guangdi uses the example of Confucius to illustrate the fact that the realization of our nature is a teleological and dynamic process of ceaseless action:

> Therefore, if one wants to act but lacks knowledge, one will wander aimlessly, not knowing what to do. If one seeks knowledge without reverence, one's mind will be confused all of the time. If one is reverent but lacks will, how can one achieve the result of daily improvement? If one has will but is not reverent, how can this will be perpetuated? If one is reverent but lacks knowledge, the mind-heart will work on empty and abstract things. If one has knowledge but does not act, then one will have no principle and lacks concreteness. Although the four things are mutually reinforcing, there is the order of priority. . . . Therefore, Confucius said, "When I was fifteen, I established the will to learn." That was establishing the will. What he said about his character's being formed at thirty referred to the achieving of reverence. As he became no longer perplexed, knowing the mandate of heaven and being

> at ease with whatever he heard, his knowledge became superior. When he could follow his heart's desire without moral transgression, he knew well how to act. Many scholars have thought that the Master was simply describing himself. In fact, he established a method for learners.[76]

According to this "method," the consolidation of moral purposes is the prerequisite for the pursuit of knowledge and action. Action is the expression of an individual's basic way of being-in-the-world. This being is first and foremost defined by the fundamental project of moral preparation. Knowledge is prior to action. As we recall, in "Principal Purpose of Honoring Zhu," Guangdi praises Zhu Xi's dictum of "prior knowledge and posterior action" as authentic and true, for it embodies "the virtues of human nature and the principle of heaven-and-earth." Just as *yang* is prior to *yin*, so too knowledge comes before action: "The order of knowledge and action, and the principle of *xing* and destiny cannot be changed."[77]

In the name of the ontologically supreme *xing*, Guangdi drains the Confucian assumption of praxis of ambiguity. *Li*, albeit the truth, nonetheless may appear as a mere simulacrum of the actual world. Its very transcendence hovers above the phenomenal reality, the firm ground of the self. But if *xing* is the very reality that we seek to realize, then no longer is moral cultivation shoved into the shadow of the metaphysical domain of transcendent truth, as the Cheng-Zhu stress on principle is wont to do. If this realization must be informed by knowledge and achieved by action, then moral quest is not the exclusively inward turn toward some essential substance in the self, as the Lu-Wang call for direct apprehension of the mind-heart is likely to engender. Rather, the elevation of *xing* provides an ontological argument and mode for being-in-the-world, for plunging the individual into involvement in the activities and events that determine a moral life. In brief, to argue on behalf of *xing* is to assert the worldliness and everydayness of reality. Otherwise, a metaphysics of the eternal or ultimate in the end can only signify one thing: an enduring nothingness, emptiness, or remoteness. Felicitous it is that Guangdi offers this summation of his own learning: "My learning has three themes: first is to preserve the concrete mind (*cun shixin*), second is to illuminate concrete principle (*ming shili*), third is to act on concrete things (*xing shishi*)."[78]

The Wholeness of *Xing*

As argued in chapter one, the late Ming and early Qing scholars came to conceive of *xing* in a more holistic fashion as the innately good *xing* was taken to be the firm ground of ultimate reality. For if *xing* seeks realization in the phenomenal and corporeal, should the affective, emotive, and sensory that constitute our existential being still be regarded as secondary nature? Should the so-called *qizhi zhi xing* (material nature) always submit to the noumenally superior *yili zhi xing* (moral nature)? To many, *xing* is holistically one. To maintain exclusively the supremacy of moral nature means the inevitable, but errant, submerging of worldly matters in a pure inner being. The acceptance of physical nature as the true nature, on the other hand, means the appropriate affirmation of a worldly reality given to the senses. As we have pointed out, this holistic conception of nature, according to Qian Mu, provides another illustration of late Ming and early Qing scholars' increasing interest in establishing and probing a reality that is the concrete and tangible.[79]

Among seventeenth-century scholars, Lu Shiyi was perhaps the most overt and explicit not only in repudiating the dualistic nature of *xing*, but also in validating the goodness of physical nature. He tells us that his "Diagrammatic Discourse on the Goodness of Nature," his final words on *xing* written just six years prior to his death, was inspired by the Donglin view on the importance of material nature. While as a matter of sectarian loyalty and philosophical conviction, Shiyi followed Cheng-Zhu learning, toward the latter part of his life, he began to develop divergent ideas on the question of *xing*. These ideas were recorded in both the aforementioned essay and in his *Selected Notes on Reflections and Disputations*, whose compilation took more than twenty years. It is useful here to recapitulate very briefly the Cheng-Zhu view on human nature which, as we recall, is premised on the dichotomy of moral nature and material nature. The former is also called *tianming zhi xing* (heaven-mandated nature) or *tiandi zhi xing* (heaven-and-earth nature). Moral nature is identified with principle, whereas material nature is a combination of principle and material force. Although principle does not exist independent of material force, it is in the realm of material force that evil arises. But the transcendent principle can be isolated from and is prior to material force. Thus the holism of *li-qi* is after all shot through with a protuberant sense of duality. In terms of human nature, the prior moral nature is always good because it is the manifestation of the fundamental ultimate reality of principle, while the posterior material nature is the repository of both good and evil.

Shiyi counters this dualistic conception by monistically seeing moral nature and material nature as one and the same: "The Song Confucians, when speaking of human nature, claimed that there were moral nature and material nature. Does nature have this duality? I say it does not."[80] *Qizhi* (materiality of being) is integrally an essential part of human nature, not posterior to moral nature which, according to the Cheng-Zhu scheme, is privileged by heaven: "Any discussion on human nature cannot depart from the materiality of being. Once there is departure from the materiality of being, there is departure from heaven-and-earth. For heaven-and-earth embodies also the materiality of being."[81] Shiyi contends, "There is no human nature outside of the materiality of being; there is no *dao* outside of *yin-yang*."[82] In fact, human nature comes after materiality: "Human nature is produced after the physical form (*xing*) has appeared and the spirit (*shen*) has developed. Thus, there must be materiality before there is nature."[83] This argument is based on his interpretation of Zhou Dunyi's "Discourse on the Diagram of the Great Ultimate" (Taiji tushuo):

> [Zhou's work states,] "Humanity alone receives the finest of [the Five Agents], therefore becoming the most enlightened. The physical form is produced, and the spirit issues consciousness." The physical form produces disposition, and the spirit issues material force. With the production of the physical form and the issuance of spirit, there is the completion of the five [moral qualities] of human nature [i.e., humaneness, rightness, propriety, wisdom, and trustworthiness]. Thus, there is first material disposition and then there is human nature. That which has not descended to the domain of material disposition cannot be called nature. Once nature is named, it is the domain of material disposition.[84]

Having established the primacy of material disposition, Shiyi redefines the meaning of principle in the Cheng-Zhu dictum of "human nature is principle": "Human nature is the principle of material disposition. The principle of humanity's material disposition is goodness. The principle of things' material disposition is the combination [of good and bad]."[85] Again, he says: "The principle that is embodied in the midst of material disposition is called human nature."[86] The Cheng-Zhu taxonomic division of human nature into the moral and material is therefore not a representation of ontological truth; it is a semantic descriptive device. Principle is the name for the fundamental nature constituted by materiality. Shiyi explains the meaning of moral nature:

> It is not that outside of material disposition, there is moral principle [in human nature] which is denied to things but is exclusively possessed by humanity. Then what is moral principle? It refers to and illumines that which is proper and organized in material disposition. What is that which is proper and

> organized? It is the four sprouts (*siduan*): the senses of sympathy, shame, humility, and right and wrong. . . . It is not that there is this one entity outside of yin-yang, physical form and material force, called moral principle, which is obtained by humanity as human nature.[87]

Shiyi situates human nature in the realm of material disposition for a reason: he wants to highlight the uniqueness of humanity and the immediacy of the human world:

> The innate goodness of human nature need not be seen in terms of heaven's mandate. It can be seen in terms of material disposition. How so? The word "nature" is universal. Human beings have nature; things have nature; animals have nature; plants have nature. If it is seen in terms of heaven's mandate, it is neither distinguished in humanity nor in things. Human nature is the same as nature of things. There is no discrimination. To speak of innate goodness in the absence of discrimination is to say that humanity is innately good and things are innately good. How can it be discerned that innate goodness ultimately rests with humanity? However, looking at material dispositions, human nature appears different from nature of things; nature of animals appears different from nature of plants. Humanity receives everything in its entirety [from heaven], while things receive parts. Humanity has intelligence, while things are dull; humanity can communicate while things are mute. Thus the completion of goodness no doubt rests with humanity. Therefore the innate goodness of human nature is like the hot nature of fire, or the cold nature of water. . . . All this can be seen in terms of material disposition.[88]

As a result, Shiyi does not accept the Cheng-Zhu interpretation of the Mencian doctrine of innately good human nature, which locates this goodness before and above the realm of material nature. He states his objection:

> Various Confucians claim that when Mencius talks about innately good nature, he talks only in terms of heaven's mandate before its descent to material nature. I used to hold this view. Now, I see that this may not be correct. Before the descent to material nature, there is only innately good mandate, and no innately good nature. If one speaks about goodness in terms of mandate, then humanity and things share the same heaven's mandate. Humanity's nature is good, things'

> nature is good. Where can there be discrimination? What Mencius calls innately good nature refers to that which comes after heaven's mandate.[89]

Thus, Shiyi's holistic view on nature as defined by materiality results from his dissatisfaction with the indiscriminate Cheng-Zhu idea that human nature is the manifestation of one universal principle, which fails to properly distinguish between humanity and the myriad things. This universal absolute intrinsically detracts from the realm of human affairs and the essential plurality of all-under-heaven. By failing to properly pinpoint the uniqueness and superiority of humanity, it dilutes the sense of urgency and immediacy needed to pursue the efforts of self-cultivation. Moral endeavor is unique to humanity. Hence Shiyi's reformulation of the meaning of principle with reference to human nature. His principle refers not to the undifferentiated universal principle but to the order and pattern discernible in human material nature. His ontology thus forges an unequivocally human locus of efforts, a space where authenticity within one's nature, material nature no less, should be asserted.

Li Guangdi, unlike Lu Shiyi, follows Cheng-Zhu and sees material force as the source of evil, as we have seen in our analysis of his general theory. But in his own way, Guangdi also painstakingly defines human nature holistically, seeking to mitigate the sense of duality and separation engendered by the pitting of principle against material force. Interestingly, Guangdi sees Han Yu as the intermediary figure who negotiated both the positions of Mencius and Cheng-Zhu. Given the fact that the question of *xing* loomed so large in Guangdi's philosophy, it is not surprising that Guangdi compiled in 1707 a work entitled *Choice Words of Master Han* (Hanzi cuiyan), an anthology of Han Yu's principal writings with Guangdi's own commentaries. It is well known that Han Yu was credited with his defense and reinvigoration of the Confucian tradition in face of Buddhist and Daoist dominance. In particular, Han propounded a theory of *xing* that stressed its concrete moral and ethical contents, as opposed to the Buddhist and Daoist conception of *xing*'s ultimate emptiness.[90] To state it briefly, Han claims that there are three "grades" (*pin*) of human nature: the superior, which is good; the inferior, which is bad; and the medium, which can be good or bad. But he also asserts that human nature consists in five cardinal virtues: humaneness, propriety, trustworthiness, rightness, and wisdom.[91]

Guangdi praises Han Yu's contribution to the Confucian discourse on *xing* for affirming that "the Way of humaneness and rightness comes entirely from *xing*."[92] Guangdi also commends him for "continuing Mencius of old and paving the way for Cheng-Zhu to come." What Guangdi means is that Han Yu, in propounding the idea of the three grades of human nature, clearly established the notion of material nature, whereas Mencius before him spoke of *xing* in terms of heaven's mandate. In other words, Han Yu's conception of *xing* is a concatenation and amalgam of both material nature and moral nature. Yet, despite his accolade for Han Yu's complex picture of *xing*, Guangdi contends that in viewing nature, the most important fact is that of the five constitutive virtues. They define the fundamental nature, the nature of heaven-and-earth: "[Han Yu's] three grades are material nature. But there are five [virtues] that make it [i.e., material nature]. They are heaven-and-earth's nature. Knowing that what constitute that nature are those five [virtues], then it is known that nature is nothing if it is not good."[93] Thus, ultimately, Guangdi singles out the heaven-of-earth nature, a la Mencius, as the only nature that really counts, thereby swamping material nature and fostering a holistic conception of *xing* as good.

Indeed, elsewhere, Guangdi proclaims that there is but one human nature encapsulating the "pure and supremely good" nature of heaven-and-earth:

> Cheng-Zhu demarcated principle and material force when discussing human nature. I feel that this was not how Mencius spoke of it. Rather, Mencius said that principle and material nature are naturally within [human nature]. If principle and material force are demarcated, it would appear that principle is simply principle and material force is simply material force. . . . The material force of heaven-and-earth originates from the principle of heaven-and-earth. When is it ever not good? . . . However, human beings . . . after all cannot be completely like heaven. But even though [their] material deposition may vary and differ, they all possess heaven-and-earth's nature. It is like the developed color of silver, which is of different grades. Although the grade may be the lowest, it is after all developed silver.[94]

Guangdi echoes Mencius in establishing the fundamental idea that all of human nature, coming from heaven, is intrinsically good. Dereliction in some people comes from the failure to develop the potentialities of this nature to the fullest. The notion of "material nature" is therefore an unnecessary "addition" by Zhang Zai and Cheng-Zhu, as Guangdi boldly argues. He takes issue with them on this point by explicating the meaning of material nature with reference to the notion of "native endowment" (*cai*) as used by Mencius.[95]

As Guangdi sees it, what Cheng Yi conceives as "material nature" is nothing but what Mencius calls "native endowment":

> Mencius said, "[If one is not good,] it is not the fault of native endowment. It is that one fails to exhaust one's native endowment. It is not that heaven bestows to those below different native endowments. Native endowment is material nature. What is wrong is the inability to extend to the utmost native endowment. If people's native endowment and nature vary, it is just that some lean toward humaneness, and some toward rightness, propriety or wisdom; there are some who are deficient in humaneness, some in rightness, propriety or wisdom. There is none who is completely without humaneness, rightness, propriety and wisdom; nor is there one who lacks completely one [of the virtues] of humaneness, rightness, propriety and wisdom."[96]

Material nature, contrary to what Zhang Zai and Cheng-Zhu maintain, does not yield the bad. Material nature is native endowment which embraces, in varying proportions, aspects of inherent goodness. According to Guangdi, it is Mencius's view that "heaven's nature, as it is endowed in human beings, is not limited by what material nature receives." Rather, it is individuals' fault that efforts are not fully exerted in such a way that nature could be fully realized. Instead of focusing on "exhausting native endowment," scholars like Cheng-Zhu rashly conclude that the problem of evil stems from a deficient native endowment.[97]

Guangdi attributes evil in humanity to uneven or inadequate development of the universally good human nature. Human "agency" (*quan*) through individual deeds, actions, and practice, after and beyond the original heaven-endowed conditions, becomes the only guarantee of the conditions that define moral living:

> Confucius says, "By nature, [human beings] are alike." This is the same as Mencius's statement that there is no nature that is not good. Therefore, it is said that whether people are different or alike is a matter of practice (*xi*). Mencius also says, "Those who prefer the major parts of their body become noble people; those who prefer the minor parts become mean people." The agency (*quan*) rests with people.[98]

To illustrate further that *xing* has the original goodness that makes possible moral perfection, Guangdi uses the analogy of creating flavors:

> It is like the blending of the five flavors. If something is not salty, it is a matter of not adding enough salt and not because there is no salt at all. If something is not sour, it is because little of the plums are added and not because there are no plums at all. Although an individual may be somewhat deficient in

> one's native endowment, with motivation and diligence, one's achievements can be limitless. Therefore, [Mencius] says that it is not the fault of native endowment. A talent of an individual can be expanded ten-fold; ten talents of an individual can be expanded thousand-fold. Although initially dull, one can become bright; although meek, one can become strong. This is what is called extending to the utmost one's native endowment. . . . The manifestations of people's native endowment may vary, but all may seek to expand and substantiate it in order to apprehend [nature] in its entirety.[99]

Human nature is replete with inherent goodness whose fulfillment awaits properly dispensed effort. One can retrieve fully heaven's bestowal on humanity and become a completely realized person: "Not everyone is Yao or Shun, but everyone can be Yao and Shun."[100] Heaven's endowment on nature is like the falling of rain from the sky: "It is never the case that rivers and streams get more, while gutters and shallow brooks get less; or that clear spots get clear [rain], while filthy places get turbid [rain]. There is the same rain everywhere."[101]

Guangdi reiterates the fact that heaven's endowment creates no eternalized human condition. Goodness has to be realized through incessant efforts to "preserve nature" (*cunxing*) and "nurture nature" (*yangxing*).[102] These efforts all boil down to the pursuit of the Mean (*zhong*), or that which is central:

> The Mean is that which completes this goodness. It cannot be said that the Mean is goodness. Analogously speaking, millet and meat are delicious, but eating too much [of them] will make one sick. Fine silk garments are warm, but wearing too much [of them] will be burdensome. Millet, meat and fine silk garments are in themselves good. If one does not overdo it, how will the problems of causing sickness and burdening the body arise? Humaneness and rightness, vis-à-vis human beings, are just like a sumptuous fare and fine silk garments. Give them concrete expression through the Mean, and [one] achieves the likeness of heaven-and-earth.[103]

People are vessels of goodness from heaven, but it is incumbent on them to realize this quality by constantly embracing and pursuing the virtues, guided by the Mean, just as they could not for a moment dispense with food and clothing, taken in moderation.

It is quite apparent that Guangdi, in diverging from the Cheng-Zhu dualistic conception of human nature, harks back to the classic Mencian one which affirms the holistic innate goodness of humanity. Now, in recent years, there has been a tendency to interpret the Mencian view of human nature dynamically. A. C. Graham has noted that Mencius, in discussing *xing*, "in particular seems never to be looking back towards birth, always forward to the maturation of a continuing growth," and "that analogies for human nature in *Mencius* are always dynamic, trees growing on a denuded mountain, ripening grain, water finding its natural channels."[104] Expanding on Graham's observations, Roger Ames expresses his dissatisfaction with the common English rendering of *xing* as "human nature," as "a 'given' that exists from birth" which "cannot be altered through human action."[105] Ames argues convincingly through a different reading of the text that *xing* in the *Mencius* "seems to come closer to 'character,' 'personality' or 'constitution' than what we generally understand by 'nature.'" In a word, *xing* is "a dynamic process which covers initial dispositions, growth, and ultimate demise."[106]

To the extent that Guangdi appeals to the Mencian position, our analysis suggests the we may also undertake a dynamic reading of his conception of human nature. Guangdi's *xing* is not entrapped statically as the unalterable innate elements established at birth. The metaphors of developing silver and blending flavors, the emphasis on moral everyday efforts to preserve and nurture nature, the pursuit of filial piety and the Mean, the complementing of heaven's decree by following the human Way, and the notion of human control in reaching destiny, all imply process, even though process is governed by the normative moral requirements originating from heaven.

Guangdi's architectonic philosophical structure was built on the centrality and primacy of human nature conceived holistically. As the philosophical motifs were concentrated into the primacy of human nature, and as individuals were weighted accordingly with ontological prominence, purposive, direct, and utilitarian human actions become paramount in testing truths and defining living. While this ontology served Guangdi's purposes well and cohered with the temper of his time, it also unwittingly recalled a besetting problem that had dogged thinkers from the Zhou to Tang times, that is, the goodness or badness of human nature. The opening lines of the *Zhongyong*—"what heaven mandates for humanity is called nature; following this nature is called the Way"—suggest that humanity is the work of heaven and so nature is seen as the natural tendency of human responses; the human Way is in essence to follow this nature. But if heaven is good, and human beings and their actions of following heaven are also good, why then is evil seemingly so naturally a part of humanity? How is one to explain the apparent coinherence of heavenly origin, which is good, and the perennial moral transgression?

Moreover, *xing* is simultaneously a fact—nature *is* good in the absence of harm—and a value—it *ought to be* good as a person lives out his or her life. This creates another source of tension. Mencius (goodness of nature), Xunzi (badness of nature), and Gaozi (neutrality of nature) all "wandered around in circles," to use A. C. Graham's description, failing in the end to find a formula that satisfactorily reconciled goodness with constant moral demands.

As Graham has shown, this fundamental dilemma was really not resolved until the appearance of the dualistic Cheng-Zhu theory of human nature, which sealed the victory for the Mencian theory. First and foremost, Cheng and Zhu conceive human nature ontologically as an entity on a par with heaven and the Way, which is good in itself. (Mencius seldom overtly states that human nature is good as such, except in his disputation against Gaozi. Rather, what is pervasively implied in the *Mencius* is that it is human beings' nature to become good.) Having explicitly ascertained the goodness of nature, Cheng-Zhu explains how and why it is so. To them, the nature which is constituted by material force can be bad, but it is not the basic nature. Above and beyond it is the fundamentally good moral nature, which is principle, or heaven itself. This scheme affirms the original and ultimate goodness of heaven-bestowed nature while simultaneously accommodating the ever-present source of evil. The enshrouding of principle by impure material force results in human wickedness. But it is an imminently tractable situation; the pall of material force can be pierced with the acquisition of knowledge, and piercing through material force by principle is knowledge. This dialectic structure of *li* and *qi* effects a coherent synthesis of the universality of goodness and the individuation of evil.[107]

Now, Guangdi, in elevating *xing* as the center of gravity of his ontology, adopts the explicitly stated Cheng-Zhu position that it is good, as principle, heaven, and the Way are good. But unlike Cheng-Zhu, he refuses to bifurcate human nature to allow for the presence of evil in human nature itself. He thus revives the classical dilemma of having to reconcile universal innate heaven-derived goodness with particular post-natal individual failure to properly nurture and develop this goodness. Guangdi's solution, as we have seen, is essentially the Mencian solution which, compared to the Cheng-Zhu one, perhaps lacks the clarity and directness of placing evil squarely within one part of nature. Once again, he is ensnared in the Mencian circular effort, having to explain why the bad so often issues from the innate moral good.

Guangdi's imputing ontological centrality to *xing* also augments the tension that is, as Donald Munro duly notes, an integral element in Zhu Xi's conception of human nature. It is the tension between the self's moral authority and efficacy on the one hand, and external guidance such as *li* (propriety, rituals, and norms) on the other. Although the most important knowable principles are innate in individuals, there is the recognition that self-revelation is not always possible. The internal principles need to be reinforced by external authorities so as to apprehend those very principles. The thorny problem is to arrive at an "optimal balance between these two sources of formative standards for the individual."[108] Guangdi's sanguine conception of the unsullied and complete *xing* logically leads to a considerable emphasis on self-discovery as the way to achieve the coalescence of all meanings. This tends to contradict his urging that one should directly engage society with all of its everyday complexities, its rituals and norms. To concentrate on the all-enveloping *xing* is in itself a veritable emphasis on introspection. His conception of investigation of things, therefore, bears an inward thrust—for to investigate things is to simultaneously illuminate and gain knowledge of the goodness of human nature. Guangdi's philosophy is ultimately not free from ambiguities and tensions with regard to the question of praxis.

The early Qing Cheng-Zhu learning, as exemplified by Li Guangdi's and Lu Shiyi's philosophies, reformulated conceptions of *xing*. But this preoccupation with human nature was no idle metaphysical pondering. The discourse on *xin* was invested with an instrumentalism and teleology that sought to narrow metaphysics to metapraxis. It established the ontological basis for individual moral and social activism. The perspective of fundamental reality was focused on the vital manifestation of human action in the experiential world. The emphasis on *xing* colonized abstract thinking on a remote absolute reality, and established an anthropocentric world where humanity became the ultimate, thereby inscribing meaning onto the very concrete things that they did, the very real actions that they undertook, from moral self-cultivation to the betterment of state and society.

FIVE

Reading the Classics

Hermeneutics and Philosophy

> A genuine higher criticism of the Bible, therefore, would be a synthesizing process which would start with the assumption that the Bible is a definitive myth, a single archetypal structure extending from creation to apocalypse. Its heuristic principle would be St. Augustine's axiom that the Old Testament is revealed in the New and the New concealed in the Old: that the two testaments are not so much allegories of one another as metaphorical identifications of one another. We cannot trace the Bible back, even historically, to a time when its materials were not being shaped into a typological unity, and if the Bible is to be regarded as inspired in any sense, sacred or secular, its editorial and redacting processes must be regarded as inspired too.
>
> —Northrop Frye, *The Anatomy of Criticism*

Our wariness of broad generalizations notwithstanding, it is easy to agree with Roger Ames that "the dominant Chinese philosophic tradition has tended to be commentarial rather than systematic, with philosophers reinterpreting the classical core in order to accommodate changing historical circumstances."[1] In a slightly different vein, while examining comparatively the varied exegetical traditions in different cultures, John Henderson informs us that in imperial China, the grounds for the contest and affirmation of truths were the classics. Flowing out of the classical hermeneutic wellspring, in the form of the commentary and annotative exegesis, was a mainstream in Chinese intellectual history.[2]

Steven Van Zoeren, in his detailed study of the history of the interpretation of the *Classic of Odes*, arrives at the conclusion that "the interpretation and exegesis of canonical texts were occasions for normative, political and speculative teaching and thinking."[3] More recently, Daniel Gardner argues that "[i]t was in commentary" that the Chinese literati "would offer their reflections on the meaning of Confucian doctrine" and "attempt to construct a philosophical or moral vision meaningful in a world far removed from that of the classical age."[4] All these authors thus suggest that there was a close interrelationship between exegetical endeavor and philosophic cogitation in the Confucian reading of the classics.

By examining Li Guangdi's exegetical works and exploring the nexus between philosophy and exegesis, we may reveal just how Confucian hermeneutics generated and expressed reflective thinking about questions of reality and existence. To put it another way, in what ways did Guangdi, the exegete (and hence the interpreter), allow his philosophical predisposition and preunderstanding to guide his interaction with classical texts? What sort of philosophic outlook can be distilled from his writings on the classics? Was he simply a custodian of the Cheng-Zhu exegetical reading of the classics? Or did he engage the classics with his own preunderstanding and preconceived ideas? Suffice it here to note that despite Guangdi's avowed allegiance to Cheng-Chu tenets, he did not refrain from critiquing Zhu Xi's earlier exegeses, particularly those of the *Mean* and *Great Learning*. Guangdi's reading of these two texts, which involved their textual rearrangement and emendation, was integrally a function of the ordering power of the principal assumptions and views of his philosophical world. He also initiated his own interpretations in his engagement with the *Analects* and the *Classic of Changes*. By examining Guangdi's endeavors, we shed some light on the fluid nature of Confucian hermeneutics undertaken within the boundary of an acknowledged orthodoxy.

We may further suggest that classical exegesis in traditional China in a general sense may not be all that different from contemporary interpretive hermeneutics, inasmuch as both involve the interpenetration of the text and the interpreter. Needless to say, the differences are also legion and crucial. On a general level, it can be argued that the Confucian exegetical project is an illustration of the "hermeneutical axiom," that is, the contention that all thought involves interpretation and is relative to the contingent context of particular historical forces and factors, including the interpreter's preunderstanding and predisposition.[5] But Confucian exegesis certainly did not cast doubt on classical truth itself, even though it might critically evaluate some of the sources in which this truth was supposedly expressed; nor did it claim to be anything more than the retrieval and reassertion of such truth. Therefore, two caveats are in order. First, in this book, hermeneutics in Confucian terms refers specifically to the study of the classics, although in illustrating the pursuit of such study, references will be made to the larger question of hermeneutics as the philosophy of interpretation. Second, it should be noted that in Confucian hermeneutics, the ultimate universality of the values embodied in the classics was taken for granted, not subject to questioning in relativistic terms. Thus, although individual authorial imprints and historico-cultural conditions did yield interpretive latitude, the timeless authority of the classical texts themselves furnished the unshakable bedrock of the hermeneutic order.

In contrast, certain contemporary hermeneutic assumptions would have been anathema in the Confucian scheme of things, namely, that words refer merely to other words, without general referential capacity; that texts are stormy linguistic seas in which truths and meanings are easily adrift; that meanings must be endlessly deferred along a string of signifiers; and that the self, both from the author's and reader's standpoints, is insubstantial at best, an ideological construction at worst. Such tenets are particularly pronounced in French poststructuralist hermeneutics, where the distrust of the explicit meanings of words effectively means the end of the communicative power of the canon with regard to the delivery of truths and traditional values. Furthermore, the French mode of interpretation views tradition as something to be overcome and surmounted, insofar as most of the ideas embraced by the past thinkers were anchored on the false consciousness of foundationalism. In the final analysis, the engagement with texts breeds merely self-referential paradoxes incapable of supporting any truth-claims.[6]

My comparative perspective is, therefore, better served by German hermeneutics which,[7] while acknowledging the incompleteness and ephemerality of apprehending human knowing through texts, affirms the meaningfulness of words as interpretations and expressions of truth.[8] In particular, I will refer to Martin Buber's and Hans-Georg Gadamer's hermeneutic arguments and principles. Both stress the interactive import of, and the dialogical approach to, reading the classics as a way to engage human responsibility, understanding, and eventually liberation.[9] Fruitful comparisons may also be drawn between Confucian hermeneutics and David Tracy's Christian hermeneutics, premised on the conviction that "no classic can be reduced to mere privacy."[10] Tracy's thesis "is that what we mean in naming certain texts . . . 'classics' is that here we recognize nothing less than the disclosure of a reality we cannot but name truth."[11] As "truth," the classics are in effect "public" and even "transcultural," embodying both "an excess and a permanence of meaning that later generations must retrieve."[12] But such retrieval must be the result of critical and rigorous interpretations on the part of the textual interrogator with his or her particular historical understanding. As interlocutors with the classics, the interpreters ineluctably bring into the conversation their preunderstanding.[13]

These hermeneutic approaches refuse to superannuate past traditions ensconced in the classics. Rather, they seek a meaningful conflation of the past and present by seeing the timelessness of the classics in relation to their temporal manifestations in the present historical contingencies. To put it another way, the truth that issues forth from the classics is indeed mediated by interpretation and therefore contextualized, but its truth-value is not at all threatened by such interpretive contextualization. The classics, because of their essential perpetuity, offer a common context, a single cultural tradition, capable of absorbing and accommodating the diversity and historicity of their interpreters. By casting Li Guangdi's exegetical endeavors in a comparative light, we hope to contribute to a better understanding of Confucian hermeneutics. It is seen not as mere repetition of the classics frozen in a timeless moment, but as constant historical restating and reinterpretation of the classical texts' apparent transtemporal claim. In other words, the Confucian quest for truths within the hermeneutic boundary involved constant remapping of the textual landscape as a result of the intrusion of philosophical interlopers.

Since Guangdi's philosophy was premised on the ontological primacy of the heaven-endowed nature, as we have shown, it follows that the basis of his hermeneutics was indeed his philosophy of *xing*. Armed with this fundamental philosophical assertion of the centrality of human nature, Guangdi sought to remedy what he saw as the principal problem of the Ming world of thought, that is, the lack of certitude in the fundamentally moral and good nature. As Huston Smith observes, in any culture that values traditions, when "people want to know where they are—when they wonder about the ultimate context in which their lives are set and which has the final say over them—they turn to their sacred texts."[14] So Guangdi did and confronted the classics. As an interpreter bound by the contingent needs of his own time, he struggled to understand the classics anew. The problem of interpretation of the classics took on added significance and importance when an interpreter, such as Guangdi, perceived his own time to be a period of cultural crisis, still grappling with the pernicious legacy of Wang Yangming's thought.[15] He therefore did not hesitate to critique Zhu Xi's hermeneutics of the classics, which had in themselves achieved canonical status. His disagreement with Zhu's exegesis was particularly pronounced with respect to the *Doctrine of the Mean* and *Great Learning*, the two canonical texts that were supposed to have encapsulated the philosophical truths of the ancient sages. Nonetheless, it should be noted that Guangdi's critical reading of the classics and his taking issue with the Song master's interpretations were in fact application of Zhu's hermeneutics, which Zhu himself called "the method of reading" (*dushu fa*). In other words, although Guangdi did not directly refer to Zhu's theory and methodology of reading, it is unthinkable that he was not familiar with and influenced by it, especially in view of the fact that, as Daniel Gardner points out, the *Zhuzi yulei* (Conversations of Master Zhu, Arranged Topically) devotes two fascicles to it.[16]

Hermeneutical Interpretations of the *Doctrine of the Mean* and *Great Learning*: Guangdi's Critique of Zhu Xi's Commentaries

Because of Guangdi's advocacy of the primacy of human nature, which was in effect his hermeneutic preunderstanding or expectation, he understood the classics differently from the original authors and their earlier audience. Inevitably, he found Zhu Xi's exegesis on the *Mean* and *Great Learning* unsatisfying. As is well known, Zhu had compiled the *Zhongyong zhangju* (Chapters and Verses of the *Doctrine of the Mean*) in thirty-three chapters, in which he accepted Cheng Yi's definition of the notions *zhong* and *yong*:

> Master Cheng said, "By *zhong* (central) is meant what is not one-sided, and by *yong* (ordinary) is meant what is unchangeable. *Zhong* is the correct path of the world and *yong* is the definite principle of the world." This work represents the central way in which the doctrines of the Confucian school have been transmitted. Fearing that in time errors should arise, Zisi wrote it down and transmitted it to Mencius.[17]

Following Cheng Yi's renditions of the eponymous key words, Zhu's *Zhongyong zhangju* aimed at expounding the "path" of "centrality" and the "principle" of "ordinariness," regarded by Zisi (492–431 B.C.), Confucius's grandson, as the "central way"(*xinfa*) of the Confucian tradition. The division of the text into thirty-three chapters, so Zhu hoped, would faithfully and strategically convey the "central way" that was originally transmitted by Zisi.[18]

However, it should be noted that Zhu Xi himself did not consider his exegetical interpretation and textual arrangement as the last word. In fact, he bemoaned the painstaking and ever-changing process of engaging the classics, whose meanings remained tantalizingly elusive. Specifically with regard to the *Mean* and *Great Learning*, he lamented:

> [My exegeses] on the *Great Learning* and *Mean* were repeatedly revised, failing in the end to reach the point where revisions need no longer be made. Recently, [my work] on the *Great Learning* appears to have a few problems. [Its] meanings and principles are best explained in lectures. But once [they] are committed to paper and brush, [I] feel that [I] have not arrived at even the most basic. Even if they are discussed in detail, there is no brilliant [insight]. Now, in order to probe the heartfelt messages of the sages, we can only look at them on paper. How can we see the very bottom? Once I think about this, I always close my books in dismay.[19]

Here, Zhu alludes to the ultimate insufficiency of words as means to apprehend the sages' truths. Yet, one has no choice but to resort to and rely on texts and their *zhangju*, the verses and sentences. Zhu, with an obvious tone of regret and resignation, explains at once the inadequacy and indispensability of textual manipulation; hence his writing the *Zhongyong zhangju*:

> Whenever I study the text [of the *Mean*], I rashly use my own ideas to divide it up into verses and sentences. But since, as Master Cheng claimed, it was that by which the central way of the Confucian school was transmitted, I wonder deep down if [its meaning] can be pursued through verses and sentences. But it is also known that one who studies the classics can only get through to their meanings by way of their words. Therefore, I dare to apply my own understanding to it [i.e., the *Mean*] as a way of studying and thinking.[20]

Thus, Zhu did not mince words in describing his interaction with the classics as an unfolding, dynamic process, fraught with ambivalence and uncertainty. While the ultimate value of the classics as the repositories of truths was an absolute given, interpreting them was a protean and tentative exercise.

Insofar as studying the classics never meant foreclosing the experience of them, there was always room for exegetical maneuvering. So it was that a devout Cheng-Zhu follower such as Guangdi would take issue with Zhu Xi's rendering of the *Mean*. Guangdi, in an essay on the *Zhongyong*, begins by first criticizing Cheng Yi's definition, the basis of Zhu Xi's own understanding of the *Mean*:

> Master Cheng uses [the ideas of] not being one-sided and not leaning toward one direction, of the correct path, and of the definite principle to interpret and explain the two terms of *zhong* and

> *yong*. [These ideas are] certainly intriguingly fine. But in speaking of the Way and principle, there should be added the idea of origin. Human nature is the origin of the Way and principle.[21]

Through such hermeneutic redefinition, Guangdi affirms the ultimacy of human nature and accordingly lays bare the significance of the *Mean* as he sees it. Curtly put, the full import of the entire text could be comprehended if this opening line is understood: "What Heaven mandates for humanity is called human nature."[22]

In another essay on the *Mean* that he completed in 1710, Guangdi again attempts to explicate the central meaning of this canon in terms of the ontological primacy of *xing*; *xing*, in a nutshell, is coeval and mutually identified with heaven (*tian*) and the Great Ultimate (*taiji*):

> *Xing* . . . refers to that which is imbued in humanity, but speaking in terms of heaven, that would be called mandate (*ming*), a term which honors heaven. . . . There is what is called heaven's virtue (*tiande*) or heaven-and-earth's virtue (*tiandi zhi de*). Such virtue is human nature. . . . Therefore, there is what is called the oneness of the principles of heaven and earth, and of heaven and humanity. Human nature is the Great Ultimate. In the movement and stillness of the Great Ultimate are seen our sentiments (*qing*) and mind-heart (*xin*). But why is it not called nature but the Great Ultimate? It is because it is also a term honoring heaven.[23]

With his avowed faith in the enveloping human nature as the source of all beings and meanings, Guangdi expatiates and amends some of Zhu Xi's annotations in the *Zhongyong zhangju*. A case in point is Zhu's explication of this verse in the *Zhongyong*: "The Way cannot be separated from us for a moment. What can be separated from us is not the Way." In order to stress the omnipresence of the Way in both spatial and temporal terms, Zhu asserts that "nothing is without [the Way], and not a moment is without [the Way]." How does Guangdi interpret Zhu's statement? According to Guangdi, many scholars think that what Zhu is saying is that all things have "the self-evident principle" (*dangran zhi li*) or "the self-evident pattern" (*dangran zhi ze*). For instance, a table has the principle of table, a chair that of chair, speech that of speech, dining that of dining, and so forth. These scholars are wrong:

> [Zhu's statement] that nothing does not have [the Way] refers to the fact that one has the immanent virtue of human nature. It is so with everyone. . . . [Zhu's] saying that not a moment does not have [the Way] refers to the fact that the mind-heart's

> substance is in motion all the time. Since everyone has it and every moment has it, [the *Doctrine of the Mean* says] that [the Way] cannot be separated [from us] for a moment. If it is separated [from us] for a moment, human nature will be terminated and the mandate of heaven will be extinguished."[24]

In brief, the Way in the *Doctrine of the Mean* is, in itself, nothing but the eternal and omnipresent human nature.

Guangdi also criticizes Zhu for presenting a truncated view of the Way (*dao*) from the twenty-second chapter on: "From the chapter 'Only those who are most sincere can develop their nature to the utmost' (*zhicheng jinxing*) onward, Master Zhu artificially separates the way of heaven (*tiandao*) from the way of humanity (*rendao*). It is not quite appropriate or proper."[25] Zhu Xi identifies human nature with the Way of heaven, and so only the sages could fully extend human nature and eradicate selfish desires. Being at one with heaven, the sages' moral force, according to Zhu, emanated outward and transformed the people, creating the "way of humanity." Guangdi counters this view by rhetorically asking: "When speaking of heaven's way, and the rise and fall of the country, can it be said that those beneath the great sages cannot know the way? . . . Originally, these were not exclusively the business of the sages."[26] Guangdi holds that the *Mean*'s idea of "developing nature to the utmost " should be viewed with reference to the holistic notion of "the myriad things as one body" (*wanwu yiti*). In other words, "all of human nature is good." Selfishness, moral transgressions, and folly are all results of "not developing nature to the utmost. . . . As one becomes aware of this in oneself, one also becomes aware of this in others. . . . To develop exhaustively nature is to develop to the utmost the nature of others and things."[27]

Since Guangdi places little store on Zhu Xi's goal of transmitting the so-called central way (*xinfa*) of Zisi, even though he subscribes wholeheartedly to Zhu's notion of "the transmission of the Way" (*daotong*), he presents his own version of the *Mean*, the *Zhongyong zhangduan* (Chapters and Sections of the *Mean*). In this 1716 text, Guangdi comes up with his own redaction of the original classic, dividing it into twelve chapters so that he can best highlight human nature as the central theme of the *Mean*. He explains the organization of this work:

> The first chapter is a general introduction, the last chapter is a general conclusion. In between, the first five chapters elaborate and illuminate the origin and development of human nature, the Way and moral teaching (*jiao*). The following five chapters elaborate and illuminate the practice and function of extending centrality and harmony.[28]

In writing this text, Guangdi first seeks clarification of the essential meaning and deep significance of the *Mean* by referring to the other classics. While explaining the purport of the *Zhongyong* in the preface, he refers to the "The Proclamation of Tang" (Tanggao) in the *Classic of Documents*, which states: "The Lord-on-High has conferred even on the inferior people a moral sense (*zhong*), the realization of which is the eternal nature (*xing*)." Whereupon Guangdi offers this gloss: "The moral sense (*zhong*) is centrality [that is, the *zhong* in the *Mean*]. That which is central is also constant, because the mandate conferred by the Lord-on-High is that which the people follow as their nature." Guangdi also refers to the *Classic of Odes*, focusing on these lines in the ode entitled "Humankind" (Zhengmin): "Heaven, in giving birth to humankind, also established in it the laws [of nature and humanity]. Since humankind is endowed with this natural disposition (*yi*), it cherishes its esteemed virtue (*yide*)." Guangdi contends that the *Mean*'s notion of centrality is the encapsulation of the meaning of these lines, which essentially affirms heaven's conferring the good nature on humanity. Thus, the *Odes*, in its own way, also "talks about the principle of nature and mandate [found in the *Mean*]."[29]

While Guangdi agrees with Zhu Xi that the first chapter of the *Mean*, preserved by Guangdi in the original form, encases the core messages that the rest of the text seeks to elaborate, he chooses to completely ignore in his commentary the supposed goals of Zisi, that is, the transmission of Confucius's messages via the "central way." Instead, Guangdi elucidates the meaning of *zhong* (centrality) and *yong* (ordinariness) in light of the paramountcy of nature (*xing*):

> The word "*zhong*" in the first chapter is specifically spoken of in terms of *ti* (substance). . . . To speak in terms of nature, it is our constant nature; to speak in terms of the Way, it is the constant Way. . . . The principles of *zhong* and *yong* originate in our mandated nature. . . . They are the laws of substance embodied in humanity.[30]

In sum, Guangdi, in this particular hermeneutic rendering of the *Mean*, done two years before his death, reaffirmed his own personal understanding of the principal teachings of Confucian philosophy, namely, the centrality of nature and its ethico-moral manifestations. The main ideas in Guangdi's *Zhongyong zhangduan* may be summarized as follows. First, nature is foundational and essential: "The way of nature is the root of moral principles. Nature is embodied in the mind-heart; the Way is seen in things."[31] Second, nature is universal: "Human nature is bestowed on me by heaven-and-earth, sharing it with all people and things."[32] Third, nature is experiential in that everyone must seek to realize the innate goodness of human nature in the everyday world: "The reception of heaven's mandate is called human nature. Human nature is the embodiment of the principle of creation and life in the mind-heart. This principle embodied in the mind-heart must be seen working in the daily practicalities. The Way is following the issuance [of principle]. The Way is the path normally followed by people." Fourth, the profundity of nature is naturally manifested in everyday ordinariness: "Nature is the embodiment of the vital principles in the mind-heart. The principles that are embodied in the mind-heart must be manifested in the midst of quotidian activity and utility."[33]

Guangdi's hermeneutic engagement with the *Mean* was in perfect accord with his philosophical premise that human nature was the ontological hinge on which all Confucian arguments turned. It is small wonder that Guangdi also read the importance of human nature into the *Great Learning*. Guangdi once again took issue with Zhu Xi, this time over the master's emendation of and addition to this classic, which Guangdi deemed unnecessary if not erroneous. In particular, Guangdi points to Zhu Xi's creation of a "supplementary chapter of commentary" (*buzhuan*), devoted to expounding the ideas of "investigation of things" (*gewu*) and "extending knowledge to the utmost" (*zhizhi*). This created text is appended to the original chapter five, which contains these words: "This is called 'knowing the root' (*zhiben*). This is called 'the completion of knowledge' (*zhi zhi zhi*)." The first sentence was regarded by Zhu Xi, following the interpretation of Cheng Yi, as redundant and he believed that it should therefore be expunged. The second sentence was most significant, but it was merely the conclusion to some missing text. Hence the need for the supplementary chapter to fill in the textual lacuna.[34]

The *Great Learning*, as is well known, was a text near and dear to Zhu Xi. In his exegetical work, the *Daxue zhangju* (The Verses and Sentences of the *Great Learning*), Zhu cites Cheng Yi, who has explicitly claimed that this one classic is "Confucius's bequeathed text" (*yishu*), which is "the gateway to initial learning of acquiring virtue." Zhu begins his discourse by reiterating that this text is the foundation of all learning. Systematically, when "the ancients sequenced learning, [they] in particular relied on preserving [the priority of] this text , followed by the *Analects* and *Mencius*. If scholars follow this in their learning, they will hardly go wrong."[35] In fact, Zhu worked incessantly on rearranging the *Great Learning*, so much so that three days before his death, he was still making changes on the chapter, "Making the Will Sincere" (Chengyi zhang).[36] Zhu Xi took the extraordinary step of actually adding words to the transmitted canon because he was committed to expounding the notions of "investigation of things" and "extending knowledge to the utmost" as centerpieces of his philosophy. Zhu's reading of the *Great Learning* in effect reinvented the text as the locus classicus of the twin ideas. He explains in his supplementary chapter the central idea that "the extending of knowledge to the utmost lies in the investigation of things":

> The intelligence of the human mind-heart is such that it is never without knowledge; all things under heaven possess principle. It is because principle is not plumbed that knowledge is not extended to the utmost. Therefore, in using the *Great Learning* to initiate learning, scholars will definitely pursue all things under heaven by increasingly plumbing them in accordance with a prior principle, so that their ultimate [principle] can be reached. As our endeavor is exerted in a prolonged manner, complete and thorough understanding suddenly arises, so much so that the exterior and interior, and the refinement and coarseness of myriad things are apprehended, and the whole substance and great function of my mind-heart are fully comprehended. This is what is called having investigated things; this is what is called having extended knowledge to the utmost.[37]

In the *Great Learning*, Zhu Xi finds logical unity of his most important precepts, from "investigation of things," through "plumbing principles" (*qiongli*), to "extending knowledge to the utmost." Indeed, in the *Daxue huowen* (Queries on the *Great Learning*), Zhu argues that "the way of investigating things lies in conceiving principle with regard to every matter, so that things are investigated." This "itemized goal" (*tiaomu*) of the *Great Learning* is the organized way of learning which the sages taught. "But since the Han and Wei," Zhu laments, "various Confucians have failed to mention it." Even Han Yu, whom he praises for revealing anew the importance of the *Great Learning*, failed to examine the idea of "extending knowledge to the utmost and investigation of things," for he erroneously concentrated on the *Great Learning*'s teaching of "rectifying the mind-heart and making the will sincere" (*zhengxin chengyi*).[38] Judging from Zhu's treatment of the *Great Learning*, it seems clear that he placed his exegesis at the service of his philosophy.

Li Guangdi, whose philosophy was premised on the ontological primacy of human nature, naturally found Zhu's hermeneutical rendering of the *Great Learning* to be less than desirable. Two years before his death, in the same year that he completed his final exegesis on the *Mean*, Guangdi also finished the essay, "A Discourse on the Ancient Edition of the Great Learning" (Daxue guben shuo), defending the integrity of the classic's "ancient edition." In this piece, Guangdi professes that in his fifty odd years of studying Zhu's works, he has developed great admiration for the master's understanding of important texts such as the *Changes*, the *Odes* and Zhou Dunyi's "Discourse on the Diagram of the Great Ultimate." Zhu's insights into these texts never cease to enlighten and inspire him, as Guangdi gratefully admits. But the master's exegetical work on the *Great Learning*, the *Daxue zhangju*, is an entirely different matter. At best, Guangdi can only agree with it in the most casual manner. He bluntly accuses Zhu of obfuscating the principal points of the *Great Learning*. Guangdi maintains that "the two ideas of 'knowing the root' (*zhiben*) and 'being sincere in self-cultivation' (*chengshen*) should especially be preserved by those who write about the *Great Learning*. They should not be sullied by the various other themes." But what Zhu did was the exact opposite: he virtually eliminated the idea of "knowing the root." To counter Zhu's redaction of the *Great Learning*, Guangdi embraces the "ancient edition" (*guben*) established by the Han exegete Zheng Xuan (127–200), which properly preserves the idea of "knowing the root."[39]

In another work on the *Great Learning*, Guangdi contends that the key to a thorough understanding of the classical text resides in the clause *ming mingde* (manifesting the clear character), which he glosses in this way: "The clear character points to human nature and not the mind-heart. Manifesting the clear character refers both to 'knowing human nature' (*zhixing*) and 'nurturing human nature' (*yangxing*)."[40] In short, the crux of the *Great Learning*'s teachings is "knowing human nature and nurturing human nature." It is not, as Zhu Xi's textual modifications suggest, "investigation of things" and "extending knowledge to the utmost." Therefore, Zhu's drastic move of adding a supplementary commentarial chapter on "investigation of things" was both superfluous and infelicitous. Guangdi concludes:

> The two Chengs and Master Zhu had all emended and edited the text of the *Great Learning*. If their interpretations were accurate, the conclusion of one master would have sufficed and lasted through the ages. Why then had Mingdao [i.e., Cheng Hao] edited it, Yichuan [i.e., Cheng Yi] edited it, and Master Zhu edited it? Master Zhu's addition of the "Commentary on Investigation of Things" especially elicited posterity's skepticism. If [the idea of] investigation of things required additional commentary, then the ideas of making the will sincere, extending its knowledge to the utmost, rectifying the mind-heart, and making its will sincere, should also have had their supplementary commentarial chapters.[41]

To Guangdi, "knowing human nature" means "knowing the root." Zhu Xi thought the latter idea to be redundant and therefore disregarded it. In Guangdi's hermeneutic engagement with the *Great Learning*, he seeks to restore the primacy of the notion of the root, whose ontological reality is human nature and whose experiential expression is "self-cultivation" (*xiushen*). It is not that Guangdi negates the importance of "investigation of things." But he firmly believes that without knowledge of the root, one will not know what and how to investigate:

> The mind-heart, body, family, state and all-under-heaven are things. Self-cultivation, ordering family, ruling the state and pacifying all-under-heaven are affairs. The root [of them all] is self-cultivation. Therefore, it is said that everyone or everything regards self-cultivation as the root. It is not true that if the root is confused, the branches can still be in order.[42]

Guangdi then proceeds to link the understanding of root and branches to the practice of investigating things:

> Things and affairs are things. That which is the root or branches, or the ultimate or beginning, is the principle of things. Investigating it will yield the knowledge of what is prior and what is posterior. . . . In investigating affairs and things, the root and the branches, and the beginning and the ultimate, must all be thoroughly understood. Only then is the entire effort of investigating things fully realized.[43]

With the realization of the comprehensive effort of investigating things finally comes the extension of knowledge to the utmost (*zhizhi*). But Guangdi makes a special point of explaining that the *Great Learning* never intended the word *zhi* (extension to the utmost) to mean "exhaustive investigation of all things under heaven." "Extending knowledge to the utmost," Guangdi opines, "means knowing the root."[44] Such knowledge of the root is manifested experientially in moral virtues, as Guangdi concludes: "Humaneness, rightness, propriety and wisdom are the investigations of things so as to extend knowledge to the utmost; [they] are the illuminations of goodness in order to know nature."[45]

In yet another earlier work on the *Great Learning*, Guangdi ties all these themes together to present a synthetic message supposedly delivered by the classics. He begins by reiterating his basic interpretation that "what is called the extension of knowledge to the utmost is what is called knowing the root."[46] But what is knowledge of the root? Guangdi returns once more to his fundamental philosophical conception: the goodness of human nature as the encapsulation of a good universe:

> Nature is just goodness. The nature of things is like the nature of humanity. The nature of another person is like my own nature. The knowledge that all nature is universally good and that the ultimate root [of such goodness] is in one's self, is the means to knowing nature and illuminating goodness, and the means to knowing the root.[47]

In sum, Guangdi's textual and exegtical engagement with the classical books turned out also to be articulation of his philosophical views. His retelling of the meanings of the *Mean* and *Great Learning* within hermeneutic bounds was not simply a repetition of time-honored and well-worn values, but was also a way to open dialogue with the ancients and intellectual forebears in a quest for truths as he saw them. Guangdi balked not at criticizing Zhu Xi's exegetical excess and error; the *Mean* and *Great Learning* became hotly contested textual terrains. In Guangdi's hermeneutical world, even the master had to be taken to task.

Hermeneutics of the *Analects* (Lunyu)

Guangdi's hermeneutic engagement with the *Analects*, documented in his *Detailed Notes on the Analects* (Lunyu zhaji), to which we referred briefly in our earlier study of his general theory, also involves disagreement with Zhu Xi's interpretations, albeit not with the same intensity and thoroughness as in the cases of the *Mean* and *Great Learning*. For instance, their glosses differ quite significantly on this passage from the *Analects*:

> Zigong said, "What do you say about the poor person who yet does not flatter, and the rich person who is not arrogant?" The Master replied, "They are all right, but they are not equal to one who, though poor, is happy, and to one who, though rich, loves propriety."[48]

Zhu's gloss goes as follows:

> Ordinary people are so mired in their wealth or poverty that they do not know that they should abide by what they have (*zishou*). Therefore, they each often have the flaws [of flattery or arrogance]. Not to be flattering and arrogant is to know to abide by what they have. However, they still have not transcended the fact that they are either poor or rich. To describe them as "all right" is to use the language that suggests that they have not done the utmost that they can. To be happy means having a broad mind and properous body that ignore

> one's poverty. To love propriety means contentedly resting in goodness. Happiness follows principle, and one forgets that one is rich.[49]

Guangdi does not mention Zhu's interpretation in his gloss, but he quite evidently addresses it:

> Not to be flattering and not to be arrogant is to exert effort on the level of action. To be happy and to love propriety is to exert effort on the level of learning. There must first be the place where one can stand before one can seek to abide by what one has. Therefore, to be happy and to love propriety requires the lack of flattery and lack of arrogance as the foundation. . . . It is just that [the latter] cannot be a life-long motto for action. . . . This [i.e., the *Analects*'s passage] discusses the progress in learning, and is not a discrimination of two types of people.[50]

Guangdi infers from Zhu's explanation a static categorization of people. First, there are those who are myopically trapped in their own state of life, committing the sin of either flattery or arrogance. Second, there are those who are able to "abide by what they have" (*zishou*) and thus eschew those wrongs. Third, there are those who, in being happy and loving propriety, truly transcend and become disinterested in their wealth or poverty. Guangdi resists such reading. He ignores the problems engendered by wealth and poverty and focuses on what we may accomplish, regardless of our station in life. He therefore sees abiding by what one has simply as a step or stage in a progressive program of learning and acting. He in effect suggests that what Confucius had in mind was not a description of the existence of two kinds of people, but a prescription for moral improvement—from acting merely acceptably to being truly exalted, transcending wealth and poverty.

This reading snugly dovetails with Guangdi's general conception of human nature as good. It is in fact echoed and reinforced in his gloss of Confucius's statement that "human beings are alike in nature." Guangdi reiterates that "humanity's nature, although uneven because of material disposition, is born of the equilibrium of heaven-and-earth. This nature is above and superior to the nature of the myriad things." As a matter of general truth, human beings, in nature, are therefore alike. "That there are the extremes between the intelligent and dull, and between the upright and immoral, is the result of practice," Guangdi postulates. If everyone practices "the right speech and right thing," then everyone will "return to goodness." He insists that Mencius's dictum of the innate goodness of nature is an extension of Confucius's original pronouncement of the likeness of humanity in terms of nature. Significantly, without specifically naming them, Guangdi rejects Zhu Xi's and Cheng Yi's suggestion that Confucius, in this instance, is referring only to "the material nature" (*qizhi zhi xing*). What do the Song masters actually say about Confucius's statement? In his annotation of the *Analects*, Zhu identifies the *xing* in the sage's statement as material nature, which "immanently possesses good and evil in varying degrees." Because there is this immanent mix of good and evil in material nature, practice becomes the crucial intervening factor. According to Cheng Yi, as Zhu proceeds to explain, Confucius refers to material nature and not the "original state of nature" (*xing zhi ben*). For "if the original nature is being talked about, then *xing* is *li* (principle). There is nothing in principle that is not good." This innately and universally good principle is what Mencius calls the good nature.[51] Guangdi begs to differ:

> Some Confucians of yore claimed that what Confucius spoke about was material nature and not the original state of nature. Only what Mencius spoke about was the nature that was the very origin and ultimate source. I say that only because human beings, by nature, are alike that nature can be said to be good; that only because it is good that it can be said that human beings, by nature, are alike. It cannot be said that Confucius and Mencius referred to different things. What both Confucius and Mencius spoke of was humanity's nature.

Here, Guangdi reaffirms the holistic nature of *xing* by rejecting the division of nature into the posterior material nature and the prior nature identified with *li*. If we "speak in terms of the princple of heaven-and-earth," Guangdi argues, we are necessarily talking about all beings, including plants and animals. As the *Classic of Changes* teaches us, all have their rightful nature and destiny with the transformations and changes of the Way of *Qian*. In other words, principle establishes the generic sameness of all beings. However, with respect to *xing*, animals must be distinguished from humanity as two different ontological kinds, or in Guangdi's word, *lei* (kinds). The nature of animals cannot be said to be similar to humanity's nature because the former does not merit the description of good (*shan*). The *Classic of Filial Piety*, as Guangdi reminds us, posits that "among the natures of heaven-and-earth, that of humanity is noble." In saying that human beings, in terms of nature, are alike, Confucius highlights and underscores their nobility and uniqueness—their innate natural goodness. This very goodness establishes humanity as "being of the same kind" (*tonglei*). For this reason, everyone can be a Yao or a Shun. To be sure, Guangdi concedes that among people, there is the difference between strong and weak, smart and dull. But these properties serve only to distinguish each individual from one's own ontolgocial kind on the level of the particular. They in no way detract from the universal under which all humanity is subsumed, namely, the ontological fact that *xing* is good.[52]

In his commentaries on the *Analects*, Guangdi not only advances his philosophical *terminus ad quem* of the goodness of nature, but he also buttresses his metapraxis of "establishing the will," "emphasizing reverence," and "knowing and acting," which he expounds in his "Principal Purpose of Honoring Zhu." In fact, Guangdi's reading here is quite close to Zhu's. Seizing upon the *Analects*'s chapter "Let the Will Be Set on the Way"—wherein Confucius says, "Let virtue be firmly grasped. Let humaneness be accorded with. Let relaxation and enjoyment be found in the arts"[53]—Guangdi declares that "learning begins with establishing the will, followed by knowing and acting." The pursuit of virtue, humaneness, and the arts is brought to fruition only as a result of seeking knowledge and acting it out.[54] Based on Confucius's reply to Zilu's inquiry about the constitution of a profound person (*junzi*)—"The cultivation of himself in reverence"[55]—Guangdi expounds on the importance of reverence: "To cultivate oneself in order to bring peace to others and the multitude naturally requires various efforts. But reverence must be the principal control. Reverence is the basis of virtue and the concrete manifestation of propriety."[56] Guangdi also introduces the question of reverence in his gloss of Confucius's opinion that a superior person stands in awe of three things: heaven's mandate, great men, and the sages' words.[57] Although there is no direct reference to reverence by Confucius, Guangdi, following Zhu Xi, interprets the classical notion of awe (*wei*) to mean reverence: "Master Zhu used to say that the meaning of the word 'reverence' is closest to that of the word 'awe.' Judging from this passage in the *Analects*, [the sense of awe] is where a scholar's effort of grasping reverence can be established." To be reverent is to bear in mind that "heaven has its correct mandate and rulers their brilliant majesty." As a result, one inevitably will "pay obeisance to those occupying a position of moral elevation, and show supreme respect to the books of the sages."[58]

In glossing the famous chapter in which Confucius charts his own moral and intellectual development in life from youth through old age, "At fifteen, I established my will in learning,"[59] Guangdi suggests that the sage's own progress is a *bona fide* exemplification of the organic unity of the metapraxis that he espouses: "What Confucians of yore said about establishing the will in order to make the origin sprout, dwelling in reverence to grasp the will, plumbing principle to extend knowledge to the utmost, and reflecting on oneself to act out the real, is sequentially congruent with it [i.e., Confucius's progress]." Such metapractical pursuit that parallels moral progress, however, is not "the exertion of effort in stages," since "knowing and acting must proceed simultaneously." Guangdi warns against separating knowing from acting, so that "today, there is adherence to action while discarding knowing, and tomorrow, there is the extension of knowledge while discarding action." Guangdi affirms the seamless cultivational web of moral exertions that unifies knowing and acting. Here, Guangdi also cannot restrain himself in giving Wang Yangming a quick jab, chiding him for erroneously imposing an artificial procedure in Zhu Xi's learning. To Wang, because the act of "making the will sincere and rectifying the mind-heart" must occur after "things have been investigated and knowledge has been extended," Zhu fails after all to accomplish the former. To Guangdi, this is a perfect example of Wang's gross misunderstanding as a result of his failure "to probe [Zhu's] words."[60] Guangdi's hermeneutic encounter with the *Analects* thus provides yet another occasion for criticizing Wang Yangming's philosophy.

Hermeneutical Deciphering of the Hexagrams of the *Classic of Changes* (Yijing)

The philosophico-hermeneutical intrication is also very evident in Guangdi's interrogation of the *Classic of Changes*.[61] Guangdi's main claim to fame in the arena of *Yijing* learning was his compilation, under imperial aegis, of the *Balanced Annotations of the Classic of Changes* (Zhouyi zhezhong). This 1715 work of twenty-two fascicles is included in the canonical *Complete Works of the Four Treasuries* (Siku quanshu). In the spirit of establishing the textual authenticity of the Classic, Guangdi adopts in this project what may be called a custodial approach. Under his editorial leadership, he and his co-compilers, while using Zhu Xi's explanations as the mainstay, copiously included other views as supplements and complements to construct a detailed summation of the multifarious readings of the *Changes* in the long exegetical history of this classical text.[62] Probably hamstrung by the format and constrained by his editorial duty in this court-sponsored endeavor, by and large, Guangdi remains rather mute philosophically throughout this compilation. But in his own writings on the *Changes*, Guangdi acts not as a custodian of old views, but as an innovative interpreter with his distinct hermeneutic voice. Particularly in his *General Discussions of the Classic of Changes* (Zhouyi tonglun), completed in 1712, Guangdi intersperses philosophical insights in his exegetical encounter with the Classic. This work, as Guangdi himself told his friends and disciples, among all his writings on the *Changes*, should be the first piece they consult, for "in it are words that one must know before one can study the *Changes* well."[63]

In the *General Discussions*, Guangdi laments that the "classical annotations" (*zhujing*) of the generations after the ancient age of the classics have been "merely textual and philological comments (*xungu*)," often failing to attain the "purport" (*yi*) of the sages. "Therefore," Guangdi opines, "one who reads the classics well swims about (*hanyong*) in the texts of the classics so as to be on cordial terms (*jiexia*) with them. Then there is the interlacing of annotations and explanations."[64] The use of such metaphoric language—swimming about in the texts to establish friendship with them—suggests direct communion with the classics and penetration into the sages' original purport, apart from the mechanistic act of textual definition and glossing. But text-reading is perforce the creative act of meaning-making. At the same time that we participate in the indisputably truth-bearing tradition forged by the classical texts, there is also the posture of, to use Paul Ricoeur's word, "distanciation,"[65] which enables the reader to achieve meaning in accordance with her or his own understanding.

Little wonder that in the *General Discussions*, Guangdi often employs the text of *Changes* as the old classical bottle into which he pours the new wine of his philosophical understanding. Guangdi's interpretive stance is that even though the *Changes* is meticulous in portraying, detailing, and dissecting the workings of the universe, its descriptions of the various parts must be understood in terms of the sum-total of its interlocking truths. In one essay, he notes that scholars, in exploring the significance of the hexagrams, *Qian* and *Kun*, often discern the two notions' intimate relation with either the "meaning of ruler-subject" (*zunchen zhi yi*) or the "learning of the sages and the upright" (*shengxian zhi xue*). In actuality, the apprehension of *Qian* and *Kun* means knowing both the former (the recognition of the social relationship), and the latter (the pursuit of moral cultivation). To begin with, the lines (*yao*) of the *Qian* hexagram show that humanity should "embody its [i.e., heaven's] strength" (*ti qi jian*), while those of the *Kun* hexagram urge humanity to "follow the path of its [i.e., heaven's] compliance" (*dao qi shun*). Strength and compliance are the virtues of "one body," which are all-encompassing. Guangdi explains the relations between *Qian* and *Kun* on the one hand, and social ties and moral cultivation on the other:

> *Qian* is heaven. In humanity, it is the mind-heart and its faculties, which engender the way of the ruler. *Kun* is earth. In

> humanity, it is the myriad bodies (*ti*), which engender the way of the subject. The embodiment of the real principle of nature (*xing*) by the mind-heart is sincerity (*cheng*), and sincerity is the virtue of the sages. The preservation of the brilliant sagacity of the mind-heart by the self (*shen*) is reverence (*jing*), and reverence is the virtue of the upright.[66]

Here, Guangdi in fact explicates the ruler-subject relation with reference to the self and its realization through the cultivation of the virtues of sincerity and reverence. Knowing the relative positions of the hexagrams of *Qian* and *Kun*, we then know not only the proper social hierarchy but also the appropriate development of the inseparable components of the self, thereby ultimately fulfilling the "real principle of nature" (*xing zhi shili*).

In fact, in the *General Discussions*, Guangdi contends that "the diagrams and images of the *Changes* are the learning of the mind-heart." To him, *Qian* and *Kun* are the "original source" of "the learning of enlightenment resulting from sincerity" (*chengming zhi xue*). They are representations of the workings of heaven in the human enterprise of moral cultivation. The concreteness of heaven's way, embodied in nature, is exemplified by *Qian*, while its vacuity is epitomized by *Kun*. Therefore, as Guangdi points out, when the *Wenyan* (Commentary on the Words of the Text)[67] pertaining to the *Qian* hexagram talks about "preserving sincerity" (*cuncheng*) and "establishing sincerity" (*licheng*), it is actually talking about "concretely developing nature to the utmost" (*shi er jin xing*). On the other hand, when the *Wenyan* on *Kun* makes reference to "reverence" (*jing*) and "rightness" (*yi*), it is referring to "quiescently complying with the Way" (*xu er shunli*). In substantiating this textual evidence from the *Changes*, Guangdi declares his moral philosophy of virtuous cultivation:

> Preserving the solid mind-heart of loyalty and trustworthiness is the beginning of sincerity; establishing the solid affairs of prudence and faithfulness is the conclusion of sincerity. Dwelling in reverence while being personally pure and clear-minded, there is the enlightenment of substance (*ming zhi ti*); concentrating on rightness while utilizing the body in peace, there is the function of enlightenment (*ming zhi yong*).[68]

From the images of the hexagram, Guangdi thus distills the metapraxis of "preserving sincerity," "dwelling in reverence," and "enlightenment as a result of sincerity," coupled with the substance-function duality. This metapraxis, as we have seen, is integral to Guangdi's general theory.

Guangdi further seeks corroboration of the philosophical notion of "enlightenment resulting from sincerity" in the "Great Commentary" (Dazhuan, alternatively known as the "Appended Phrases," Xici zhuan) of the *Changes*:

> The Great Commentary also says that *Qian* provides the mastery of knowledge while *Kun* provides capability. How so? [*Qian*,] being spiritually clear, pure, and vacuous, is therefore the lord of knowledge. But [its knowledge] must also be honestly concrete and plainly straighforward before [it] can connect with the ambitions of all-under-heaven. Therefore, [the *Changes*] says, "*Qian* through ease provides the mastery of knowlege." With sincerity, there is enlightenment.
>
> [*Kun*,] giving rise to shapes, colors and concreteness, is therefore the lord of capability. But [its capability] must also be clearly understandable and concisely summed up before [it] can complete the tasks of all-under-heaven. Therefore, [the *Changes*] says, "*Kun* through simplicity provides capability." With enlightenment, there is sincerity.[69]

In the *General Discussions*, Guangdi also finds the occasion to expound his conception of *xing* by devoting an essay to the notion of "continuing [heaven's] goodness to complete nature" (*jishan chengxing*), a notion found in the "Great Commentary." In the *Analects*, it is recorded that Confucius remained mute on the questions of nature and heaven's Way. Guangdi postulates that what the master did not actually say is fully revealed in the *Tuanzhuan* (Commentary on the Judgments) and the *Wenyan* of the *Changes*. Moreover, the *Changes*'s statement—"Profound is the fundamental nature (*yuan*) of *Qian*! The myriad things owe their beginning to its resources"—is tantamount to this pronouncement by Zhu Xi: "The mind-heart of heaven-and-earth is the production of things. The people and things born each obtain heaven-and-earth's mind-heart to produce things as their own mind-heart." The *Changes* makes it clear that this "fundamental nature" of *Qian* is "good" (*shan*), which is in turn manifested as "humaneness" (*ren*). This humaneness, Guangdi avers, is the virtue (*de*) of heaven-and-earth's production of things. This virtue, obtained by humanity and things, is the solid substance (*shiti*) of the mind-heart. This process of "giving" by heaven, and "receiving" by things and humanity, constitutes what the *Changes* calls "continuation." Since what is given and what is received is invariably good, there is consequently the idea of "continuing [heaven's] goodness."[70]

Yet if the endowed nature is good as the continuation of heaven's goodness, the *Changes* also states that "the change and transformation of the Way of *Qian* in each instance imbue things with their correct nature and destiny," thereby asserting the differences among things. Guangdi elucidates this onto-genetic phenomenon with Zhu Xi's idea that although the universal principle is the controlling master, the workings of yin-yang and the Five Agents mean that in the production of things and people, there will be differences in material disposition (*qizhi*). In short, the creative fundamentality of *Qian* confers on all humanity the good nature, but the flux of the Way of *Qian* results in the particularities of material nature. Guangdi concludes that the theory of material nature espoused by Cheng Yi and Zhang Zai can be traced directly to the *Changes*.[71]

Specifically, in the *General Discussions*, Guangdi devotes a series of essays to unpacking the meanings of various hexagrams in terms of "the learning of the mind-and-heart" (*xinxue*), that is, his moral philosophy premised on nature. In the essay on *Fu* (Return),[72] the hexagram becomes a sort of eidetic recall of the famous sixteen-character core message of the *Classic of Documents*, in which there is the juxtaposition of the mind-heart of the Way (*daoxin*) and the mind-heart of humanity (*renxin*): "The mind-heart of humanity is prone to error. The mind-heart of the Way is subtle. Remain discerning and single-minded. Keep steadfastly to the Mean." Guangdi posits that the capability to reveal the subtlety of the mind-heart of the Way is indicated by the first line of the *Fu* hexagram, which refers to "return from a short distance." Despite momentary lapses and waywardness, there is always the return to the correct Way. Guangdi goes on to say that "keeping steadfastly to the Mean" in the *Documents* is what the hexagram's second line calls "quiet return" because it is blessed by the "good fortune" of persistent retrieval of the good. It can also be equated with what the fifth line calls "noblehearted return without remorse."

The third line, which states "repeated return from danger," echoes the *Documents*'s assertion that errors are imminent when human desires are not curbed. The fourth line, which refers to "one's returning alone from walking in the midst of others," actually also refers to the fact that the goodness of *yang* resides in the surrounding *yin*. It highlights, so Guangdi reasons, the subtlety of the moral person who possesses the mind-heart of the Way. As for the sixth line at the top, it points to "missing the return" and the resulting "misfortune." Guangdi attributes this phenomenon to the "extinguishing of heaven's principle and the flourishing of human desires." Therefore, the *Changes* claims that in this circumstance, there is "misfortune from within and without," and "great defeat when armies are deployed." This, Guangdi elaborates, is the result of "the inability to triumph over the strength of human desires." Because of this moral failure, misfortune spreads to the ruler and the state, whose exalted position of leadership can no longer be secured. Guangdi concludes that all this begins with

> the mind-heart's failing to discharge its duty. If the mind-heart comes to grips with its duty, then there is the control of the self and certain victory. Both heaven and the ruler enjoy peace and the myriad bodies will follow orders. How in the first place will there be misfortune and defeat?

Thus, in this essay on the *Fu* hexagram, Guangdi espouses his moral philosophy of the mind-heart in the course of explicating a cosmic symbolization in the *Changes*.[73]

In another essay, Guangdi bases his gloss of the hexagram, *Wu Wang* (No Errancy),[74] on this statement by Zhu Xi: "Heaven's principle flows where human desires are exhausted." To Guangdi, Zhu's assertion encapsulates the moral message of the hexagram's judgment that if one is not righteous, there will be disaster, and it will not be "appropriate for one to set out to do something." Under this circumstance, Guangdi adds, one should "preserve that which is constant." This constancy is heaven's principle, or our nature (*xing*). While the No Errancy hexagram advises caution in springing into action, it also counsels setting out at the right time under the right circumstance. Regarding the lower trigram (*Zhen*) of the *Wu Wang* hexagram, the "Commentary on the Judgment" (*Tuanci*) says: "[No Errancy] is such that the hard and strong comes from without and becomes the ruler within." The first line of the hexagram says, "If one sets out with No Errancy, one will attain one's goal." Guangdi explains that No Errancy is the condition under which one should go forward into action, and the goal that one attains is none other than "the nature to which there can be no addition." If we do not set out to do something because we are not in a righteous state, we are then "preserving our immanent nature so that it will not be harmed." Guangdi concludes that since No Errancy is "the straightness of heaven's mandate," or nature, its realization in action always brings profit. But it is our sense and awareness of "rightness" (*yi*) that makes the initial decision of whether to act or not to act. In other words, we must be certain that desires, or the calculations for profits and losses, not be the motivating force behind our action.[75] It is quite apparent that Guangdi boils the meaning of the No Errancy hexagram down to the goodness of nature, which is only realized in action untainted by selfish desires.

Looking at Guangdi's *General Discussions of the Classic of Changes*, it can be clearly seen that he philosophizes in the exegetical domain, seeking to ferret out the real meanings beyond the apparent words. Instead of subscribing to the epistemological credulity of the philological endeavor of taking words to mean what they say on the surface, he probes the classic's words so as to affirm, substantiate, and invigorate his own moral philosophical preunderstanding. To the extent that his engagement with the classics' words is mediated by his philosophy, this examination of Guangdi's hermeneutics heuristically invites some pondering on the nature of the Confucian enterprise of classical exegesis in light of contemporary hermeneutics.

Confucian Exegesis Seen in the Light of Contemporary Hermeneutics

A Confucian such as Li Guangdi, as with a Hebrew theologian, a Christian thinker, or a contemporary philosopher of the interpretative enterprise, plays the role of a Hermes (from which the word "hermeneutics" is derived), the messenger of the gods, a prophet of sorts, who, in the words of Martin Buber, "represents the Lord . . . [and] enunciates the message and commands in his Name."[76] The messages of the "gods" and "the Lord" are canonical and scriptural texts, or in other words, the classics that ineluctably impart a sense of the sacral. Just what are the classics? In the broadest terms, they are, in David Tracy's definition, paradigmatic and exemplary texts that "have helped found or form a particular culture."[77] Hence their paradigmatic "public status" and "public meaning."[78] They are the most important element in a community's cultural inheritance, the central testament to its imaginative and mythological universe, comprising the basic assumptions and beliefs; they form "the Great Code," as Northrop Frye describes the Bible, for instance.[79] The Bible, like other classics, so Frye tells us, consists of stories and other narratives that a society must know: "its gods, its history, its laws, or its class structure." These stories are "mythological" in the sense that they are "charged with a special seriousness and importance," and mark off and "outline a specific area of human culture." Hence their historically and culturally acknowledged sacrality.[80]

As exemplary, public, and sacred texts, the classics, to begin with, possess lasting qualities. But more important, their longevity and their refusal to disappear readily from a culture are also a consequence of their "openness to accommodation," in the words of Frank Kermode, welcoming readers and interpreters across time to assume their share of the production of the classics' meanings.[81] This openness is possible because of the general recognition of what David Tracy calls the classics' "excess of meaning," which "demands constant interpretation and bears a certain kind of timelessness—namely the timelessness of a classic expression radically rooted in its own historical time and calling to . . . [the interpreter's] own historicity."[82] To put it another way, the classics have no future other than their invitation to constant historical and finite reinterpretation; otherwise, their fate is death. The vital classics are capable of staking a strong and irresistible claim to attention both as the encompassing timeless framework and as repositories of universal values. At the same time that they imbue individual passing phenomena with meaning and significance, they demand the hermeneutic intrusion spearheaded by the interpreter's own questions and history.

Following Gadamer, David Tracy outlines the four major characteristics of this inevitable hermeneutic interpolation. First, the interpreter initially arrives at the reading of the text with some strong preunderstanding, determined by the interpreter's particular and contingent historical concerns. But these concerns are in turn informed by the memories of the traditions and also animated by the inquirer's fiduciary relationship with the community of other investigators. In brief, there is no fully autonomous interpreter above history, severed from tradition and exiled from the wider community of other readers. Second, the classics, with their strong claim to attention, draw to them the interpreter. But instead of turning the interpreter into an unquestioning eulogist, the classics provoke a confrontation between their identity as immanent transhistorical texts and the interpreter's radical historical alterity. Third, a dialogue then ensues, a dialectical process of engaging the realities and questions disclosed by the texts, marked by the interpreter's negotiations with them. Such negotiations, as in any meaningful dialogue, involve acceptance, rejection, modification, and compromise of viewpoints. Fourth, this dialogue inexorably spills over into the large community of interpreters, insofar as the individual interpreter's preunderstanding is forged by other understandings of the classics. Intersubjectively, the dialogue becomes a broad dialogue with other inquirers, so that a single individual reading acquires the stamp of relevance.[83] In short, the classics cannot be understood by repeating them; they must be interpreted. Only then, as Kierkegaard has insisted, can they be really "repeated."[84]

To state this in Martin Buber's hermeneutic terms, the Word of God in the Bible, and not the rite, is the principal point of "contact between godhead and manhood." Through such Word, God becomes a person who addresses human beings in a human language. Such address demands response, so that the "human person not only adopts the word, he also answers, lamenting, complaining to God himself, disputing with Him about justice, humbling himself before Him, praying."[85] The person, as the "I," a particular being, in such communication with the Word of

God, the "Thou," the universal framework, gains larger insights that transcend limited individual visions. Nonetheless, the Bible, as Buber reminds us, should not be treated as "absolute, sufficing, immutable," although it must be read as "sacred text." The thawing hermeneutic act forestalls such texts from being frozen in time. Through interpretation, their living quality is invigorated and enlivened.[86]

In light of the foregoing description of the classics and their inescapable hermeneutic corollaries, some palpable commonalities may be discerned between Confucian exegesis and the Western hermeneutic tradition. Both conceive the understanding of particular phenomena in terms of a larger overarching framework. Both strive for understanding of the classics' words through dialogic communication. Both, notwithstanding their acceptance of the classics' cultural function as the preservation of truths, subject these truth-bearing texts to constant interrogation. Both make no assault on the classics' claim to ultimate value, but they dissect the particular ways in which the classics served as the vessels of the ancient sages' pleas and teachings in finite historical moments.

A case in point, as we have shown, is Li Guangdi's reading of the classics. Guangdi's disagreement with Zhu Xi, across time, via hermeneutic pondering on the *Mean* and *Great Learning*, is an example of the tripartite dialogic relation among the sacred texts, Zhu Xi's commentaries, and Guangdi. As the interpreter, Guangdi inevitably brought his vision to bear on the canons themselves and on prior canonical interpretations. As finite historical subject, he approached the classics with his preunderstanding of the Confucian teachings based on the primacy of the goodness of human nature, which was a distinct response to the historical development of Confucian thought addressing the rise and growth of Lu-Wang thinking. Hence, willy-nilly, the timelessness of the classics was qualified by this specific historical insight. Just note the juxtaposition of the following two statements in the preface of his *Zhongyong zhangduan*.

On the one hand, Guangdi claims that "Because nature is constant, the Way is constant, without the caprice of fads. Is it not true that the sages' teachings, which established the ultimate for human living and which resist changes in the ten thousand generations, are based on this?"[87] On the other hand, Guangdi asserts that although "the myriad principles are replete in the classics bequeathed by Confucius," individuals can only apprehend them after "painstaking thinking and exhaustive quest."[88] In fact, "the sages, while adopting the ways of the ancients [before them], forged their own individual molds."[89] Thus, even if the classics were timeless monuments, they invited constant questioning, thereby staking their claim to attention. Guangdi responded to the provocation of the classical texts and entered into hermeneutical dialogues with the ancients and their words, involving in the process the wider community of interpreters.

To the extent that a dialogic relation existed between the hermeneut and the classical text, Confucian exegesis also brings to mind Gadamer's philosophical hermeneutics, which rejects what he calls "Romantic hermeneutics," the sort that sees understanding of classical texts as an "empathic" and "divinatory" process that bypasses history. Such a process renders hermeneutics into psychological interpretions, the intuitive retrieval of the original.[90] Gadamer also faults the sort of mechanistic programmatic hermeneutics that is based on the all-too-sanguine notion of the liberating thrust of critical reason unburdened by tradition. This approach claims that the way to read meanings out of texts is to treat them as objects in themselves, to be approached without preconceptions of the interpreter. Pruned of present prejudices, unencumbered by presuppositions, released from the current time, this mythical interpreter leaps into the past and thus makes his or her presence felt in the objectified text.[91] In so doing, the temporal and chronological gap between the reader and the text can be bridged.

While one may well argue that eighteenth-century Qing *kaozheng* (evidential textual studies) came close to the purport and aim of such programmatic hermeneutics,[92] the sort of Confucian hermeneutics examined here would have found much more common ground in Gadamer's philosophical hermeneutic, which affirms that every interpreter enters into the hermeneutic act bearing the historical effects of tradition. To be sure, Guangdi's hermeneutics did bear the rhetorical stamp of what Gadamer would have labeled as "Romantic." It is interesting to note what one of Guangdi's junior relations, in a preface he wrote for a collection of Guangdi's exegetical writings on the *Four Books*, had to say about the elder Li's hermeneutic aim:

> The difficulty of glossing the classics lies in the difficulty in gaining access to the minds of the authors. Since the Han and Tang, there had been many prominent individual schools which had developed their own expertise in strictly adhering to the philological annotations of the original verses and sentences. But often, they could not avoid hairsplitting debates about minutiae. It was only with the emergence of Cheng [Yi] and Zhu [Xi] in the Song that the hitherto ignored ideas in the classics were apprehended. Using their understanding of moral meanings and principles, they explained the mistakes and lacunae in the terse classical texts, and scholars were

> relieved to learn that they obtained the real messages which were closely in tune with the minds of the sages. . . . [Guangdi] delved into the essence of the classics and plumbed the Six Classics and Four Books not only by broadly studying the exegeses of the Han and Tang, but also synthesizing their central ideas via [the learning of] Cheng and Zhu. . . . His extensive studies of the various books were always guided by the classics, while his careful investigations of the various ideas were always rooted in moral principles.[93]

From this description, it can be seen that Guangdi sought to be in "tune with the minds of the sages," the goal of "Romantic hermeneutics." But it is also evident that he invariably complemented formalist philological hermeneutics, or in Dilthey's hermeneutic terms, *Erklären* (explanation), with *Verstehen* (understanding), or the preunderstanding of the classics based on Confucian moral principles.[94] Guangdi himself, in studying the *Changes*, claimed that one must thoroughly know the lines and images so that even if all the commentaries and judgments are no longer available, one would still know exactly what they meant, just as the sages would.[95] The attainment of such undertanding could only come with painstaking study of the words themselves, as Guangdi revealed his own struggle with the *Changes*:

> When I first studied the *Changes*, after a few years of effort, I had examined every one of the lines (*yao*). I felt that all the three hundred and eighty-four lines did not quite cohere with one another. Thereupon, I forged individual essays out of every hexagram, after which I tried to correlate every word and every sentence with the hexagrams. At first, I thought that when there were one or two places where I did not have understanding, I could just muddle through with the correlations. But how could I know that these one or two black spots were not exactly the places that mattered the most? Even if there is one word or sentence in the way, the overall thinking cannot be right. It is only when no word stands in the way, so that even the particles strike responsive chords, that the overall thinking can be correctly verified and corroborated. Only then can each word and each sentence exert its great effort. The establishment of the overall thinking, and the seeking of the meaning of each word and sentence, are compatible with each other as surface and interior are.[96]

Thus, understanding, after all, in Guangdi's hermeneutic scheme, could not be "pure" in the sense that it directly intuited the minds of the sages.

It could not be "romantic"; it must be guided by critical methods (*kaozheng*); philology went hand in hand with philosophy (*yili*). On this score, one is also reminded of Paul Ricoeur's formulation of the hermeneutic process when he suggests that "explanation *develops* understanding" and "understanding precedes, accompanies, closes, and thus *envelops* explanation."[97]

Given Guangdi's hermeneutic stance, he would have agreed with Gadamer's assertion that "[h]ermeneutic experience is concerned with *tradition*. . . . But tradition is not simply a process that experience teaches us to know and govern; it is *language*—i.e., it expresses itself like a Thou." Without citing Buber, Gadamer goes on to clarify the nature of text-reading via the I-Thou relation: "A Thou is not an object; it relates itself to us. Rather, I maintain that the understanding of tradition does not take the traditionary text as an expression of another person's life, but as meaning that is detached from the person who means it, from an I or a Thou. . . . For tradition is a genuine partner in communication, with which we have fellowship as does the 'I' with a 'Thou'."[98] The clearest expression of the transmitted tradition as language is the classics, in which is ensconced a culture's "normative sense." Through these texts which impart a sense of the norms, we gain "a consciousness of something enduring, of significance that cannot be lost and is independent of all the circumstances of time—a kind of timeless present that is contemporaneous with every other present." The great canons, albeit once written in the distant past—hence their ineluctable "temporal quality that articulates it historically"—will always yield some significant insight into the particular situation of the reader.[99] Thus, to read the classics is to realize the communicative dialogic relation between the enduring texts as transmitted tradition and the hermeneut. In this interactive process, in which the reader and the text are locked in a "hermeneutic circle" where their questions and answers interpenetrate and unfold,[100] Gadamer sees the affirmation of the reader's own biases in the hermeneutic enterprise. Indeed, he sees the fusing of the interpreter's own historical horizons with that of the texts as the ontological basis of understanding. Our cognizance of the historical role of the texts is the very condition of our understanding of the texts.

For instance, it would be quite a futile effort to attempt to understand the Bible without prior knowledge of the paramount influence of the scriptures in the historical life of the West. The understanding of any text is the result of the dynamic fusion of one's own "effective historical consciousness," consisting of one's prejudgments and the tradition of interpretation that preceded one, and the texts'. This "fusion of horizons" finally yields "effective history" for the hermeneut.[101] Guangdi, the hermeneut, had his own prejudgments, namely, his philosophy predicated on the goodness of human nature. Also, he had Zhu Xi's works on the *Mean* and *Great Learning* and other classical commentaries as the preceding interpretive tradition. In Buber's terms, the reader as the "I," "without forfeiting anything of the felt reality of his activity, at the same time lives through the common event from the standpoint of the other [i.e., the text as 'Thou']."[102]

This "common event" means that the fullness of the hermeneut's horizons must be appreciated in the dialogue with the texts. The I and Thou enter into "a new community," as Gadamer puts it:

> When we try to examine the hermeneutical phenomenon through the model of conversation between two persons, the chief thing that these apparently so different situations—understanding a text and reaching an understanding in a conversation—have in common is that both are concerned with a subject matter that is placed before them. . . . To reach an understanding in a dialogue is not merely a matter of putting oneself forward and successfully asserting one's own point of view, but being transformed into a communion in which we do not remain what we were.[103]

In light of this notion of a "common event" or "communion," developed through dialogic contact with the classics, we may develop a different perspective in appreciating the meaning of these familiar words uttered by Guangdi: "The Way of all-under-heaven is fully embodied in the Six Classics. The Way of the Six Classics is fully embodied in the Four Books. The Way of the Four Books is entirely within my own self."[104] Customarily, these oft-repeated words are interpreted as an expression of the mystical and holistic Confucian conception of the organismic cosmos. Now, we may explain them more specifically in hermeneutic terms as the fusing of the horizons of the reader and the classical text.

However, we must take note of the fact that the fusion of horizons in the Confucian sense took place in the presence of the unshakable conviction of the correctness and wisdom of the classics, as I pointed out at the outset of this exploration on Confucian hermeneutics. In other words, the status of the sacred texts in terms of their ultimate truth and meaning was never destabilized, decentered, and thereby questioned. To be sure, Guangdi did bring his philosophic preunderstanding, most notably the notion of the ontological primacy of *xing*, to his hermeneutic act. But the notion of *xing*, to begin with, was an important and time-honored one in the classics, and indeed in the Confucian tradition as a whole. He certainly did not bring some notions *other than* those available in the unalienably Confucian structure. This deep veneration for the canon was a vital and crucial element in the Confucian hermeneutics. Moreover, the ontological conception of *xing* as the root and essence of all Being, at once endowed by and coeval with heaven, presumed the ultimate oneness of the reader and the sages (authors of the classics).[105] Thus, Guangdi's dialogue with the classics did not begin with the view of their strangeness and distance, but rather with their familiarity and closeness. The Confucian fusion of horizons suggested no bridging of a chasm of ultimate meanings between the reader and the text. The classics might be rigorously interrogated, but the hermeneutic circle must also be drawn in acceptable Confucian terms.

Furthermore, this fusion of horizons not only brought about change in understanding, but it also in effect created an occasion for existential transformation. Indeed, Confucian hermeneutics saw understanding as integrally tied to action and commitment. The comprehension and elucidation of texts was an existentialist encounter with the living, vital messages of the Confucian classics. As Li Guangdi sought understanding of the classics in terms of "knowing the root," that is, awareness of the goodness of our nature, he also prescribed a way of living anchored on individual moral-ethical self-cultivation (*xiushen*), which was the existential result of exegetical understanding of the *Mean*, *Great Learning*, *Analects*, and *Changes*: "Knowing that all-under-heaven and the state both take the self as the root, it is also known that one's self and mind-heart must not be indulgent, slothful and selfish."[106] In point of fact, this Confucian conviction in praxis resonates with David Tracy's conception of hermeneutics as praxis. Tracy asserts that "[e]very time we act, deliberate, judge, understand, or even experience, we are interpreting. To understand at all is to interpret. To act well is to interpret a situation demanding some action and to interpret a correct strategy for that action," leading to his conclusion that hermeneutics must be used "as they should be used: as further practical skills for the central task of becoming human."[107] Such praxis would have elicited a hearty endorsement from Guangdi.

As with Gadamer, Buber, and Tracy, a Confucian hermeneut like Guangdi took the classics or scripture, the textual embodiment of a vital cultural tradition, as the locus of understanding. Their hermeneutic reflection on the classics was engagement with and participation in a cultural tradition. An avowed Cheng-Zhu follower like Guangdi would readily diverge from Zhu Xi's reading of the classics. With his preconceived notion of the centrality of human nature as the ontological center of gravity of reality, Guangdi communicated with the classics. His hermeneutic project achieved the intended agreement with the classics, and vice versa, about a shared reality, a reality defined by the primacy of human nature as the origin of human actions.

If we may generalize from our understanding of the particular case of Li Guangdi's hermeneutics, Confucian exegesis was an interactive dialogue with a living past ensconced in the classics. Hermeneutics led not only to a better understanding of the words of the sages, but also to their integration in the interpreter's philosophy and life. As Gadamer contends, engaging and understanding the classics does not simply refer to the interpretative relation between the classics as an "object" and the reader as the inquiring subject. The central relation is between the inquirer and whole history of the effects of the classics. To know the classics is to act in accordance with them, or with their spirit. Guangdi would have agreed with Gadamer's assertion that "understanding belongs to the being of that which is understood."[108] To know is to act.

SIX

Vita Activa

Action in the Political and Social Realms

> In human finitude we have need both of work and of the word in order to situate ourselves in the direction of a creative world which we are not. . . . Hence, every human civilization will be both a civilization of work *and* a civilization of the word.
>
> —Paul Ricoeur, "Work and the Word"

With intended economy, Guangdi, as we recall, offers this summation of the major themes of his learning: "first is to preserve the concrete mind (*cun shixin*), second is to illuminate concrete principle (*ming shili*), third is to act on concrete things (*xing shishi*)."[1] There is an unmistakable gravitational tug toward the practical in his philosophy. From his metaphysics to his hermeneutics, the abiding conviction is that truth is experienced, that investigation is lived, and that theory is, after all, practice. This leitmotif runs through Guangdi's ruminations on the forging of ethico-moral character and quality in an individual through concrete action. But if we have shown that his general philosophical theory yields meta-practical apodicticity, we have not explored what he says about practice and policies specifically in the workaday political and social realms. Aristotle's definition of praxis is germane here, for its most consequential thrust is ultimately a political and social one. Praxis in the Aristotelian sense is directed toward the accomplishment of the virtuous life of individuals not in a vacuum, but ineluctably in the context of the *polis* as citizens. The *polis*, as the intricated ethico-socio-political web of people's lives, is the very site on which practical wisdom is realized and fulfilled.[2] To be sure, we are not here in any way referring to Aristotle's views on ethics and politics particular to his conception of the Greek *polis*. What we do say, however, is that in appropriating the term "praxis," we perforce subscribe to the notion that a political and social community provides the inescapable institutional context in which action acquires meaning.

It is also significant to note that despite the Aristotelian emphasis on the institutional *topos* (locality) for the exercise of practical ideas, there is, in the Western tradition, a pronounced endorsement of *theoria*, contemplative knowledge of pure theory, for its own sake and on its own terms, as we have pointed out earlier. As Paul Ricoeur remarks, a "man of culture is not concerned with *political* efficacy (which is the measure of all projects by means of the capture of power or the exercise of power). . . . [T]he man of culture is not concerned with the political realization of his ideas."[3] Small wonder that René Char, with a notable sense of pathos, uttered this terse jeremiad on the European intellectuals' experience in the four years in the Resistance: "Our inheritance was left to us by no testament." Testament here was the Western tradition, one that demanded no active and direct participation in public affairs. A generation of European men of culture found themselves suddenly enmeshed in the public realm. Unaccustomed to playing politically relevant roles, these unprepared men of letters felt that their newfound obligations in the world of political reality were burdensome and irksome, at least initially.[4]

In contrast, the Confucian men of culture, the literati, not only saw the state and society as providing the context that regulates and vitalizes human interaction, but they were concerned with the political and social efficacy of their ideas and therefore sought to actively participate in the officialdom. In point of fact, they *were* the state and government. The Confucian *junzi*, or the "noble men," as Wm. Theodore de Bary contends, took on what he calls "the prophetic role," that is, the assumption of the ultimate responsibility to transform and bring order to the world. They were held accountable for the well-being and the suffering of the people.[5] Thus, among themselves, a public space was created, wherein transformative social and political actions were implemented. Given the worldview of the Confucian noble men, study of the ancient texts of the classics invoked not nostalgic distance but presentist involvement. In the *Doctrine of the Mean*, for instance, the *junzi* is described as one who "reverently realizes one's virtuous nature, and pursues inquiry and learning." The aim of such endeavor was to consummate the trichotomous goals prescribed in the *Great Learning*: self-cultivation (*xiushen*), ordering state and society (*zhiguo*), and bringing peace to all-under-heaven (*ping tianxia*). Thus, private ethico-intellectual endeavors happily conjugated with their public realization; the world of elevated ideas was closely related to that of common human affairs. In short, for a Confucian man of culture, the inner efforts of achieving sagehood (*neisheng*) was never severed from the outer concerns of implementing the Way of the ruler (*waiwang*).[6]

To the extent that by outer concerns were meant rulership and leadership (the Way of the ruler), the public function of the Confucian men of culture was first and foremost the political organization and exercise of power in the context of the state. Wm. Theodore de Bary has made it crystal clear that this political role began with assuming the burden of self-cultivation on the part of the *junzi*, that is, both the ruler and his assistants, followed by the creation of humane government (*renzheng*), the raison d'être of which was "to have compassion on Heaven's people" and "doing what is right (*yi*) by them."[7] Indeed, this prime concern for the people, and the definition of the state and government in terms of conferring benefits on the people from above, constitute the main ingredients of Li Guangdi's political vision.

While it is important to note that Confucian praxis envisaged the erection of benevolent governance *for* the people in the political realm, one must not ignore the Confucian practical concerns with the social organization of human relations through rituals (*li*). De Bary has aptly acknowledged these concerns as the other principal motifs in Confucian discourse.[8] As Kai-wing Chow's recent study has argued, particularly from the late Ming through the high Qing periods, the literati sought to establish a social order by revivifying and codifying the correct rituals. This "ritualism," as Chow puts it, was seen as the most concrete basis on which a moral-ethical society could be constructed.

In short, this chapter, with a view to exploring Li Guangdi's praxis in the political and social realms, focuses on two subjects: first, his people-based political ideas; second, his discourse on rituals as the foundation for the ethico-moral strengthening of the social fabric.

People (*Min*) as the Basis of Governance: The Moral Foundation of Statecraft

Li Guangdi does not offer us a systematic political philosophy, but from his various writings it is not difficult to piece together a coherent picture of his conception of a political order. For instance, in his *Recorded Sayings*, there are two fascicles entitled "The Way of Governance" (Zhidao), in which we catch clear glimpses of his views on rulership. Here, Guangdi expounds the fundamental Confucian doctrine that governance is the moral Way in action, which ideally involves all individuals: "That there is the Way of all-under-heaven does not only mean that the court is clear and bright, but also that the literati and the common folk all follow the Way and principle in action." However, it is undoubtedly the court above that sets the example and leads the way: "That the clear and bright are above, and the heavy and turbid are below, form a dialectical relation of constant mutual responses. When the material force of heaven is pure and expansive, the myriad things on earth below multiply; when a person's countenance is bright and nourished, there is no ailment inside the body. So when the court is pure and bright, the multitude is loyal and honest."[9] The state is a natural, all-encompassing order whose moral force nevertheless emanates from the court above. Referring to the Twentieth Book of the *Analects*, "Yao Said" (Yao Yue), Guangdi maintains that in the business of "ruling all-under-heaven, everything must be investigated, but there must be the basic root (*genben*)." This basic root is spelled out in King Tang's proclamation: "If I myself commit offenses, they are not to be attributed to you of the myriad regions. If you in the myriad regions commit offenses, these offenses must rest on my person."[10] In other words, the ruler, de Bary's "prophet" who stands at the apex of the political order, takes ultimate responsibility for the transgressions of the people under his rule.

This palpably paternalistic vision of the political community, while affirming the prophetic role of the ruler, also celebrates the ideal importance of the people. "The establishment of the state," Guangdi declares, "invariably has as its foundation the people." But in between the ruler at the pinnacle and the people at the base is the "intermediary stratum of the literati and officials (*shi dafu*), who are most crucial." Their paramount importance comes from the need of communication between the ruler and the people:

> For example, when the generalissimo commands the generals, and the generals in turn command the soldiers, it is like the arm's connecting with the fingers. But if [the ruler] does not have the confidence and loyalty of the generals, in times of crisis, it is unlikely that he can bypass the generals and appeal to the soldiers for protection. Therefore, it is an established truism that the cultivation of the upright [i.e., the *shi dafu*] will involve the multitude.[11]

Order comes into existence when a multiplicity of individuals are brought together under the moral folds of the ruler, whose benevolent, commanding authority is disseminated via the intermediaries of the literati. Through them, the people's sentiments (*minqing*) may properly be gathered and known. In fact, the principal responsibility of the local officials is to acquire a thorough understanding of the sentiments of those under their jurisdiction. A truly good local official must first "personally experience the meanings of the two words of '*fu*' (father) and '*mu*' (mother)," so that he can discharge his duties as though he were the parents of the people. It is Guangdi's view that one should first serve in the provinces and localities before becoming a high-ranking official precisely because of the invaluable experience gained from direct and close contact with the people.[12]

Thus, Guangdi sees the political order as a tripartite organic community composed of the ruler, the *shi dafu*, and the people. However, it is in effect bipartite, in that only the ruler and the literati are the active agents in the political domain. The plurality of the multitude of people is drained of differentiation and rendered into the inert masses, the object at which the exercise of the power, albeit altruistic and benign, is directed. An organic relationship exists between the top and the bottom, which is construed by Guangdi as a microcosm of the interaction between heaven and earth:

> When heaven and earth have intercourse, there is great peace. When those above and those below have intercourse, there is orderly rule (*zhi*). When heaven and earth do not communicate, there are impediments and clogging that become winter. When the ruler fails to broadly accommodate the sentiments of the people, there can be no state established all-under-heaven. Heaven's material force shoots through to the core of earth, and the ruler's mind-heart pervades the multitude.[13]

This political worldview may be described as what Hao Chang terms "moral statesmanship," which was a sort of normative statecraft predicated on the metaphysico-cosmological tenet that heaven and humanity were one (*tianren heyi*). The ideal ruler was the moral sage who realized his essential nature and achieved oneness with the universe. Participating in public life was simultaneously cultivating ultimate spirituality. Such moral-metaphysical conception of the political order regarded existing institutions as the manifestation of the Way and the moral capacities inherent in humanity. The *Great Learning*'s triple-goals of self-cultivation, ordering the state, and bringing peace to the world were a naturally contiguous progression rather than functionally separate pursuits.[14]

Guangdi's "moral statesmanship," as an ideal-type in Confucian political culture, was enlivened by what Thomas Metzger calls the dominant "ethos of interdependence," by which he refers to the conviction that the selves, interdependently or intersubjectively, in their moral assertions, could realize their immanent potentialities by identifying with the transcendent source such as heaven or the Way, thereby totalistically transforming the world.[15] When Guangdi waxed philosophic that harmony reigned as the mind-heart of the ruler penetrated the multitude, he in fact proclaimed the totalistic apprehension of the world through the moral assertion of the self. The political accomplishment of orderly rule was the cosmic commerce between heaven and earth. Safeguarding the welfare of the people was the moral exercise of the ruler and the *shi dafu*.

Examples of Guangdi's moralistic rendering of statecraft abound in his reading of the *Classic of Documents*, a classic that deals much and directly with the formation of the ancient polity. In his hermeneutic engagement with this classic, Guangdi finds once again the occasion to expound his philosophy, this time around his understanding of the workings of the political regime. Much of this understanding can be gleaned from his *Reading Verses of the Classic of Documents* (Shangshu judu). In this work, Guangdi glosses selected passages from the classical text and in the process reveals sketches of his political ideas. First and foremost, Guangdi seeks to establish the principle of diligent and generous rulership. It is no accident that he chooses to illustrate the meaning of this proclamation by the duke of Zhou in the *Documents*:

> My young son, promulgate (*ban*) everywhere my tireless assiduity and listen to my directions to you regarding how you may help the people observe what is always right. If you do not exert yourself in these matters, you will not last long. If you studiously implement the correct course of your father by following his example, no one will venture to go against you. Go and act reverently. Henceforth I will retire and teach farmers about rightness. Rule our people generously, and no matter how great the distance, they will come to you.

The message of this passage is self-explanatory. It urges the ruler to be unwearily industrious in his duty to help people follow the right course. By reverently enacting beneficent rule, people's loyalty and obedience can be secured. Guangdi provides an interesting gloss. Apart from recapitulating the message of benign and conscientious leadership, he also highlights the idea of the division of labor between the ruler and the officials. He postulates that the character *ban* (to promulgate) also means "to divide" (*fen*). Thus, while the king did his part in heeding the advice of the duke of Zhou, who had labored ceaselessly on behalf of the royal family and consolidated his rule, the duke also fulfilled his role by not abandoning even for a moment the king's mandate (*ming*) on him. While the king "reverently pursued his affairs, the Duke retired to husbandry and to teach the farmers rightness so as to help them, in hopes that the people live (*minsheng*) a correct and plentiful life and that they would not stray far from the path."[16] The ruler and his officials shared collaborative roles in the enterprise of rulership, both devoted to bettering the lives of the people.

Guangdi next addresses the question of the legitimacy of rulership in terms of the notion of the mandate of heaven (*tianming*). He refers to the chapter entitled "Prince Shi" (Jun Shi), wherein the duke of Zhou explains the fall of the Shang as a result of its loss of heaven's mandate and cautions the Zhou, the new recipient, that heaven's favor is not granted in perpetuity. Guangdi seizes upon one sentence from this chapter, "It depends on ourselves!" (*shi wo*), and treats it as the *idée maîtresse* of the duke's discourse, and therefore also of his own understanding of political legitimacy and dynastic longevity. Although, as the duke of Zhou made clear—"I dare not say, as though I knew, that our foundation will forever abide in prosperity. . . . Nor do I dare say, as though I knew, that the end will issue in our misfortunes"—the mandate of heaven cannot be easily fathomed, Guangdi reiterates that "what can be known lies within ourselves." He proceeds to unpack the meanings of the *Documents*'s statement, "It depends on ourselves!" He writes:

> [As for] the meaning of "It depends on ourselves!," it is that if we dare not rest content with having heaven's mandate and fail not to ponder its majesty, people's hearts will surely not turn against us, and so heaven's mandate can be perpetuated. What [the *Documents*] says about "our foundation's forever abiding in prosperity" is only a matter of what people summon for themselves. If our descendants and offspring fail to revere heaven, be in awe of the people, and maintain the bright glory of the forefathers of the family, thereby bringing an end [to such glory] and blithely ignoring the fact that heaven's mandate is difficult to preserve and hard to be trustful in, then they will certainly lose the mandate, unable to pursue and carry out for long the forefathers' virtues of reverence and wisdom. Is it not that case that what [the *Documents*] says about "the end's being issued in our misfortunes" is the result of our own flawed actions?[17]

Guangdi's reading thus plays down the apparent determinism of the notion of the mandate of heaven and reduces it to a voluntarism of choice. A regime's future is malleable, controlled by our chosen actions.

Guangdi sees orderly and prolonged rule as the consequence of the plurality of appropriate actions by both the ruler and his assistants. The

Documents tells us that the longevity of the Shang dynasty owed much to its ministers, in particular these six: Yiyin, Baoheng, Yizhi, Chenhu, Wuxian, and Ganpan. Guangdi quotes the classic:

> Because of [these six ministers] . . . , the rituals of the Yin were promoted so as to be in tune with heaven, and so it lasted for many years. Heaven thus sincerely maintained its mandate, and the Shang became abundant. The various officials and members of the royal family in employment all adhere to their virtue and show their heartfelt concern for the regime. The lesser officials and the lords of the Hou and Dian domains rushed to fulfill their duties. They manifest their virtue in aiding their ruler. So when the one man, the ruler, had affairs at hand, they became affairs of the four quarters of the empire. It is like conceding confidence to all in accordance with the divinatory indications of the tortoise shell and milfoil.[18]

Guangdi's gloss of this passage hammers home two notable points. First, although the six ministers "are specifically named so that their virtues are advertised to the world, they are in actuality only the outstanding representatives of the numerous officials and feudal lords." Therefore, the *Documents* makes a point to talk about the officials' and royal relatives' "sharing the worries" of the ruler. In other words, to celebrate the six famous officials is to underscore the importance of the entire officialdom. Second, according to Guangdi's interpretation, heaven's "sincerely maintaining its mandate" with the Shang means heaven's offering assistance to the Shang by providing it with "able subordinate officials." Thus, to him, the phrase "resolute maintenance" (*shunyou*) used in the *Documents* really means "able subordinate officials" (*liangzuo*).[19] Guangdi here may also be engaging in some kind of wordplay with the respective homonyms of *you* (right) and *zuo* (left). Idiomatically, "left and right" refers to close and able assistants. In any case, Guangdi's message is clear: the maintenance of heaven's mandate requires the good work and help of officials.

With this articulation of the importance of the officials comes naturally the imperative to employ able persons. In the chapter entitled "Establishing Government" (Li zheng), the *Documents* talks of the care that the ruler must exercise in making appointments. The Xia dynasty was great precisely because it remained anxiously vigilant in the matter of appointing officials. It did not judge candidates by their appearance but by their virtues. Only when their "nine virtues" (i.e., amicability coupled with sternness, tenderness coupled with firmness, bluntness coupled with respectfulness, craftiness coupled with reverence, submissiveness coupled with boldness, straightforwardness coupled with mildness, simplicity coupled with discrimination, strength coupled with sincerity, and courage coupled with rightness)[20] were proven would they be recommended for the "three appointments" (*san zhe*): high officers, pastors, and legal officers. Jie, the last king of the Xia, failing to follow this practice, used cruel men, and brought his house to an ignoble end. King Tang of the Shang, on the other hand, revived the efficacious Xia precedent and thus succeeded in implementing the imperative of heaven. He appointed those with the appropriate "three grades of ability" (*san jun*) to fill the "three appointments." He not only monitored but also emulated them. The result was that harmony reigned in all the cities, and "the different quarters of the empire all emulate[d] the manifested virtues." Guangdi's various glosses of this classical narrative boil down to his assertion that proper appointments and emulation of those appointed constitute the "profound rule" (*dafa*) in establishing government. With the enactment and enforcement of this profound rule, "virtues are visible all-under-heaven."[21] The paramountcy of this rule stems from the fact that "the principal concern of establishing government and making appointments is to enable the officials to help us in the management of the trust of the people which we have received."[22] The people are ultimately the basis of governance.

This government for the people relies not on punishments but on virtues, as the *Documents* teaches: "The profound gravity of the ruler above and the illuminating wisdom of those above shine brightly throughout the four quarters of the regime, so much so that all are influenced to become assiduous in cultivating virtue. But if need be, punishments are clearly meted out to manage the people, aiding them in discharging the constant correct duties." Guangdi elaborates: "Virtue is the basis of punishments. The bright shining forth of [the ruler's] profound gravity and [the officials'] illuminating wisdom is what is called the illumination of the bright virtues all-under-heaven. With the follow-up of administering fair punishments, virtue is illuminated and virtue's power is revealed. There is no one who does not retrieve one's constant nature. Hence the statement that bright wisdom helps people discharge the constant correct duties."[23] People-based governance is also virtue-based governance, the supplement of punishments notwithstanding.

From Guangdi's interpretations of the *Documents*, it can be seen that his ideal of the polity was a moral one. It may also be noted that Guangdi's moral-political rhetoric and philosophy, in both tone and substance, was concordant with the imperial instructions and admonitions of the Kangxi emperor. This is hardly surprising since Guangdi was a trusted official close to the throne. For instance, the emperor proclaimed, "The way of maintaining the country rests solely on cultivating virtues and appeasing the people. When the hearts of the people are happy, then there is the foundation of the regime, and the boundaries will naturally be consolidated."[24] Within the limits of this moral framework is ensconced the eternal hierarchy—those above, the ruler and his indispensable assistants, and those below, the people. Those above were enjoined to maintain the government, and hence also the cosmic order, primarily by their virtue, expressed as their unwearied devotion to the people. To conduct government was to accept the constant self-counsel that the ruler, aided by officials, must carry out heaven's imperative, virtuously exercising his prerogatives to achieve happiness for the people.

Practical Statecraft: Using Talents and Implementing Beneficial Policies

If the geometry of the aspirations of this moral statesmanship was ultimately vertical, pointing upward to heaven as the manifestation of the realized immanent self, there was the practical task of acting horizontally in the domain of the earth where the ruler, the *shi dafu*, and the people commingled. In other words, what should the ruler and the state do on behalf of the people, the foundation of the ideal polity? How should morals and virtues be manifested? In short, what policies were to be pursued? On this level of actual policies, Guangdi's political praxis involved what Hao Chang calls "the ethics of social orientation." Guangdi's ideas regarding sociopolitical actions may thus be studied in terms of an alternative ideal-type, one that Chang labels "practical statesmanship." This mode of operation stressed the utility of human action. It was more apt to perceive political and social actions in secular institutional terms and be more attentive to nonmoral ends and profits.[25] Needless to say, such statecraft was not bereft of the sacral and normative imperative of conducting humane and virtuous government. It was indeed pursued in the name of moral imperative. Yet, its very objective of ameliorating the physical lives of the people inevitably meant direct confrontation with the profane aspects of the body-politic, as it were. Specifically, Guangdi's practical statesmanship, directed to the material betterment of people's daily living, consisted of several major interrelated themes: employing the capable and talented; lightening the burden on and bestowing leniency toward the people; generating profits for the people; curbing corruption among the officials.

Guangdi, as shown in his expositions of the political import of the *Documents*, emphasizes the crucial roles played by ministers and officials in bringing about orderly rule. We find reiteration of that conviction in his elucidation of the *Analects*: "To recommend and recruit the upright and the talented is the principal function of government. Not only will the government positions be appropriately filled, but by promoting persons of talents and abilities, customs and traditions are forged."[26] Elsewhere, he contends that "to truly know men and to properly use men is the main business of the ruler."[27] Therefore it was not simply by chance that Guangdi took seriously the necessity and practice of identifying and recruiting the able and talented to serve the dynasty. *Rencai* (persons of talents and abilities), he remarks, lay the foundation and set the tone of a new dynasty: "All-under-heaven, persons of talents serve completely as the mainstay. At the beginning of a dynasty, if there were upright personages, then a whole era of good customs and traditions would be established."[28] In his view, "if the purity and honesty of the court, and the great peace all-under-heaven were to be achieved, none other than the persons of talents would do."[29]

Guangdi took great delight in identifying and knowing those he considered to be good men. In his *Collected Sayings*, his observations and judgments of his dynastic contemporaries are culled and grouped under the heading of "Personages of Our Current Dynasties" (*Benchao renwu*). Guangdi, the connoisseur of good people, said, "Throughout my life, whenever I know of or meet a good man, I become so elated that I cannot sleep. Even those who excel in only one narrow skill have that effect on me. They may not have anything to do with me, but it is just that I am born with this propensity. . . . I treat the goodness I see in others as though it is my own goodness. When I hear of evil in others, it is like thorns on my back."[30]

Who are these good men? Who are the *rencai* whom the ruler should employ? Guangdi takes virtues as the fundamental qualification: "In ancient times, only virtues are considered when officials were appointed. Those of great virtues were given great offices; those with merits were given rewards. Those with merits ended up with rewards, but offices were not extended to them." This ought to be the case because, as Guangdi asserts, "the root of ruling the country and bringing peace to the world lies in not indulging in pleasures and in not producing material profits. The exercise of office begins with honesty and integrity."[31] These virtuous officials act in the name of public fairness (*gong*), and eschew selfish interests and private connections (*si*). They seek not to be popular by currying favors with people. They may even have to remain aloof from the masses and deprive themselves of company, for fear of undue influence. For they must make decisions and act conscientiously on their own. If they are egotistically bent on having "everyone shout approval" of them, they inevitably end up "doing an extremely bad job."

This stress on uprightness and honesty was a reflection of Guangdi's keen awareness of the pervasiveness of corruption throughout the officialdom. As Thomas Metzger argues, it was also in keeping with the Qing administrative and bureaucratic outlook, according to which the officials were often viewed as moral failures, prone to transgressions and deserving punishment.[32] Whether Guangdi's rhetoric was prompted by the actual rifeness of corruption or mirrored the bureaucracy's mistrust of its own ranks, or both, he spoke most passionately about the need to curtail dereliction and dysfunction brought on by the avarice, selfishness, and sloth of the officials. For instance, in 1700, he submitted a lengthy memorial detailing the corruption endemic in the examination system. Because the system itself is laden with corruption, Guangdi contends, it breeds malfeasance perpetrated by the degree-holders themselves. He proposes five solutions. First, the examination officials themselves must be subjected to testing to ensure their ability to perform. Second, the system must be rid of sinecures. Third, the examination system is to be fundamentally reformed by "rectifying the practices of the literati (*shi*)." In particular, Guangdi impugns the practice of the sale of offices, which produces a host of semiliterate *shengyuan* (lowest degree-holding gentry). Since their goal in joining the ranks of the gentry is to acquire the wherewithal for selfish aggrandizing, few "embark on right actions." Instead, they engage in tax resistance, tax evasion, tax-farming (known as *baolan*, which is strictly proscribed by law), pettyfogging, and so forth.[33] If the examinations truly promote only those who are versed in learning, such gross misconduct will not arise. Guangdi thus urges the educational officials and the schools to foster a climate of hard work and discipline among the pupils, so that "old customs are changed, and *rencai* will emerge." Fourth, as far as the examination curriculum is concerned, there should be the strengthening of the subjects on the classics. Fifth, cheating is to be weeded out. All in all, Guangdi's point is that if the system of recruitment of officials is restored to good health, there will be no dearth of men of impeccable moral qualities in the government.[34]

Just as the virtuous and incorruptible officials must discharge their duties with honesty and uprightness, so too they must approach their tasks with knowledge of the present and the past. A great official, according to Guangdi, knows both the "ancient purport" (*guyi*) and "current affairs" (*shiwu*). Ignorance of one is ignorance of the other. Moreover, to be aloof does not mean rejecting cooperation and collaboration with others. Guangdi explicitly warns against taking on everything by oneself, thereby becoming tyrannical. An official's work should be fairly shared and delegated. Last but not least, he should know when to retire. Guangdi writes of retirement as a graceful withdrawal from active public life:

> When the *shi dafu* grow old, they should themselves ask to retire. Even heaven and earth have their time of rest. Things wither and die when the cold winter arrives. This does not mean that things become useless, but that they serve their function in the process of regeneration. In ancient times, the old were emulated even though their words were not asked for. They were looked upon as models but were not burdened by requests for their words and speeches. . . . If after an aged official has retired from office, his virtuous reputation is still admired by all-under-heaven, is it not compensation? It is not the case that one must hurry about resisting misdeeds before one is considered to be useful.[35]

This utterance might well have been made when Guangdi himself was an aged official who had retirement in mind. As we know, at the urging of the Kangxi emperor, he continued, perhaps willy-nilly, to serve the court until his death. This musing about retirement as part of the way of governance might have been prompted by his own yearning to withdraw from active public life in his old age.

Rencai, whom the ruler should seek, do not emerge out of the blue. They have to be produced and cultivated, as they should be, because even in the age of "small peace" (*xiaokang*), able men are needed. Therefore,

> even though the quest for the upright is absolutely necessary, it is not just a question of the quest for the upright. There must be the promotion of teaching and moral transformation, and the emphasis on teachers and scholars. Only when *rencai* are cultivated and produced can they be chosen for employment. The *Classic of Changes*, represented by the hexagrams of *Qian* and *Kun* and their commentaries, focuses on honoring the upright. With the honoring of the upright, there will be no misfortune. It can therefore be seen that honoring the upright is the unsurpassed supreme way.[36]

To honor the upright and to value the scholars did not mean exclusion of people with other skills. Guangdi informed us that when he was the director of education in the greater capital area of Zhili, he examined the "junior students" (*tongsheng*) preparing for both the civil and military examinations. Some were well versed in the classics while others excelled in the military arts and displayed great physical prowess. With regard to the latter group, as long as the candidates demonstrated some general understanding of the texts, they would be passed. To Guangdi, this was "the method of encouragement and enticement. In time, all the candidates will naturally be at home with practical learning, and the tradition of pursuing the Six Arts [of rituals, music, archery, charioteering, writing, and mathematics] will be revived."[37]

Given his emphasis on broad-based and practical learning, albeit construed in terms of the traditional ideal Six Arts, it is not surprising that he displayed some keen interest in mathematics, technology, and even Western learning. For instance, in an essay entitled "Calendrical Rules" (Lifa), he praises the precision of the "new calendar," that is, the Western calendar. With its basic postulation that the earth is a rotating globe, it explains the change of seasons and the succession of night and day. Guangdi admits that from the Han, many Chinese scholars have not been able to come up with such exact and elegant explanations of the various natural phenomena. He confers on the Western calendar the ultimate compliment, namely, that it captures "the intention of the sages, whose thousand-year-old truth is now illuminated with one stroke."[38] In his discourse on "The Three Texts of the *Classics of Rites*" (San Li), Guangdi remarks that what Westerners produce cannot be simply branded as "novel skills and indulgent tricks." Many of their creations are actually useful, such as clocks and other instruments. In an effort to domesticate and render familiar the innovations of the West, Guangdi appeals to the *Classic of Changes*. In this classic, he reminds us, the narratives on the cultural heroes of ancient China, such as Paoxi and Shennong, invariably make mention of their invented implements, and so "it can be seen that the utility of technology is most profound." Similarly, Guangdi reminds us, in the chapter "Institutions of the Zhou" (*Zhou guan*) in the *Rites of the Zhou* (Zhou li), there is a section entitled "Recording the Investigations of Technology," which is devoted to the making and operation of vehicles.[39]

Moreover, Guangdi was very much attracted to mathematics. He wrote on the subject and developed a close friendship with the eminent Qing mathematician and astronomer, Mei Wending (1633–1721), who actually was his house-guest for a while. In his essay, "Mathematical Methods" (Suanfa), he discusses the progress in mathematics and sees the new superior mathematical knowledge in trigonometry and geometry as the key to unraveling the secrets of the physical universe. He hypothesizes in the broadest of terms, claiming that such know-how is the means "by which heaven and earth are surveyed and measured, and in narrow terms, it gauges the myriad things and makes calculations. There is nothing that is sought after that is not obtained."[40]

Guangdi, himself a polymath, not surprisingly regarded *rencai* in very broad terms, his celebration of moral excellence notwithstanding. In any event, to the extent that *rencai* had to be nourished, schools had to play a pivotal role: "Those who are in charge of government must establish as the priority the renewal of schools and the nurturing of persons of talents and abilities."[41] "The son of heaven sweeps aside disasters and disorder to achieve universal peace, and is ever bent on extending the Way, the beginning of which lies in the schools."[42] Guangdi, having served as the director of education in Zhili, naturally held schooling dear and near to his heart. In 1685, at the age of forty-four, he set up a place of study which he called the "*Rongcun shuwu*" (The House of Books in the Village of Banian Trees), so named because the establishment was situated in an area of "several tens of *mou* (Chinese acres) shaded by quite a number of banian trees." There in his hometown, he provided a place for study, lectures, and scholarly exchanges.[43] Judging from the fact that Guangdi was often posthumously addressed as Mr. Rongcun, this place of study must have exerted considerable influence on his kin and occupied a special niche in the intellectual landscape of his native land. In 1699, he set up a charity school, which was apparently a school of strict discipline and high academic standards.[44]

A government staffed by *rencai* was one that was unobtrusive, one that imposed no burden on the people, so Guangdi argued. Sound governance meant not turning government into a crushing onus on the people. Prosperity of the regime began with allowing the people their appropriate rest. He opined:

> If the world wants festivities, it must first patiently put up with a few years of calm and quiet. A person is first frugal before becoming wealthy. In teaching the people to be frugal, they must also be taught diligence. . . . When the government honors and respects simplicity and plainness, resting together with the people, the strength of the people will naturally be revived. If [the government] seeks only outward festivities, extending itself fully to everything by embarking on building and creating everywhere, with the funds coming after all from the fat and blood of the people, then how can the families adequately provide for their members?[45]

The surest way to lighten the burden was the levying of reasonable taxes. Thus Guangdi wrote nostalgically about the ancient Zhou institution of revenue-collection. In his "Written Notes on the 'Institutions of the Zhou'," he praises the simplicity of the practices of yore:

> In the eras of the ancient rulers, what were collected from the people were only three: *gong, fu* and *shui*. *Gong* was the presentation of the produce from the land as tribute; *fu* was calculated in accordance with the production of weapons,

> vehicles, horses, cattle, tools and implements; *shui* was the duties levied on the ownership of fields and lands, and on the transactions of the market-towns. There were no other items apart from them, unlike the oppressive ways of the governments of the later ages.[46]

It is noteworthy that this rhetoric of light government was shared by the Kangxi emperor whom Guangdi faithfully served. The emperor admonished, "I always seek to rest with the people, following the way of noninterference. To add one thing is not as good as subtracting one thing. When I look at the rulers of the previous dynasties, I see that many enjoyed great glory and delighted in establishing merits, so much so that people had to labor hard, and resources as a result dwindled. The established practices were chaotically overturned; the original vital force of the domain was wasted away; those above and those below were in discord. Daily, the livelihood of the people became more miserable. This is a lesson to be deeply reflected upon."[47]

This principle of not disturbing the people molded the language and contents of Guangdi's policy-proposals. On one occasion, when the officials of his home province, Fujian, requested contributions to fill the granaries, Guangdi opposed the venture. He was not against the act of filling the granaries per se, but he was worried that such contributions would simply go to waste. His rationale was that since Fujian had a humid climate, much of the stock had already rotted due to poor care. To put more rice in the existing granaries meant more spoilage. More pressing was the problem of official corruption. Half of the granaries in the various localities had become looting grounds for the covetous officials. They embezzled the inventory and handed out rice according to their whims. Moreover, the initiation of such a project afforded opportunities for official aggrandizement. For instance, in the name of financing the endeavor, officials might solicit unnecessary funds, not to mention the proliferation of paperwork and other administrative chores. All this business would end up "inflicting harm on the people."

In the same memorial, he also spoke against the governor-general's proposal to ban vessels from engaging in deep-sea fishing in order to curb the activities of the pirates. Guangdi explained that most of the pirates these days, unlike the remnant Ming loyalist forces who established strong footholds in the various islands in the areas of Xiamen and Taiwan, were based on the mainland. They did occasionally head to the seas and attack the fishing boats. But since they were land-based, the task of weeding them out must take place on land. To implement the prohibition meant massive unemployment since much of the population of both

Fujian and Guangdong fished for a living. Worse still, with the banning of fishing vessels, the waters would become the exclusive domain of the pirates. It was no different from, Guangdi reasoned, imposing a curfew on the populace, which would result in the monopoly of the night hours by bandits and the colluding soldiers. To illustrate the potential devastation of such a proposal, Guangdi raised the specter of the early Qing policy of moving entire coastal populations inland for the purpose of rooting out the Ming loyalist forces by isolating them. In those days, he lamented, "hundreds of thousands of innocent folk completely lost their houses and fields. There were countless [people] who perished from cold and hunger as they were dispersed." In short, no benefits at all could come out of the plan, which instead enhanced illicit opportunities for the thieves and their unscrupulous official collaborators. Protection of the people came not from carrying out draconian measures but began with "employing honest men who, by implementing the sound existing rules, will naturally extend profits to the people."[48]

For several years from 1701 on, Guangdi oversaw a series of flood-relief projects in Hubei, but he did not indiscriminately called for aggressive and costly dike-building everywhere. For instance, he argued against such an effort in the Guangping district. He exempted the district from expensive dike-building after he had surveyed the land and found that historically, neither embankment nor dredging had worked, because of the loose soil and deep water in times of flooding in that particular locale. The gentry and the villagers themselves were not in favor of such public works because of their costs and probable ineffectiveness. After consultation with them, he further established the fact that the extent of the flooding resulting from the change of the course of the river had not been great, usually covering only one district and sparing the nearby ones, meaning that the affected population could temporarily relocate in times of deluge. In view of the expense and ineffectiveness of erecting dikes and dredging, and the relatively minor extent of flooding, Guangdi petitioned that the district be granted a tax-waiver for the year, and if the fields were judged to be uncultivable after the water had receded, the waiver would be extended for another year.[49] It may also be mentioned here that Guangdi, as the overseer of the flood-control projects in the nearby Yongding River area, argued strongly for cost-cutting by reducing the number of sinecures in the administration. Many unqualified persons on the payroll were to be dismissed, and the district magistrate, who had not been held responsible for flood-control, would be required to provide help in times of serious flood crisis.[50]

Connected with flood-control and river administration was the question of military installations. On this matter, Guangdi made his adjudication from the vantage point of one principle, namely, minimizing the financial burden heaped on the people. He suggested that with the exception of the strategic points along the rivers in question, local militias made up of farmers, instead of regular military garrisons, should shoulder the responsibility of maintaining law and order. "The urgent business of government at this time," he contended, "is to save on military spending."[51] Guangdi agreed that it would not be possible to revive the sort of ancient system that merged soldiery into the peasantry, but he insisted that, particularly in time of peace, civilians could double as soldiers in many parts of the country. Often, Guangdi wrote of the employment of soldiers and military pursuits disapprovingly:

> During the Three Dynasties [of Xia, Shang, and Zhou], soldiers were regarded as misfortune and so they were restrained and not used lightly. Even when they were used, their military prowess was not the emphasis. Therefore, soldiers could be integrated into the peasantry. In the Han and Tang, they were activated any time. Their tenure lasted years, their campaigns covered thousands of miles. Poets sorrowfully wrote about them. Therefore, it was because of changed circumstances that soldiery and peasantry were separated.[52]

Guangdi concluded, "People who do not farm may be supported by the profits from natural resources and commerce, and so likewise, since soldiers are no longer to be kept, the pursuit of convicts and the business of garrisoning can be taken over by the people."[53] Curiously, Guangdi did not seem to think that the incorporation of soldiery into the citizenry was a burden. In any event, his advocacy for reducing the military certainly stemmed from the desire to reduce spending on behalf of the people.

To argue for light government, however, was not the same thing as endorsing an inactive one. The welfare of the people had to be actively promoted and defended, as Guangdi urged. In the matter of government, instead of seeking perfection or being mired down in detailed calculation, a certain bravado was necessary:

> The implementation of action cannot be too rash, nor can it be too restrained. If the deliberations are too minute and finicky, not only will others be hindered, but even ourselves will find it hard to act. The result is no action at all. We try to calculate thoroughly the benefit and harm of every matter while also calculating the impact on our reputation. But how can there ever be such a perfect arrangement? Therefore, if there is a seventy or eighty percent chance that the people will be benefited, we must take action.[54]

Where benefits for the people were discerned, prompt measures should be applied. Just as Guangdi argued against dike-building in the Guangping district for lack of evidence of its potential benefit, so he pressed for activist intervention in other parts of Zhili exactly because of its perceived effectiveness. Along the Yongding River, which was sometimes known as the little Yellow River, he oversaw the construction of embankments and supervised the digging of channels. For instance, in the Anci district, such flood-control works spanned a distance of 200 *li* (miles). For such a colossal accomplishment, he earned both verbal accolades and gifts from the Kangxi emperor.[55] In other locales, he proposed the reclamation of flood-prone areas as a means of creating arable land.[56]

Guangdi was a strong supporter of maintaining government granaries. In 1700, he memorialized the throne, pleading for the reinvigoration of the operation and maintenance of these granaries, known as ever-leveled granaries (*changping cang*). His memorial pointed to wastage due to improper storage, lax management, and embezzlement by officials. Once again, he urged that the local authorities be required to strictly observe the government regulations that granaries be established and operated properly. These granaries served to guard against fluctuation in the prices of rice and various grains, and also functioned as a relief tool. When the system was working well, grains would be purchased by government funds, and the grain-reserve would be sold to the needy at below current price. Purchases were made each year after the autumn harvest when the abundance of crops meant relatively low prices. To mitigate the problem of spoilage as a result of prolonged storage, in the spring and summer, portions of the reserved grain would be sold under market value, to be replenished during the autumn harvest.[57] Early in 1703, two more memorials were submitted concerning the mismanagement of the granaries and its rectification.[58] Toward the end of the same year, Guangdi sent a memorial detailing the dispensation of relief for the victims of flooding by opening up the grain-reserve.[59] In a 1704 memorial, he expressed his enthusiasm about the creation of the community granaries of the countryside (*she cang*), which built up the reserve of grains for rainy days and thus "benefit the livelihood of the people."[60]

In 1700, entrusted with the task of taking stock of the Banner lands designated for grazing horses, Guangdi, together with local officials, surveyed the lands in question. He discovered that many areas were unofficially, and therefore illegally, claimed by people for farming purposes. Some left their own lands, for reasons such as insect-infestation and floods, and moved into unauthorized regions. He memorialized the throne that these people who might have violated the laws be spared since all they did was seek opportunities to eke out a living. He proposed that they be allowed to stay and continue to farm, registering them as taxpaying households. He further suggested that the various Banner land administration authorities actively revive abandoned fields and develop hitherto undeveloped lands, so that "the little people can promote agriculture at an opportune time." By such measures of forgiving past offenses and encouraging the expansion of arable land, the ideal governance of "being sympathetic toward, worrying on behalf of, and aiding the people" could be realized.[61]

If tending to the needs of the people was one side of the coin of good government, curtailing corrupt practices on the part of the officials was the other. Of the instances of malfeasance, none was more widespread and ingrained than the problem of having deficits and shortages in the treasury funds (*kueikong*) in the various localities, as Guangdi pointed out in a 1700 memorial. Sometimes, the deficiencies were quite understandable and excusable, being consequences of the reduction of the tax-base or unforeseen spoilage of the granaries. But more often than not, such shortfall was the result of reckless spending or embezzlement by local officials. Worse still, such shortage was often covered up by false bookkeeping. Since the problem was endemic, many supervising officials simply turned a blind eye to the whole situation. Needless to say, Guangdi was most forceful in pushing for imposing harsh and prompt punishment on the culprits.[62] In a 1701 memorial, he reported that among the officials themselves, there was a good deal of procrastination and delay in meting out judgments against their corrupt colleagues. He therefore proposed that in cases of bankrupting and embezzling public funds, there should be a four-month period in which the cases must be properly adjudicated and resolved. In view of the fact that many officials, in trying to defend themselves, blamed the loss of public funds on their required involvement in public projects such as "repairing city walls, fixing leaks in the granaries, constructing irrigation dikes and refurbishing schools," the only way to deprive them of excuses and establish the veracity of their defense in the future was to place the accounts of such public works under strict scrutiny. All these endeavors, including those financed by private contributions, must be reported to the provincial authorities of the governorship before they could be carried out.[63]

Judging from the political ideas of Guangdi in theory and in action, several conclusions may be drawn with regard to their ideal-typical attributes. First, the proposed political order was quintessentially the exercise of moral directive, not coercive power. It was guided by the rule of morality, whose supreme expression was the tireless and ceaseless effort on the part of the ruler and his helpers, the *rencai*, of tending to the needs of the people, heaven's people. The abiding beneficence of the emperor, distilled, mediated, and communicated by the upright and incorruptible *shi dafu*, reached the multitude and transformed them, thereby forging a state of peace and harmony, an organic whole.

Second, this vision of the harmonious organic community was paradoxically lodged within an antipodal paradigm in which the ruler and his assistants were clearly demarcated from the people. Authority and moral dispensations flowed one way, from the top to the bottom. This subordination to authority by the people was in accord with nature. Just as, to use Guangdi's words, "in the case of a tree, there is first the root before there is the trunk," so in the case of government, "even though we must know that the officialdom is set up for the people, the officials must come first before the people. Otherwise, the people will not stay peaceful. . . . There must first be the cultivation of the upright before there are the people. . . . If those of small virtues rule over those of great virtues . . . , it is like those below usurping those above. . . . Then the laws of the ruler (*wangfa*) will be no more."[64]

Third, both the organic and antipodal paradigms presumed a closed political order in which there was no genuine public space for either the *shi dafu* or the people. On the one hand, in the vision of an organic community, everyone was, as it were, massified. The ruler, the officials, the literati, and the people behaved as if they were all but numerically indistinguishable. One merely duplicated and multiplied the other's perspectives. There was no public world when it was seen as speaking in one voice and possessing one perspective. On the other hand, in the antipodal scheme, the assumed natural hierarchy of high and low meant primarily the subordination of all to the imperial sway, and secondarily, people's obedience to the officials. The clear and rigid classification of roles and status nullifies plurality and openness.

Fourth, while it can be safely argued that in a political order such as that conceived by Guangdi, the people were the voiceless and passive recipients, the *shi dafu* operated in a tension-ridden workaday world of government. At the same time that they were touted and praised as the *rencai* aiding the imperial quest for a morally inspired order, weeding out corruption in the officialdom, and guaranteeing the welfare of the people, they were the first to be chastised as exemplars of moral transgressions, perpetrators of corruption. At the same time that tremendous responsibility was given to them, they were viewed with enormous mistrust. While they were not supposed to focus on the conventional deliberations of motives and aims on the one hand, and consequences and achievements on the other, they had no choice but to engage in utilitarian statecraft. Thus we find in Guangdi's political ideas evidence of what Thomas Metzger calls "the sense of predicament" in the Confucian political culture—

just as internal moral praxis was suffused with the anxiety of the imminent possibility of failure, so too political praxis was animated by the pervading sense of inadequacy as "the officials were confronted with an external barrage of official rhetoric and administrative sanctions defining them as moral failures."[65]

Fifth, to the extent that morality was the wellspring of orderly rule, *li*, the rituals and norms, morality's very embodiment, manifestation, and prescription, necessarily played an instrumental role. Indeed, many of Guangdi's thoughts on rituals and norms were subsumed under the rubric of "the way of rule" (*zhidao*) in his *Recorded Sayings*. Thus by way of this conclusion of Guangdi's political ideas, we introduce the corollary question of rituals and norms as crucial ingredients in the recipe for peace and order. To Guangdi, *li* was also statecraft.

The Ideal and Practice of *Li* (Ritual-Norms): Ritualism as Praxis

A number of years ago, the eminent historian of British and European political thought, J. G. A. Pocock, intrigued by the Chinese conceptions of government of society by *li*, was prompted to reflect on the apparent political meanings in ancient Chinese philosophy. He characterized such government predicated on rituals as rule by "nonverbal means," in contradistinction to the Western orientation toward laws, or government by verbal command. *Li* is nonverbal in that "the performance of ritual is the display of virtue in a form which ensures that it acts upon, and is transmitted to, those before whom it is displayed." He further argued that "because rituals have no contraries, the values of a ritual-controlled society cannot be questioned or doubted, and the Confucian world, being without moral alternatives, is a closed society."[66] Indeed, Guangdi and, for that matter, most Confucians, did see the *li*-regulated society as the society par excellence. This emphasis on *li* as the definition of the best society gained great momentum in the late Ming and early Qing, as revealed by Kai-wing Chow's recent work on the pervasive ritual purism of that period. Often, particularly in the early years of the Qing, the reassertion of rituals was conceived as a cultural counterweight against Manchu rule, a means to safeguard the Chinese cultural identity. But as Qing rule became an inescapable reality and as it acquired the imprimatur of a Confucian monarchy, *li* posed itself as a supra-ethnic normative system. To the extent that the Qing had fully subscribed to the Confucian *li*, political service to the Manchu regime was ultimately cultural service to the Confucian norms.[67] Guangdi, as a loyal official in the

Kangxi court, certainly perceived *li* in the most generic and universal cultural terms. *Li,* in his worldview, was the foundation of peace and the concrete tool instrumental to the betterment of state and society.

To Guangdi, rituals and music constitute not only what Pocock describes as "nonverbal" government, but they do so because they exude mystical qualities and possess mysterious power, penetrating the very core of the universe, moving heaven, humanity, and the spirits alike:

> The rituals and music of the ancient sages all had their reasons for being. In instituting rituals, even the feelings and circumstances of the ghosts and spirits were most intimately and appropriately embodied within them. Music came into being because in ineffable and mysterious ways, it moved heaven and humanity, and probed ghosts and spirits. With the making of a few bamboo flutes with the twelve tones, there came the most intriguing mutual response with the vital forces of heaven-and-earth.[68]

With respect to music, Guangdi in particular stresses its nonverbal nature by referring to the fact that "among the Six Classics, that on music has no texts." Although we have a general record of musical instruments and the institutions pertaining to music and musical rites, we do not have a classic on music as such because, according to Guangdi, the ancient officials realized that "the subtlety and mystery of the sounds and their moods cannot be written out. Therefore there is the so-called demise of music."[69]

In any event, given the putative power of rituals and music to move the hearts and minds of the people, Guangdi declares that "as for appeasing those above and governing the people, there is nothing better than rituals. As for moving the moral climate and changing customs, there is nothing better than music." But rituals, he contends, must be simplified and rendered easy to follow so that people will happily abide by them. Moreover, ritual and music must not be performed in isolation, apart from the people. Otherwise, no matter how properly the rituals are conducted or how finely the music is played, only heaven and the spirits can enjoy such munificence. They must exert their transformative power squarely in the midst of the people: "It is only when they are seen and heard by everyone that they can move the moral climate and change customs. It is like watching a drama. When people see acts of loyalty and filiality, or pain and suffering, they sob and weep. Thus it can be seen that moving the moral climate and changing customs are not difficult."[70] In addition, although rituals must be "congruent with the ancient ways," there must also be contemporaneous social felicity, "following the sentiments of the people and in accord with the circumstances of the time."[71]

What exactly is *li*? It is that by which "the human relationships are ordered," and it entails proper rites and ceremonies: "Only when there is marriage does the distinction between husband and wife become strict. Only when there are funerals is the intimacy between father and son extended. Only when there is schooling is the hierarchy of the mature and the young made clear. Only when there is appointment by the court is the loyalty between the ruler and the officials made solemn."[72] These ceremonial choreographies based on the keen awareness of relative status, these physical and bodily actions required of respective members of society, while regulating the human relationships, in fact express and mobilize a field of virtues, norms, and ethics. Thus Guangdi refers to the so-called "three categories of virtues" (*san de*) in the *Rites of Zhou* (Liji). In other words, the performance of rituals is undergirded by three kinds of virtue and is their very manifestation. The first sort of virtue is "ultimate virtue" (*zhide*), whose basis is the Way itself. Insofar as it centers "on the business of being loyal to trustworthiness and preserving sincerity," it manifests our nature, and hence also the Way. The second is "sagacious virtue," which is the basis for earnest action. With "learning, inquiry, thinking and discriminating," it furnishes the starting point for correct actions. Third is "filial virtue," which leads all other various virtues because inherent in filiality is the knowledge that humanity will go against evil and has the ability to be transformed. This virtue is therefore also the basis of governance.[73]

In another essay on the question of the intrication of virtues and rituals, Guangdi elaborates on the multivocality of the three classes of virtues as explained in the *Rites of Zhou*. To begin with, they find foremost expression in the universally important "three obligations of conduct" (*san xing*): "the act of filiality to effect intimacy with parents," "the act of friendship to honor the upright and honest," and "the act of obedience to serve our teachers." These paradigmatic acts are further distinguished as the "six acts" (*liu xing*): "filiality, friendship, kindness, love of kin, endurance on behalf of others, and charity." They in turn correlate with the "six virtues" (*liude*): "wisdom, humaneness, sageliness, rightness, moderation and harmony." Interestingly, Guangdi claims that the word "sageliness" (*sheng*) here is an error. It should be the word "propriety" (*li*). It goes against reason that the "six virtues" include only three (wisdom, humaneness, and rightness) of the commonly known "four cardinal virtues" (*side*), leaving out "propriety." Moreover, according to Guangdi, the main teaching of the *Doctrine of the Mean* is precisely to link together (*guan*) the four cardinal virtues with equilibrium (*zhong*) and harmony (*he*). In any event, all these virtues and moral conduct begin with the practice and learning of the "six arts" (*liuyi*): rituals, music, archery, charioteering, writing, and mathematics.

In so defining these three virtues as the underpinning of rituals, and in so identifying their moral ramifications and practical requirements, Guangdi establishes the correlation among the performance of rituals, the cultivation of virtues, the pursuit of learning, and the commitment to action. On the basic level as propaedeutics, there are practice and learning through which we become gradually but inexorably in tune with living life as a moral undertaking. There are then true understanding, knowledge, and wisdom, which in turn breed further correct actions, the advanced practice of rituals, and profound quest for learning. But whether it is the rudimentary or the advanced, the root of moral acts in accordance with knowledge and practice of rituals lies within our "body, mind-heart, nature and sentiments," or in short, in our internalizing external actions.[74] Thus, with reference to the teachings of the *Rites of Zhou*, Guangdi argues for an ever-deepening and continuous process of moral celebratory production of virtues through their performance and internalization, the inescapable requisites of which are knowing and acting. Hence, *li* is ultimately metapraxis. This integration of *li* into the metapraxis of knowing and acting is clearly revealed in Guangdi's explication of the *Analects*'s statement: "The profound person studies extensively all learning, and restrains himself with rituals and propriety." He contends that "ritual is the site where learning is immediately and actually realized. Learning, via-à-vis one's very self, may be somewhat remote and impertinent, and so it must be scrutinized and investigated through our personal daily functions and social relationships."[75] What we learn and know has immediacy, urgency, and relevance only when it is realized in *li*, and *li* is nothing but that which lends order and meaning to those quotidian activities we undertake in the entangling social web.

Accordingly, whether *li* is seen as social choreography (the performance of rituals) or perceived as social sensibility (the virtue of propriety), it has its ineluctable political figuration and usage. Again, taking his cue from the *Analects*, Guangdi postulates the hegemonic role of *li* in effecting orderly rule. He, needless to say, agrees with Confucius's mistrust of laws. The sage famously voiced his dissatisfaction with a state of affairs in which "the people are led by governmental promulgation so that uniformity is established by punishments." Guangdi remarks that such governance reverses the proper course of rulership. It begins with the secondary instead of the primary. It is secondary because it "lacks virtue as the root [of governance], offering no implementation of ritual and its instruction." On the other hand, if, as Confucius said, "the people are led by virtue so that uniformity is established by rituals," there is then governance which is erected with a firm root. Guangdi concludes:

> In using *li* to rule, all-under-heaven is brought entirely within the domain of the profound person. Although we do not say that laws and punishments are thus abandoned, laws are incorporated into rituals merely as restraining stipulations, and punishments are for the rectification of those who violate rituals. Therefore, when uniformity is established among the people by rituals, nothing that is right is ignored, and so there is no need to argue for the assisting of rituals by laws and punishments. . . . Moved by virtue, there is the sense of shame; adhering to rituals, there is the move toward goodness.[76]

In short, the sense of shame, induced by the performance of rituals and internalized by the performer, renders politics and governance into a normative activity. Ironically then, in this political universe of moral suasion effected by *li*, the homogeneity and the unity that are to be engendered by moral sense are perforce absolute and total. Ideally, there can be nothing that surpasses virtues expressed in rituals. An alternative better world is not possible. Governance by *li* is a closed system in theory, although in practice, the imminent failure to abide by it animates much of the Confucian moral and existential discourse. By contrast, the uniformity that is elicited by laws and punishments can only be an ephemeral armature. Verbal enactments and commands presume disobedience and therefore seek to launch a preemptive strike against it. In both theory and practice, rule by law, to begin with, is premised on imperfection. It peddles and preaches order but simultaneously accepts the fact of ever-simmering and imminent recalcitrance.[77]

Such was Guangdi's affirmation of the essential efficacy of *li* as governance. How was this ritualism carried over into the realm of action? What were the correct and authentic rituals? In what way could they actually foster a social order that was truly Confucian? Such questions were often asked in the early Qing in terms of the discourse on lineage and the related ancestral rites, seen to be the crucial institutions in preserving and promoting Confucian values.[78] Indeed, Guangdi contributed to this discourse. In an essay entitled "A Brief Account of the Rites of Offering Sacrifices in the Official Family Shrine" (Jiamiao jixiang li lüe), Guangdi asserts that among the rituals, none is more important than making sacrifices to the ancestors, and in order to properly observe this rite, there must be a clear understanding of both the "great descent-line system" (*da zongfa*), which includes all agnates and all ancestors, and the "lesser descent-line system" (*xiao zongfa*), which limits the depth of descent to only five generations. Without a sound knowledge of them, all the minute ritual prescriptions become irrelevant and insignificant for lack of a sense of origin and place.

Guangdi begins his discourse with the rebuilding of the family shrine in 1665. Upon the completion of the new shrine, his father gathered the agnates there and talked about the institution of the descent-line ancestral rites. He told the assembled agnates that in the Ming, their forebears contemplated the possibility of designating descent-line heirs (*zongzi*) in accordance with the ancient great descent-line system. But they discerned several difficulties in such attempted revival of the ancient practice. First, in antiquity, only those with inherited rank and emolument bestowed by the court could become heirs and perform sacrifice. Now that there was no longer the practice of such inheritance, no one really merited the ancient official designation. Second, in ancient times, the heirship was conferred by the ruling house on the nobility, who all knew the rituals well. But in their own time, many of the first sons had lowly professions and were quite ignorant. They would be truly hard pressed if they were asked to discharge the duties as masters of the familial and ancestral ceremonies. Third, as the principal of the multifarious rites, the descent-line heir ought to be of some illustrious stature. Otherwise, it not only went against common human sentiment for decency, but it also violated the ancestral spirits. In light of this family anecdote, Guangdi concludes:

> The world has changed and customs have altered. Rituals arise from reason. Nowadays, the elevated status of members of the families are not determined by whether they are firstborns or secondary sons. Therefore, we should not obstinately conform to the written rule that secondary sons do not perform sacrifice. We should surely follow the way that only those with government stipend perform sacrifice. Moreover, in recent times, the practice of conferring awards on ancestors does not make such bestowal in accordance with their positions in the main or secondary lines of descent.[79]

In short, social and political status derived from degree-holding and government position overrides the biological order in determining the qualification of the descent-line heir who officiates in the familial and lineage rites. Guangdi's rationale is that since his lineage, which maintains a family shrine honoring the first ancestor (*shizu*), has a large number of agnates, it is a good practice to assemble the lineage to show their respects under the guidance of a worthy heir, namely, one with government position.

However, even if a secondary son becomes the official heir, a place should still be established for the biological descent-line heir. In prayers or pronouncements, for instance, the name of the natal heir will follow that of the designated heir with government rank. In the actual performance of ceremonies, the officiating descent-line heir will stand in the middle, with the natal heir on the left and the assistant master of ceremony, a lineage member of advanced age, on the right. Guangdi also specifies what should be done in the case where both the first son and the secondary son hold government ranks. If the secondary son holds only a slightly higher rank, then he should defer to the firstborn. But if the secondary son possesses a much higher rank, he should claim the honor of the descent-line heir. In families where there is no one with official rank, Guangdi calls for the observance of the simplest form of rites, over which the elders will preside. Such should be the ritual arrangements as far as the great descent-line system is concerned.

With respect to the lesser descent-line system, it is the quaternary system of worshiping the immediate four ancestors: great-great-grandfather, great-grandfather, grandfather, and father. But if the ancient practice of the lesser descent-line system were to be strictly followed, considerable difficulty would arise, as Guangdi points out. First, individual shrines would have to be maintained for each of these ancestors. Second, the descent-line heir must be from the line of firstborns traced back to the great-great-grandfather. The maintenance of such an uninterrupted and continuous succession is very difficult. It is often broken. Small wonder that in his day, as Guangdi observes, there is, among the gentry and officials, the prevalent practice of erecting temples dedicated to the first ancestors but not that of establishing shrines for the four immediate ancestors of a lineage. However, it is not unusual that individual households each worship their own quaternary forefathers. Nevertheless, even if the ancient rituals may not be fully revived, it is still important that the "ancient intentions be preserved." Guangdi refers to the actions and ideas of Cheng Yi, the Song master. He claims that Cheng, although lacking the support of classical precedents and evidence, nonetheless proposed the worship of the first progenitor (*shizu*) and the four immediate ancestors. He did so precisely because he wanted to preserve and honor the ancients' intentions. Criticisms have indeed been leveled against Cheng's advocacy, but since his intention was admirable, Guangdi concludes that the Song master's proposals should be followed. He thus argues that in accordance with the great descent-line system, there should be the establishment of the temple for the first ancestor. In addition, if possible, the descent-line heir should be also be designated with reference to the lesser system honoring the four immediate ancestors. At the very least, the descent-line heir of the individual households should make sacrifice on the anniversaries on the death of the quaternary ancestors.[80]

In another essay, "Briefly on the Rites and Sacrifices of the Temple of the First Ancestor" (Shizu ciji li lüe), Guangdi clearly invests in the gentry members of the lineage unmistakable leadership position and role. The ancestral rites within the framework of the lineage are the domain of the gentry, and within the gentry stratum of the lineage itself, there is a hierarchy. In antiquity, as Guangdi observes, those who enjoyed emolument from the ruler maintained special fields, the produce from which were used for making sacrifices to the ancestors. The high-ranking officials (*dafu*) used special sacrificial animals and made the most elaborate sacrificial offerings. The reason for such distinction was to show that the rites did not extend down to the common folk. Guangdi tells us that in the ancestral shrine of his family, apart from ancestral tablets of the first ancestor and the early ancestors (*xianzu*, that is, those who came after the progenitor and before the great-great-grandfather), there are also tablets for those kinfolk who served in government, those who established a great moral-ethical reputation, and those who made contributions to the ancestors, such as erecting buildings and developing farmlands. As far as the sacrificial offerings are concerned, ancestors of the first to fifth ranks are honored by both lamb and pig. For those of the sixth to the eighth ranks, either lamb or pig is called for. As for those below the eighth rank, any sacrificial meat will do. Commoners do not require the killing of animals at all.[81] In the *Recorded Sayings*, Guangdi also makes it clear that a separate shrine may be established for those who have attained government positions of the third rank and above, regardless of their natal positions in the lineage. In fact, those of lower ranks may also do the same, as long as the rituals are simplified. However, the common folk may not do so and should only worship ancestors at the graves. Guangdi, in particular, urges those with official status to create shrines for their four immediate ancestors in accordance with the lesser descent-line system.[82]

It is therefore quite apparent that Guangdi sought to integrate the practice of rituals with the exercise of gentry power within the framework of the lineage. *Li*, as we have argued, was statecraft in that, generally speaking in terms of the Confucian conception of governance, it constituted nonverbal commands. But in the particular context of the pervasive late Ming and early Qing local gentry effort of lineage-building, the definition and implementation of correct rituals assumed added sociopolitical poignancy. To define *li* was to operate the informal local government of the lineage, and the gentry must be in charge.[83] Guangdi's family produced many officials and it was therefore a family of high local standing. It may reasonably be conjectured that Guangdi's discourse on rituals pertaining to the lineage was not merely a fictive construction by dint of the time-honored respect for *li*, but was also a functional program of local control. But he also clearly reminded his kin that as members of an official family with prestige and wealth, they must not abuse their status. In an admonitory essay, "Warning the Offspring" (Jie zisun), written when he was seventy years old, he cautions the young that family fortunes cannot be taken for granted. To safeguard the interests of the family, one does not aggrandize and take advantage of the humbler folk. The less fortunate and the elderly must be taken care of, embracing the virtues of filiality and friendship. In short, local power, buttressed by the ritual order of the lineage, carries moral responsibility.[84]

Another ritual that engaged Guangdi's attention was one concerning the temple dedicated to the worship of Confucius. While the imperial cult of Confucius, established in the course of the Han dynasty and centered around the honoring of the sage-teacher, might have experienced considerable vicissitudes throughout the ages, the idea that Confucius should be honored was by and large unproblematic and straightforward.[85] However, the picture became complicated when in A.D. 72, Emperor Ming of the eastern Han performed sacrificial rites not only to Confucius but also his famed seventy-two disciples. Thus began the institution of "accessory sacrifice" (*congsi*) in the Confucian temple. Illustrious scholars and other meritorious personages were admitted to membership in the temple through the practice of "matching sacrifice" (*peixiang*). It became an officially stipulated institution in the Tang. Successively in the ensuing dynasties, many figures in history deemed to be worthy by the various courts and regimes were inducted into the temple, particularly in the Ming.[86]

In an essay entitled, "My Private Opinions on the Admission to Membership in the Confucian Temple through Matching Sacrifice" (Wenmiao peixiang siyi), Guangdi begins briefly by recapitulating the aforementioned history of inducting worthies. He then promptly launches a scathing attack on the Ming corruption of the institution. In particular, he excoriates the Ming act of massively overhauling the Confucian temple in 1530, which banished many learned classical scholars of the Han and Jin periods.[87] Guangdi defends the contributions of the banished, arguing that even though "they might not have virtues that were unrivaled in the world, they had the achievement of transmitting the classics." Most important, they preserved the teachings of the classics and Confucian scholarship after the disastrous destruction of learning by the Qin. Thus, if Confucius's seventy-two disciples, many of whom did not possess scholarly distinction anyway, deserved to be in the temple, so should these Han-Jin exegetes.

Just as those who contributed to the "transmission of classics" (*chuanjing*) should be properly honored, so should those who played crucial roles in "transmitting the Way" (*chuandao*) and "defending the Way" (*weidao*). In these two latter groups, Guangdi includes Yan Hui and

Zengzi, the two best disciples of Confucius, Zisi, Confucius's grandson, together with other worthies such as Mencius, Dong Zhongshu, Zhou Dunyi, Shao Yong, Zhang Zai, the Cheng brothers, and Zhu Xi. With regard to their respective positions in the temple, first, Guangdi specifies that these stalwarts of the Way be placed to the left and right of Confucius. Second, in the southern end of the temple, four shrines should be established, two on the eastern side and two on the western side. One of these shrines is devoted to honoring the seventy-two disciples of Confucius. One honors those who transmitted the classics. The other two are dedicated to worthy scholars. According to Guangdi, such configuration based on the left-right and east-west positioning serves to mitigate the sense of order (*xianhou*) as a means of differentiating the degree of importance.[88]

But, after all, these were Guangdi's own private feelings about the ritualistic ordering of the Confucian temple, as he himself made clear in the title of his essay. In 1712, Guangdi completed the compilation of the collected works of Zhu Xi. The Kangxi emperor, upon reading the assembled writings of Zhu, was so moved and impressed that he intended to place Zhu right next to the so-called four matching associates (*sipei*, that is, Yenzi, Zengzi, Zisi, and Mencius) in the temple, so as to illustrate the fact that Zhu had truly captured the essence of Confucius's teachings. Guangdi memorialized against such an elevation of Zhu Xi's position. His rationale was that although Zhu's scholarly accomplishments and moral stature rivaled that of the illustrious quartet, Zhu came much later in time. Moreover, such promotion would also mean that Zhu would surpass the so-called ten wise men (*shizhe*, referring to ten of Confucius's accomplished disciples) who conventionally came after the "four matching associates." Guangdi thus concluded that Zhu should be placed after the "ten wise men" so as to show clearly that Zhu Xi belonged to a different era, quite remote from that of Confucius. Zhu Xi himself, he maintained, would not have felt comfortable with the ascension of order. Kangxi, on second thought, accepted Guangdi's reasoning and propelled Zhu to a position that came after the "ten wise men."[89]

This episode clearly shows that Guangdi, despite his ardent championing of Cheng-Zhu orthodoxy, sought not to subvert existing protocols. Although he most explicitly claimed that in terms of moral and intellectual accomplishments, Zhu played no second fiddle to the ancients, as long as the conventional positions and categories were in place in the Confucian temple, Zhu's status must not usurp those of the ancient sages. Perhaps it was because of the discrepancy Guangdi perceived between Zhu's profound achievements and his necessary secondary status in the official temple that he wrote in private about reconfiguring and recategorizing the positions of the inductees.

In sum, whether it was in the political arena of governance or in the social realm of ritual propriety, Guangdi was a man of action and practical ideas. If the primary issue of his metaphysics and metapraxis is how to live, the issue of his praxis and actions is how to live together in an ordered community. If the self, with its innately good nature, is the site of ultimate fulfillment, it is because that which is humane is realized in terms of *les autres*, the larger whole composed of other people. Hence the inescapable attention to *zhi* (rule) and *li* (ritual), the outer dimensions of inner self-cultivation.

CONCLUDING REFLECTIONS

Li Guangdi was unquestionably one of the most important keepers of the Cheng-Zhu flame in the early Qing. Obliged as a scholar-official devoted to the court, patronized by the emperor, he upheld and promoted the imperial Cheng-Zhu orthodoxy. Throughout his long and rather distinguished, albeit at times precarious, career as an official, he conscientiously performed his bureaucratic and administrative duties. As a scholar and thinker, impelled by his faith in the Song masters' teachings, he reworked their original ideas and came to be their prolific and thoughtful exponent. Yet, in many surveys of Ming–Qing thought, he was barely mentioned, if at all. He has indeed been unjustifiably neglected as a bona fide thinker and active contributor in the intellectual universe of seventeenth-century China. Some of the plausible reasons for this neglect have been rehearsed but are worth recapitulating here.

To begin with, there is the seldom challenged historiographic apriorism that Song learning was a nonentity, repulsed and then overwhelmed by the call for concrete and practical learning in the early Qing. Consequently, scholars identified with it have been readily judged to be insignificant. Moreover, Guangdi's many roles as a court official and the political imbroglio in which he was embroiled certainly have not helped to build and consolidate his reputation. He had to confront the venomous tongue of suspicion that lashed out at him when he was alive. After his death, there came the damning criticisms that the celebrated eighteenth-century scholar, Quan Zuwang, heaped on him. To these reasons one may add the fact that Guangdi was not a truly systematic thinker. He did not produce any magnum opus; nor did he pen any lengthy and well-organized treatises. The well-known works with which he was associated, such as the *Xingli jingyi* (Essential Ideas on Nature and Principle) and *Zhouyi zhezhong* (Balanced Annotations of the *Classic of Changes*), earned him only the distinction of editorship. Indeed, he was often seen merely as a hack court scholar, a compiler of orthodox canon. But, as I have attempted to show, Guangdi was a learned man, an enormous reader, a productive if somewhat unsystematic writer, and, most important, a genuine thinker. This study has been dedicated to providing a balanced, if not comprehensive, assessment of his achievements. In these final pages, it is fitting that we take stock of Guangdi's historical significance as a thinker, and ponder the relevance and meaning of his thought.

Notwithstanding the lack of any coherent major works, and despite the occasional awkwardness of his prose, he was an insightful and innovative thinker, developing some very notable and easily identifiable motifs that were his own. He was a true Confucian in the Cheng-Zhu vein in the sense that he was a man possessed by such learning, as evidenced by so many of his writings. The effect of this devotion was perhaps all the stronger because he was exalted by neither his contemporaries nor later commentators. A devout follower of Cheng-Zhu learning, he understood his devotion to the Confucian way to be a destiny and a passion. However, his rootedness in such learning meant no intellectual servitude. Far from simply reconstructing and reciting a received philosophic catechism, he developed in his thought a protuberant and persistent sense of relevance to the intellectual tone and tenor of his age. Thus in evaluating Guangdi's importance and significance in the intellectual history of seventeenth-century China, one may justifiably argue that with his early Qing Cheng-Zhu learning, he did not stand outside the ambit of history, but was an active contributor to the intellectual developments of the age. As a Cheng-Zhu partisan, he nevertheless also had the distinct imprimatur of a Qing thinker. In short, through him, we may develop and gain a meaningful view of the Ming–Qing intellectual transition and early Qing thought.

Guangdi tackled, and thereby reformulated, what was generally perceived to be empty and vacuous Song learning at its very root—propounding a fundamental philosophical ground on which the advocacy for practicality and concrete learning could be confidently and securely erected. He began with the domain of ontology, concentrating in particular on the conception of nature, *xing*. Building on the late Ming repudiation of the ambiguous conception of nature as beyond good and evil, Guangdi reasserted the fundamental goodness of nature. By offering us his metaphysical pondering, often elaborate and finicky, he meant not to fuel any allure for abstruse introspection but rather the impetus to act. He sought the establishment of an ontological basis for our moral and social activism. By replacing the apodictic Cheng-Zhu *li* (principle) with *xing* (nature) as the ontological anchor, Guangdi narrowed the metaphysical gap between ultimate reality and humanity. This perspective of fundamental substance would now focus on the vital manifestations of reality, namely, human actions in the experiential world; anything that in any sense partook of reality stemmed from the individual. In so elevating an individual's nature as the universal predicate, however, Guangdi did not mean to render it ontologically nomothetic, a law-governed entity. Rather, it provided the presupposition and demand that every domain of reality must involve direct immediate individual action. In other words, the goodness of nature was not some static inborn innocence, but the destructive overcoming of evil and the constructive enactment of good. Thus, his ontological language was invested with an experiential syntax, and nature was not some transcendent faculty. Although nature was determinate in the sense that it was inexorably good, humanity was essentially self-transforming, inherently unfinished and incomplete in the existentialist sense. Hence Guangdi's metapraxis.

His philosophy is primarily a metapractical program of moral cultivation that seeks to verify metaphysics (nature, heaven, principle) in lived experiences (knowing and acting, dwelling in sincerity, establishing the will, and emphasizing reverence). What controlled Guangdi's authorship was this metapractical grammar of action, written on the basis of the original Cheng-Zhu vision. Enacting the ultimate reality of nature in purposeful actions meant not only moral self-cultivation but also engagement with the quotidian world of political affairs and social entanglements. Hence his ruminations and policies on the management and betterment of state and society. In short, despite, and in fact because of, nature's ontological primacy, human agency reigns supreme: engagement with oneself through ceaseless self-cultivation, association of one's pursuits with other individuals in the web of social relationships, and confrontation with affairs of the state and the world.

If Guangdi as a subject matter sheds historical light on both the Ming–Qing transition and Cheng-Zhu Song learning in the early Qing, his thought also affords us an opportunity to contemplate the meaning and relevance of Confucianism from our contemporary vantage point. P. J. Ivanhoe, through his recent study on the "rich and vibrant [Confucian] ethical tradition," hopes to make some contribution to "contemporary debates on the nature and status of ethical traditions in general." For in this tradition, we see not only ideals and conceptions of virtues but actually the ways of their enactment, the ways to do good.[1] Likewise, Anne Birdwhistell, focusing on the early Qing figure of Li Yong (1627–1705), analyzes Confucian philosophy in systematic and theoretical terms with specific reference to its epistemology, seeking in the process to establish a framework for comparative philosophy.[2] In this study, my examination of Guangdi's exposition and elucidation of the classical texts has similarly drawn attention to the import and purport of the Confucian exegetical act by bringing in some comparative perspectives from the Western hermeneutic traditions. Therefore, I quite concur with Ivanhoe and Birdwhistell that present-day interpretation and reading of Confucian ideas should not eschew thinking about their implications for our engagement with philosophical questions in general, although as I cautioned at the very outset of this history of ideas, to "impose" our contemporary standards would be unreasonable, ahistorical, and anachronistic.

In its essentials, Guangdi's metapraxis is a moral philosophy, cogitation, and prescription of the ways to live well in accordance with a community's shared sense of values, that is, normative rules of conduct and normative standards of evaluation. In other words, it is teachings of ethics, defined generally as the philosophical exploration in morality. We may take the well-known Socratic question—how ought I to live—as the very entry point for ethical reflection, regardless of whether we are talking about the Confucian or Western ethical traditions. For in origin, the question need not be taken to be a philosophical one. It is a question that anyone might pose to oneself at a certain time in one's life. Yet, when it is pursued seriously and pondered deeply, it invites and ultimately demands critical examination, and generates answers that deliberately seek to be persuasive in terms of reasonableness and reflective in terms of generality. Whence emerges moral philosophy, or ethical reflection.[3] Whence there is also the parting of ways between the Confucian and Western ethical traditions. In the latter tradition, what follows the Socratic question of "how should one live?" are these corollary inquiries: "What is the good life?," or indeed, "What is the good?," to begin with.

Therefore, then, in moral philosophy as we generally know it in the West, there are two basic purposes and approaches. First is substantive or normative ethics that aims at discovering and constructing a universally consistent account and system of moral norms, in the process erecting a rational basis for moral acts. Explicated are the fundamental grounds of morality, upon which an edifice of justifiable moral imperatives and yardsticks may be built. The anticipated end result is the molding and consolidating of a comprehensive conception of good life, an ideal, according to which all good reasonable people should and would live. Second, there is meta-ethics, devoted to analyzing the concepts and language used in moral discourses, and to exposing the logic, rationale, and methodology that define the truth and falsity of moral claims. In brief, it interrogates semantically, logically, and epistemologically the presumptions of substantive ethics. In contemporary philosophy, there is in fact a tendency to privilege meta-ethics, based on the ideological stance that the role of philosophy should merely be to elucidate the various and varied nomenclature and arguments used, and not so much to admonish, exhort, and advise people to live in a certain moral way. The choice of life is an individual's.[4]

Looking at the Chinese tradition as exemplified by Li Guangdi's Cheng-Zhu Confucian thought, one will be hard pressed to discern the lineaments of meta-ethics. Although Guangdi's exposition of the meta-practical dictum of "knowing-acting," for instance, comes close to a sort of rigorous epistemological ratiocination regarding why moral knowledge precedes moral action, its ultimate goal is to enjoin people to act morally in accordance with the accepted Confucian norms. On the other hand, Guangdi's moral philosophy, expressed in terms of his metapraxis, does embody those constitutive elements of substantive or normative ethics described above. It does describe what right conduct is and what an ideal moral world is. But in the final analysis, the Confucian ethical tradition goes beyond both the purposes of normative ethics and meta-ethics. It transcends the Western paradigm in several ways.

First, to begin with, as Benjamin Schwartz points out, in the ancient axial age, whereas the Greeks were preoccupied with the question "What is the good?," the Chinese were concerned with the query "Why do people depart from the good?" They asked different questions because the former were not sure what defined and constituted goodness in humanity, while the latter were already convinced that the good had been "revealed" and "mandated" by heaven, which was intimately meshed with the human order.[5] Thus, in the West, ethical traditions are cultural conventions. Even with the intervention of the Judeo-Christian religions, ethical ideals are still construed as things constructed by humanity first and foremost, albeit with reference to the laws and commandments issued by God. It is so because God is the *other* impersonal God. There is the unbridgeable ontological chasm between humanity and God and his/her aseity. Human ethics may follow or even stem from the divine commands, but they cannot be organically or naturally derived from God. By contrast, in the Confucian case, the ethical tradition is not just a conventional order—it is certainly that, since the Way is a language of discourse that is culturally formed, transmitted, and cumulative—but it is also a natural order. As we have seen, according to Guangdi, following and inspired by the *Doctrine of the Mean*, the Way of humanity, via the realization of the fundamentally good nature (*xing*), endowed by and coeval with heaven, *is* the very Way of heaven. Goodness, or ultimate reality itself, is inherently and integrally our very being. There is the panglossian optimism and quixotic confidence that morality is what we *are* and not just what we seek to know and possess.

Second, this fundamental ontological understanding of the oneness of the good nature and ultimate reality means that the theoretical concern with what is good, insofar as it is taken for granted, must play second fiddle to the practical act of moral cultivation. How we practice and act on what we know to be good is more important than describing what we ought to know to be good. Theoretical description of virtues, that is, the dispositions of character to embrace or repulse certain actions, is far outweighed by the practical programmatic prescription to realize them. In Guangdi's metapraxis, we do find references to the genetics and ontology of cardinal virtues, in particular, wisdom, humaneness, and courage, but they are invariably discussed in terms of the inescapable human existential design to realize them in the province of everyday living. To know and to act, to establish the will, to dwell in sincerity, and to abide by reverence are all practical and immediate means by which we get to be moral and virtuous.

Third, if early Qing Cheng-Zhu Confucianism is a polysemic theory of moral cultivation founded on both a metaphysical conception of humanity's nature as driven by its own inner purpose and a meta-practical program that demands humanity's self-fulfillment, it may then be argued that a certain religiosity lies in this very simultaneity of metaphysics and metapraxis. The latter, as subjective-introspective activity of self-cultivation inspired by the utmost reverence and sincerity, is deeply committed to the inquiry of and commerce with the former. To put it another way, as praxis and logos achieve their organic conflation in the highest goal of moral cultivation, ultimate reality is apprehended. This apprehension of the ultimate can be described in no other terms than the religious one. In short, Confucianism, as represented by the seventeenth-century Cheng-Zhu school, dubs the voices of metaphysics into the calls of metapraxis, yielding in the process an unmistakable religiosity. The quest for human self-fulfillment is a religious pursuit.

It is useful here to remind ourselves of Tu Wei-ming's definition of Confucian religiousness in terms of "ultimate self-transformation as a communal act," culminating in the realization of the coevality and co-creation of humanity and the cosmos.[6] In Rodney Taylor's words, this transformed self, this sage, "not only hears the ways of Heaven but manifests, reveals, or discloses them to man."[7] Most recently, Mary Evelyn Tucker argues that the Confucian sense of the religious stems from the dialectic conflation of moral self-cultivation and the larger cosmological processes. As she puts it: "Confucianism can certainly be regarded as religious in the sense that the primary activity of Confucians is the establishing of moral reflection and spiritual awareness within the changes of cosmological processes."[8] I myself have written elsewhere that a religious mystique is inherent in the Confucian meditational praxis aimed at the apprehension of ultimate reality.[9] Given these definitions and characterizations of Confucian religiosity, Guangdi's meta-practical program of self-cultivation is patently animated by a religious impulse, for it aims at nothing short of the fulfillment of our nature, and the cosmos is the self writ large.

And so, this much seems clear so far: Confucianism is a practical learning concerned with how to live and to achieve, in the process, the ultimate identification with the grand cosmological processes; its anthropocentrism is imbued with religious sensibilities and goals. But how do we, as contemporary beings with our cultural preunderstanding and predisposition, relate to such an anthropology? In coolly dissecting its unique qualities, we may have ascertained a certain degree of fidelity to the Confucian way, and we may have established an alternative taxonomy of religiousness. But paradoxically, such intellectual endeavor may have also served to augment the alterity, the radical otherness, of Confucian religiosity. It is something *other than* what we have, what we have had, what we know, and what we have known. Although we may arrive at an intellectualist understanding of it as an object of discursive analysis, we may not have accomplished what Gadamer calls the "fusion of horizons." It seems to me that this hermeneutic act of breaking onto the other side requires our establishing some notion of commonality concerning the religious, that is, the sense, experience, and awareness of transcendence.

This epilogue offers some very preliminary thoughts on this question. I do not use the word "transcendence" as a paradigmatic term that presumes a positive and analytic theory of religiosity. (Mary Evelyn Tucker has duly cautioned us of the problematic nature of employing a transcendence-immanence paradigm to study Confucianism.) I use it simply as a term of art referring to the sense of going beyond and rising above the mundane and the humdrum, a sense of uplift that even though one is squarely immersed in the common and ordinary, one enjoys a feeling of elevation. This sense of transcendence may be construed and understood as what the well-known and influential psychologist Mihaly Csikszentmihalyi calls "flow," an optimal mental and spiritual state that arises out of ordinary experiential engagements with the world at large, in which one finds the expansion of the boundaries of the self and the mysterious feeling of universal harmony, so much so that the personal is integrated with the social, the communal, and ultimately, the universal.[10]

In fact, Csikszentmihalyi surmises that a Confucian sage is one who has found "flow," although he does not offer empirical evidence. Let us then briefly examine the conditions and prerequisites for achieving "flow" and determine if we can hear their echoes in Li Guangdi's meta-practical program of moral self-cultivation. According to Csikszentmihalyi, the eventuation of "flow" is governed by certain "external" factors. Activities that are most likely to yield "flow" embody clear goals and definite rules, provide information on our progress, adjust possibilities for action to our capacities, and exclude distractions and enable concentration. There is also the "internal" factor, referring to a person's ability and skill to control consciousness, thereby focusing intently and intensively on the matters at hand. All this is facilitated by having "faith in a system of meanings that gives purpose to one's being." The end result of flow is, after all, knowing ourselves, so that in our individual existence, we find oneness with the power that is the universe, in possession of knowledge and wisdom that deal not with the superficial appearance of experiences but with the underlying universal truths. We have become "transcenders," or "T-persons."[11]

Li Guangdi's meta-practical program of self-cultivation consists of all these ingredients. In defining the triumvirate of cardinal virtues—wisdom, humaneness, and courage—Guangdi sets the goal and prescribes the unalienable rules. Virtues and wisdom are the bonds of nature that we ineluctably seek to realize and fulfill, while courage both enables and manifests their experiential fructification. His discourse on the nature of, and relationship between, "knowing and acting" (*zhixing*) charts a sequential course for both pursuing and gauging our moral learning and progress. His dictum of "establishing the will" (*lizhi*) consolidates the proper orientation toward the goal by constituting a proper psychological state. Further, his injunction of "emphasizing reverence" (*zhujing*), coupled with the exercising of "sincerity" (*cheng*), calls for the deepest and most internal concentration of one's entire being on moral cultivation, effecting transformation of not only our outer countenance, posture, and speech, but also our inner thought and will. The end is "enlightenment" or the attainment of a sense of transcendence: the wisdom that knowledge and truth are the ceaseless inclination to inquire into what ought to and can be known, and earnestly act on what is known.

In sum, this slight comparative exercise juxtaposing "flow" and Confucian cultivation is engendered by my proposition that a discursive representation of Confucian religiosity in provincial Chinese cultural and historical terms, no matter how veridical, runs the risk of being frozen in its alterity. Therefore, we need to apprehend it by appropriately bringing in our contemporary resources, including our sensibilities and feelings for the transcendent. To fully appreciate the religious charisma of Confucianism, we have no choice but to resort to our contemporary cognitive imagination for the high and profound. After all, to ponder religiosity, be it Western or Confucian, present or past, is to contemplate the invention or reinvention of a universal fundamental, to wit, humanity. Indeed, whether we are talking about a Confucian sage or Csikszentmihalyi's "transcender/T-person," we are only human.

NOTES

Introduction

1. On the meaning of the terms "Song learning" and "Han learning," see Yü Ying-shih, "Some Preliminary Observations on the Rise of Ch'ing Confucian Intellectualism," *Tsing-hua Journal of Chinese Studies* 10.1–2(December 1975):105–36, and He Youshen, "Qingdai Han Song zhi zheng pingyi" (A Balanced Discussion of the Debate Between Han Learning and Song Learning in the Qing), *Wenshizhe xuebao* 27(December 1978):97–113.

2. Quoted in Wm. Theodore de Bary, "Introduction," in Wm. Theodore de Bary, ed., *Self and Society in Ming Thought* (New York: Columbia University Press, 1970), p. 1.

3. Quoted in Ian McMorran, "Wang Fu-chih and the Neo-Confucian Tradition," in Wm. Theodore de Bary, ed., *The Unfolding of Neo-Confucianism* (New York: Columbia University Press, 1975), p. 474.

4. Qian Daxin, *Qianwentang wenji* (Collected Writings from the Qianwen Studio) (Shanghai: Commercial Press, 1935), p. 347.

5. Quoted in dc Bary, "Introduction," p. 2.

6. Liang contrasted Song–Ming thought, which was in his words "vague," "intangible," and "abstract," with Qing learning, which he described as "enlightened," "solid," "practical," "utilitarian," "sound," and "scientific." See his *Intellectual Trends in the Ch'ing Period*, translated by Immanuel C. Y. Hsu (Cambridge, Mass.: Harvard University Press, 1959), pp. 21–48. Hu shi similarly constructed two antithetical modes of learning. The Song–Ming one was marked by "subjectivism," "idealism," and "emptiness," while the Qing mode was suffused with a "scientific," "exact," and "impartial" spirit. See Hu's *Dai Dongyuan de zhexue* (The Philosophy of Dai Zhen) (Shanghai: Commercial Press, 1927), pp. 1–4. For a discussion on their theses, see Yü, "Preliminary," p. 111.

7. Qian Mu, *Zhongguo jin sanbainian xueshushi* (The History of Chinese Learning in the Past Three Hundred Years) (Taipei: Shangwu, 1937), p. 1.

8. Apart from the article by Yü already cited, see also his "Cong SongMing ruxue de fanzhan lun Qingdai sixiangshi" (A Discussion of Qing Intellectual History in Light of the Developments of Song-Ming Confucianism), *Zhongguo xueren* 2(September 1970):19–41, and "Qingdai sixiangshi de yige xinjieshi" (A New Explication of Qing Intellectual History), in Yü Ying-shih, *Lishi yu sixiang* (History and Thinking) (Taipei: Lianjing, 1976), pp. 121–56.

9. Hoyt Cleveland Tillman, *Confucian Discourse and Chu Hsi's Ascendancy* (Honolulu: University of Hawaii Press, 1992), pp. 9–11, *passim.*

10. *From Philosophy to Philology: Intellectual and Social Aspects of Change in Late Imperial China* (Cambrdige, Mass.: Harvard University Press, 1984), p. 29.

11. Ibid., pp. 28–29.

12. He, "Qingdai," *passim.*

13. Elman, *From Philosophy*, pp. 233–48.

14. Tu Wei-ming, "Perceptions of Learning (*Hsüeh*) in Early Ch'ing Thought," in his *Way, Learning, and Politics: Essays on the Confucian Intellectual* (Albany: State University of New York Press, 1993), p. 123.

15. Thomas Metzger, *Escape from Predicament: Neo-Confucianism and China's Evolving Political Culture* (New York: Columbia University Press, 1976), p. 52.

16. He Yousen, "Qingdai jingxue sichao" (The Tides of Thought of Classical Learning in the Qing Period), in *Qingdai chingxue guoji yantaohui lunwen ji* (The Conference Proceedings of the International Meeting on Classical Learning in the Qing Period) (Taipei: Institute of Literature and Philosophy, Academia Sinica, 1994), pp. 18–21.

17. Kai-wing Chow, "The Development of Sung Learning in Ch'ing Thought, 1660's-1830's," *Hanxue yanjiu* (Chinese Studies) 13.2(December 1995):47–76.

18. On the early Qing implementation of the examinations and the curricula, see Huang Dezhao, *Qingdai keju zhidu* (The Examination System in the Qing Period) (Beijing: Zhonghua, 1984), pp. 17–24, 40–41.

19. Wing-tsit Chan, "The *Hsing-li ching-i* and the Ch'eng-Chu School of the Seventeenth Century," in Wm. Theodore de Bary, ed., *The Unfolding of Neo-Confucianism* (New York: Columbia University Press, 1975), pp. 545–46, 555–56.

20. Yamanoi Yû, "Mimmatsu Shinsho ni okeru keisei chiyô no gaku," in Yamanoi Yû, *Min Shin shisô shi kenkyû* (A Study of Ming–Qing Practical Learning) (Tokyo: Chubun, 1980), pp. 229–31. This book also includes two other essays on the question of the Ming–Qing intellectual transition. See pp. 239–67.

21. Wing-tsit Chan, p. 561.

22. Ibid., pp. 543–79. Tu Wei-ming has also referred to some of the Cheng-Zhu scholars' emphasis on "solid scholarship" and "concrete human affairs." See "Perceptions," pp. 123–31.

23. Wm. Theodore de Bary, *The Message of the Mind in Neo-Confucianism* (New York: Columbia University Press, 1989), p. 161. Another work by Hou Wai-lu and his associates is noteworthy: *Song Ming lixue shi* (A History of Confucianism in the Song and Ming) (Beijing: Renmin, 1987). It gives the late Ming and early Qing Cheng-Zhu learning a fairly substantial treatment, but there is no concerted effort to situate this learning in, or to discuss it in terms of, the altered intellectual context of the period.

24. John B. Henderson, *Scripture, Canon, and Commentary: A Comparison of Confucian and Western Exegesis* (Princeton: Princeton University Press, 1991), Steven Van Zoeren, *Poetry and Personality: Reading, Exegesis and Hermeneutics in Traditional China* (Stanford: Stanford University Press, 1991), and Daniel K. Gardner, "Confucian Commentary and Chinese Intellectual History," *Journal of Asian Studies* 57.2(May 1998).

25. Hoyt Cleveland Tillman, *Confucian Discourse*, Hoyt Cleveland Tillman, *Utilitarian Confucianism: Ch'en Liang's Challenge to Chu Hsi* (Cambridge, Mass.: Harvard University Press, 1982), Hao Chang, "On the *Ching-shih* Ideal in Neo-Confucianism," *Ch'ing-shih wen-t'i* 3.1(November 1974):38–46, Chung-ying Cheng, "Practical Learning in Yen Yuan, Chu Hsi and Wang Yang-ming," in Wm. Theodore de Bary and Irene Bloom, eds., *Principle and Practicality* (New York: Columbia University Press, 1979), pp. 37–38. Statements specifically on the practical import of Chu Hsi's learning can be found in Wm. Theodore de Bary and John Chaffee, eds., *Neo-Confucian Education: The Formative Stage* (Berkeley: University of California Press, 1989). For instance, the introduction states, "Unrecognized too is the fact that, even as originally expounded by Chu, his teaching was meant to serve the needs of his own times—as a method of learning to be practiced rather than as a doctrine to be imparted or dogma to be imposed" (p. 2). Another useful collection of essays on the subject is Conrad Schirokauer and Robert Hymes, eds., *Ordering the World: Approaches to State and Society in Sung Dynasty China* (Berkeley: University of California Press, 1993).

26. Tillman, *Confucian Discourse*, p. 9.

27. In an earlier essay, I have examined the underlying metaphysical concerns of some late Ming and early Qing scholars as the foundation of their practical worldview. See "Toward an Interpretation of Ch'ing Ontology," in Richard J. Smith and D.W.Y. Kwok, eds., *Cosmology, Ontology, and Human Efficacy* (Honolulu: University of Hawaii Press, 1993), pp. 35–58.

28. Cf. Wm. Theodore de Bary, "Introduction," in de Bary and Bloom, *Principle*, p. 22.

29. Karl Jasper, *The Great Philosophers*, translated by Ralph Manheim (New York: Harcourt, Brace & World, 1962), pp. viii, xi.

30. See Wm. Theodore de Bary's translation with an introduction: *Waiting for the Dawn: A Plan for the Prince: Huang Tsung-hsi's Ming–I tai-fang lu* (New York: Columbia University Press, 1993).

31. *Mingru xue'an* (Records of Ming Scholars) (Beijing: Zhonghua, 1985), p. 9. This source is hereafter cited as MRXA.

32. On the intellectual reorientation of the Lu-Wang school in the early Qing, see Zhan Haiyun, *Qingchu xueshu lunwenji* (Anthology of Essays on the Learning and Scholarship of the Early Qing) (Taipei: Wenjin, 1992), pp. 73–105.

33. For a good recent synthetic treatment of Liu's philosophical reformulation and critique of Wang Yangming's ideas, see Tao Qing, *Ming yimin jiu dajia zhexue* (The Philosophies of Nine Great Ming Loyalists) (Taipei: Hongye, 1997), pp. 157–231.

34. Li Yong, *Erqu ji* (Anthology of [Li] Yong's [Writings]) (Beijing: Zhonghua, 1996), p. 149.

35. Chin-shing Huang, *Philosophy, Philology, and Politics in Eighteenth-Century China: Li Fu and the Lu-Wang School under the Ch'ing* (Cambridge: Cambridge University Press, 1995).

36. De Bary, *Message*, pp. 163, 175–85.

37. An example of the growing historiographic awareness of Li Guangdi's importance is the recent publication of a volume of essays devoted to him in mainland China, commemorating the 350th anniverary of his birthday: Yang Guozhen et al., *Li Guangdi yanjiu* (Studies on Li Guangdi) (Fujian: Xiamen daxue, 1993). However, it should be noted that this collection of essays was published by Xiamen University in Fujian, the native province of Guangdi. Thus, this effort owed much to the Chinese provincial sense of respect for and celebration of a historical personage who was a native son.

38. Cf. John Patrick Diggins, *The Promise of Pragmatism: Modernism and the Crisis of Knowledge and Authority* (Chicago: University of Chicago Press, 1994), pp. 7–8.

Chapter One. A Philosophical Dimension of the Ming–Qing Intellectual Transition

1. *Xinti yu xingti* (The Reality of the Self's Nature and the Reality of the Mind's Nature) (Taipei: Zhengzhong, 1968), pp. 21–41. The first quote

is from p. 31, the second, from p. 37. On the main differences between classical Confucian and Neo-Confucian conceptions of human nature, see P. J. Ivanhoe, "On the Metaphysical Foundations of Neo-Confucian and New Confucianism," *Journal of Chinese Philosophy* 22(1995):81–89.

2. On the self and its nature as embodiment of the organismic "moral universal," see for instance, Tu Wei-ming, *Confucian Thought: Selfhood as Creative Transformation* (Albany: State University of New York Press, 1985), pp. 19–28, 35–50. For a succinct examination of the important views on human nature in the history of Chinese thought, see Zhang Dainian, *Zhongguo zhexue dagang* (An Outline of Chinese Philosophy) (Beijing: Zhongguo kexue, 1982), pp. 183–232.

3. See, for example, Ortega y Gasset's *History as a System*, translated by William Atkinson (New York: W.W. Norton, 1941), pp. 165–233. My discussion on Ortega y Gasset's idea of *creencias* is based on Karl Weintraub, *Visions of Culture* (Chicago: University of Chicago Press, 1966), pp. 260–74, and Oliver Holmes, *Human Reality and the Social World: Ortega's Philosophy of History* (Amherst: University of Massachusetts Press, 1975), pp. 122–24.

4. Cf. also Collingwood's doctrine of *speculum mentis*, which sees philosophy as expatiation upon known experiences. In the words of Louis Mink: "Philosophy is not a specialized form of experience but the self-consciousness of experience in general. . . . The doctrine of *Speculum Mentis* . . . [is] the doctrine that the 'conclusion' of philosophical thinking and the 'experience' on which they are based are names for any two successive stages on a philosophical scale of forms." See Mink, *Mind, History, and Dialectic: The Philosophy of R. G. Collingwood* (Bloomington: Indiana University Press, 1969), pp. 253–54.

5. For illustrative examples of such perspective on learning and thought, see Chang Dainian, pp. 497–527.

6. MRXA, pp. 854–55, 861, 975–76. See also Huang Tsung-hsi, *The Records of the Ming Scholars*, edited by Julia Ching (Honolulu: University of Hawaii Press, 1987), pp. 199–201, 204–6.

7. I have provided a much more detailed description of both Xu's "Nine Scrutinies" and Zhou's "Nine Explanations" in a paper I delivered at Columbia University's Regional Seminar on Neo-Confucianism, March 1993. However, in view of the fact that Zhao Jie has repeated much of the same material in his doctoral dissertation, "Chou Ju-teng at Nanching: Reassessing a Confucian Scholar in the Late Ming Intellectual World" (Princeton University, 1995), I see no compelling reason to present my earlier, lengthier examination of this debate here. For the original texts by Xu and Zhou, see MRXA, pp. 861–68. The outline here is a summarization of the arguments of the two texts.

8. On Wang's dialogue with his pupils on this matter in the context of the "four maxims," see Wang Yang-ming, *Instructions for Practical Living and other Neo-Confucian Writings*, translated with notes by Wing-tsit Chan (New York: Columbia University Press, 1962), pp. 241–45.

9. On Wang Ji's and Qian Dehong's explanations of the "four maxims" and Wang Yangming's response, see Wing-tsit Chan, *Instructions*, pp. 243–45; Okada, pp. 126–29; Tang Chun-i, "The Development of the Concept of Moral Mind from Wang Yang-ming to Wang Chi," in de Bary, *Self*, pp. 112–13; and Huang Tsung-hsi, *Records*, pp. 115–16.

10. On Wang Ji's view on the "four nonbeings," see Wing-tsit Chan, *Instructions*, pp. 241–42. See also Takehiko Okada, "Wang Chi and the Rise of Existentialism," in de Bary, ed., *Self*, pp. 126–29.

11. MRXA, pp. 867–68.

12. On Guan Zhidao, see Huang Tsung-hsi, *Records*, pp. 171–73.

13. Heinrich Busch, "The Tung-lin Academy and Its Political and Philosophical Significance," *Monumenta Serica* 14(1949–1955):85.

14. Collected in *Gu Duanwengong yishu* (Bequeathed Writings by Gu Xiancheng) (n.p., 1877 edition).

15. Guan was described by Jiao Hong (1540?–1620), another syncretist, as one who "attempted to encompass the Three Teachings and fuse the Nine Schools of thought in order to formulate a doctrine of his own." See Edward T. Ch'ien, *Chiao Hung and the Restructuring of Neo-Confucianism in the Late Ming* (New York: Columbia University Press, 1986), p. 39. On the late Ming syncretism, see pp. 14–30.

16. "Zhiyi shang," 5b.

17. Ibid., 14b.

18. Ibid., 2b–3a.

19. "Zhiyi xia," 3a.

20. "Zhiyi xia," 2a–b.

21. "Zhiyi shang," 17a–b.

22. "Zhiyi xia," 24b.

23. "Zhiyi xia," 10a.

24. "Zhiyi xia," 14b–15a.

25. Qian Mu, *Zhongguo*, pp. 9–14, 18–19.

26. The significance of the Ming–Qing intellectual transition as represented by these Song learning figures has yet to be studied. On Gao Panlong, see Gu Qingmei, "Gu Jingyang Gao Jingyi sixiang zhi bijiao yanjiu" (A Comparative Examination of the Thoughts of Gu Xiancheng and Gao Panlong) (Ph.D. diss., National Taiwan University, 1979). On Liu Zongzhou, see T'ang Chun-i, "Liu Tsung-chou's Doctrine of the Moral Mind and Practice and His Critique of Wang Yang-ming," in de Bary, *Unfolding*, pp. 305–31, and Tu Wei-ming, "Subjectivity in Liu Tsung-

chou's Philosophical Anthropology," in Donald Munro, ed., *Individualism and Holism: Studies in Confucian and Taoist Values* (Ann Arbor: University of Michigan Press, 1985), pp. 215–38.

27. T'ang Chun-i, pp. 308–10; Qian Mu, pp. 9–10.

28. *Xiaoxinzhai zhaji* (Notebook from the Studio of the Prudent Heart) (Taipei: Guangwen, 1975), 7/1a.

29. *Gaozi yishu* (Surviving Works of Master Kao), Siku quanshu edition (hereafter GZYS), 3/31b, 32a–b.

30. GZYS, 4/39a.

31. *Donglin shuyuan zhi* (Records of the Donglin Academy) (Taipei: Guangwen, 1968 reprint), 5/1a.

32. Ibid., 9/14b.

33. Ibid., 9/16a–b.

34. Ibid., 8 (*shang*)/24a.

35. Liu Zongzhou, *Liuzi quanshu* (Complete Works of Master Liu) (Kyoto: Chubun, 1981), hereafter LZQS, 19/14a–b.

36. LZQS, 19/13b.

37. LZQS, 19/4a–5b.

38. T'ang Chun-i, p. 326. Tu Wei-ming also stresses that, according to Liu Zongzhhou, "human nature is ultimately good." See Tu, "Subjectivity," pp. 219–20, 228.

39. Ibid., p. 228.

40. LZQS, 25/1a.

41. LZQS, 8/24b–25b. For a detailed discussion on Liu Zongzhou's critique of Wang Yangming's idea of innate knowledge of the good, see Gu Qingmei, "Liu Jieshan dui Yangming zhiliangzhi shuo zhi jicheng yu fazhan" (Liu Zongzhou's Continuation and Development of Wang Yangming's Teachings on Innate Knowledge of the Good), in her *Mingdai lixue lunwenji* (Collection of Essays on Neo-Confucianism in the Ming Period) (Taipei: Da'an, 1990), pp. 237–48. See also T'ang Chün-i, pp. 310–3, 324–26.

42. LZQS, 19/54b–55a.

43. "Xingjie shang" (An Explication of Human Nature, Part One), in *Chen Que ji* (Collected Works of Chen Que) (Beijing: Zhonghua, 1979), p. 447.

44. "Xingjie xia" (An Explication of Human Nature, Part Two), in *Chen Que ji*, p. 451.

45. "Yu Liu Boxing shu" (Letter to Liu Boxing), in *Chen Que ji*, p. 466.

46. *Rongtan wenye* (The Enterprise of Inquiry and Learning in a Fuzhou Academy) (Taipei: Guangwen, 1975 reprint), 10/16b–17a.

47. *Rongtan wenye*, 14/9a.

48. *Shang* (Part One), 9b–10a. This essay is included in *Essays on Corroborating Human Nature*.

49. *Xiaoxinzhai zhaji*, 11/4a.
50. "Zuiyan," (*shang*), 8b–9a.
51. MRXA, p. 1396.
52. *Xiaoxinzhai zhaji*, 1/5b.
53. *Xiaoxinzhai zhaji*, 18/11a.
54. *Xiaoxinzhai zhaji*, 12/12a–b.
55. *Jinggao canggao*, 4/17a–18b.
56. *Jinggao canggao*, 11/2b–3a.
57. *Jinggao canggao*, 10/8b.
58. *Xiaoxinzhai zhaji*, 2/1a–b.
59. *Jinggao canggao*, 2/20b.
60. GZYS, 9 (*shang*)/24a.
61. GZYS, 8 (*shang*)/61a.
62. GZYS, 8 (*shang*)/24b.
63. MRXA, v. 2, p. 1417.
64. GZYS, 8 (*xia*)/61b.
65. GZYS, 3/17a.
66. GZYS, 8/46b. On Gao's teachings on quiet-sitting, see Rodney Taylor, "Meditation and Ming Neo-Orthodoxy," in his *The Religious Dimensions of Confucianism* (Albany: State University of New York Press, 1990), pp. 93–114.
67. GZYS, 3/17a.
68. GZYS, 4/61a–b.
69. GZYS, 3/23b–24a.
70. GZYS, 3/23a.
71. MRXA, v. 2, p. 1420.
72. GZYS, 3/4b–9b.
73. GZYS, 3/26b–27a.
74. Tu Wei-ming, "Subjectivity," p. 219.
75. T'ang Chün-i, p. 320.
76. LZQS, 13/47b.
77. LZQS, 13/21b.
78. LZQS, 19/7b–8b.
79. Tu Wei-ming, "Subjectivity," p. 231.
80. LZQS, 13/35a.
81. LZQS, 29/28a.
82. LZQS, 10/18a.
83. LZQS, 19/25a.
84. "Zhixing" (Knowing Nature), in *Chen Que ji*, p. 443.
85. "Xingjie shang," p. 447.
86. "Yuanjiao" (Fundmental Teachings), in *Chen Que ji*, p. 457.
87. *Daxue bian* (Disputation with the *Great Learning*), in *Chen Que ji*, pp. 553–54. In fact, Chen rejects the *Great Learning* as a genuine Confucian

text and characterizes it as a piece of Chan-inspired writing. On Chen's hermeneutics on this classic, see Huang Chin-hsing, "Lixue kaozhengxue yu zhengzhi: yi Daxue gaiben de fazhan wei lizheng" (Learning of Principle, Evidential Scholarship and Politics: Using the Developments of the Textual Alterations of the *Great Learning* as an Example), in his *Youru shengyi* (Entering the Master's Sanctuary) (Taipei: Yunchen, 1994), pp. 378–80.

88. *Rongtan wenye,* 15/1b.

89. *Rongtan wenye,* 15/11a.

90. *Rongtan wenye,* 15/1a–3a.

91. On Zhu Xi's conception of this duality in human nature, see, for instance, Wing-tsit Chan, *A Sourcebook in Chinese Philosophy* (Princeton: Princeton University Press, 1963), pp. 612–26.

92. For a succinct discussion of the Cheng-Zhu conception of human nature and its illustration by the use of "this-worldly analogies," see Don J. Wyatt, "A Language of Continuity in Confucian Thought," in Paul Cohen and Merle Goldman, eds., *Ideas Across Cultures: Essays on Chinese Thought in Honor of Benjamin I. Schwartz* (Cambridge, Mass.: Harvard University Press, 1990), pp. 50–57. For a more thorough treatment of Zhu Xi's ideas, see Donald Munro, *Images of Human Nature: A Sung Portrait* (Princeton: Princeton University Press, 1988), especially chapter three. For an overview of the question of the mind-heart in the Confucian philosophical tradition, see my "An Early Qing Critique of the Philosophy of Mind-Heart (*Xin*): The Confucian Quest for Doctrinal Purity and the *'Doxic'* Role of Chan Buddhism," *Journal of Chinese Philosophy* 26.1(March 1999):89–120.

93. Qian Mu, p. 13. For a discussion on the early Qing tendency toward the accommodation of the ontological value of material force, see my "Toward an Interpretation," pp. 35–39.

94. MRXA, p. 1444.

95. MRXA, p. 1442.

96. MRXA, p. 1440.

97. MRXA, p. 1443–44.

98. MRXA, p. 1441.

99. MRXA, p. 1445. For an interpretation of the dynamic nature of *xing* in Mencius's thought, see Roger Ames, "The Mencian Conception of *Ren Xing*: Does It Mean 'Human Nature'?" in Henry Rosemont, ed., *Chinese Texts and Philosophical Contexts: Essays Dedicated to Angus C. Graham* (La Salle, Ill.: Open Court, 1991), pp. 143–75. For an opposing view, see Irene Bloom, "Mencian Arguments on Human Nature (*Jen Xing*)," *Philosophy East and West* 44.1 (January 1994):19–53.

100. MRXA, p. 1444.

101. MRXA, p. 1457.

102. MRXA, p. 1461.
103. MRXA, p. 1447.
104. MRXA, p. 1448.
105. MRXA, p. 1467.
106. *Xiaoxinzhai zhaji*, 2/1a.
107. *Xiaoxinzhai zhaji*, 9/6b–7a.
108. "Zhiyi xia," 11a.
109. GZYS, 3/32a–b.
110. *Donglin shuyuan zhi* [Records of the Tung-lin Academy] (Taipei: Guangwen, 1968 reprint), 5/9a.
111. GZYS, 4/53b.
112. GZYS, 3/33a–b.
113. GZYS, 1/21b.
114. GZYS, 3/35b–37a.
115. LZQS, 11/12a.
116. MRXA, p. 1521.
117. LZQS, 8/11a–b.
118. MRXA, p. 1554.
119. LZQS, 10/22b.
120. LZQS, 6/1a.
121. LZQS, 5/26a–27a. For a concise examination of the role of *qing* in the Confucian philosophical tradition, see my "Is Emotion (*Qing*) the Source of a Confucian Antinomy?" *Journal of Chinese Philosophy* 25.2(June 1998):169–90.
122. "Xingjie xia," p. 451.
123. *Chen Que ji*, pp. 451–52.
124. "Wuyu zuoxing bian" (Disputation with [the Idea of] Becoming a Sage in the Absence of Desires), in *Chen Que ji*, p. 461.
125. "Qingbing qing zhuo shuo" (Discourse on the Purity and Turbidity of Material Endowment), in *Chen Que ji*, p. 455.
126. *Rongtan wenye*, 17/7a.
127. *Rongtan wenye*, 17/6a.
128. *Rongtan wenye*, 17/7a.
129. *Huang Zhangpu ji* (Anthology of Huang Zhangpu's Works) (n.p., n.d.), 30/28a–b.
130. *Huang Zhangpu ji*, 30/32a.
131. Qian Mu, pp. 9–14, 18–19.
132. On the practical import and orientation of early Qing Cheng-Zhu thought, see Wing-tsit Chan, "The *Hsing-li ching-i*," pp. 543–72, and my "*Hsing* (Nature) as the Ontological Basis of Practicality in Early Ch'ing Ch'eng-Chu Confucianism: Li Kuang-ti's (1642–1718) Philosophy," *Philosophy East and West* 44.1(January 1994):79–109.

Chapter 2. The Life of a Scholar-Official

1. Li Qingzhi, *Wenzhen gong nianpu* (Biographical Annals of Li Guangdi) (Taipei: Guangwen, 1971), 1/1b–3b. This source is hereafter cited as NP. Peng Shaosheng, "Gu Guanglu dafu Wenyuange daxueshi Li Wenzhengong shizhuang" (Recordings of Significant Events in the Life of the Grand Secretary Li Guangdi), in Qian Yiji, comp., *Beizhuan ji* (Anthology of Tomb Inscriptions and Biographical Sketches) (preface 1826), 13/6b.

2. NP, 1/3b–6a; Peng Shaosheng, 13/6b.

3. NP, 1/6b–7b; Yang Mingshi, "Guanglu dafu Wenyuange daxueshi jian libu shangshu shi Wenzhen Li Guangdi mujie" (The Tomb Inscription of Li Guangdi, the Grand Secretary and Vice President of the Board of Works) in Qian Yiji, *Beizhuan ji*, 13/4a.

4. NP, 1/8a–15a.

5. On the rebellion, see Lawrence Kessler, *K'ang-hsi and the Consolidation of Ch'ing Rule, 1661–1684* (Chicago: University of Chicago Press, 1976), pp. 81–90, and Frederic Wakeman Jr., *The Great Enterprise: The Manchu Reconstruction of Imperial Order in Seventeenth-Century China*, vol. 2 (Berkeley: University of California Press, 1985), pp. 1099–1115.

6. NP, 1/14b–15a.

7. NP, 1/15a–16a.

8. On Chen's life, see Arthur Hummel, ed., *Eminent Chinese of the Ch'ing Period* (Taipei: Ch'eng Wen Publishing Company, 1970 reprint), pp. 93–95.

9. Ibid., p. 93, 473.

10. NP, 1/16a. On the two Zhengs, see Hummel, *Eminent Chinese*, pp. 108–10, 111–12.

11. A complete text of the "wax ball memorial" constitutes fascicle (*zhuan*) 26 of the *Rongcun quanji* (Anthology of Writings by Li Guangdi). This anthology is included in the *Rongcun quanshu* (Complete Works of Li Guangdi) (n.p., preface 1829). A slightly abridged version can be found in NP, 1/16a–18b.

12. NP, 1/18b–20a. See also *Da Qing Shengzu Ren Kangxi huangdi shilu* (The Veritable Records of the Reign of the Kangxi Emperor) (Taipei: Huawen, 1964), 66/12b.

13. Hummel, *Eminent Chinese*, p. 93.

14. Ibid.

15. Cai Guanle, *Qing dai qibai mingren zhuan* (Biographies of Seven Hundred Eminent Personages in the Qing Period) (Beijing: Zhongguo shudian, 1984 reprint), p. 16.

16. Hummel, *Eminent Chinese*, p. 93.

17. A complete text of this 1705 memorial, which gives a picture of the entire affair through Chen's eyes, can be found in *Fujian tongzhi* (The Gazetteer of Fujian) (Taipei: Huawen 1968), 7/12a–b.

18. 1/37a–41a. This work, hereafter cited as RCPLHK, supplements the information in the NP by using material from the *Rongcun yulu xuji* (A Sequel to the Recorded Sayings of Li Guangdi), hereafter cited as RCYLXJ, and unpublished letters. Both these works are included in the *Rongcun quanshu* (Complete Works of Li Guangdi).

19. NP, 1/20b–31b.

20. NP, 1/31b–32b.

21. Kessler, pp. 90–93.

22. For Guangdi's role in and his ideas on the pacification of Taiwan, see RCYLXJ 11/1b–11b.

23. NP, 1/33a–36a.

24. NP, 37a–38b.

25. NP, 38b–39b, and RCYLXJ, 11/10b–11b.

26. NP, 39b.

27. Hummel, *Eminent Chinese*, p. 577. See also Kessler, pp. 129–30.

28. Hummel, *Eminent Chinese*, p. 311.

29. NP refers to Xu simply as the "jealous one," but the RCPLHK made it very clear that the jealous official was Xu. See 1/49a.

30. NP, 47b–48a.

31. NP, 40a–43b. The official in power could very well have been Xu Qianxue.

32. NP, 1/41b–43b, RCPLHK, 1/49a–b.

33. NP, 43b–48a, RCPLHK, 1/50b–55b.

34. RCPLHK, 2/5b–6a.

35. Hummel, *Eminent Chinese*, p. 311.

36. Hummel, *Eminent Chinese*, p. 938.

37. RCYLXJ, 14/10b–11a.

38. RCPLHK, 1/59b–60a.

39. NP, 1/54b.

40. NP, 1/53b–55a, RCPLHK, 1/65b–67b, and *Qing shi gao* (A Draft Dynastic History of the Qing) (Taipei: Guofang yanjiu yuan, 1971), p. 3909, and Hummel, *Eminent Chinese*, p. 547.

41. Hummel, *Eminent Chinese*, pp. 701, 253.

42. RCPLHK, 2/45b–46a, Hummel, *Eminent Chinese*, p. 253.

43. Fang Bao, *Fang Bao ji* (Shanghai: Guji, 1983), pp. 686–87.

44. Cai Guanle, *Qing dai qibai*, p. 17, NP, 1/55b–56b.

45. RCPLHK, 2/5a–b.

46. RCPLHK, 2/5b.

47. NP, 1/56b–57a.

48. Hummel, *Eminent Chinese*, p. 474.

49. Wm. Theodore de Bary, *Neo-Confucian Orthodoxy and the Learning of the Mind-and-Heart* (New York: Columbia University Press, 1981), pp. 190–91.

50. De Bary, *The Message*, p. 175.

51. It is a highly condensed version of the Ming text by Hu Guang (1370–1418) and others, the *Xingli daquan* (Philosophy of Nature and Principle in Its Completeness) of 1415. See Wing-tsit Chan, "The Hsing-li ching-i," pp. 543–79.

52. Hummel, *Eminent Chinese*, pp. 924–25.

53. RCPLHK, 2/37b–38a.

54. RCPLHK, 2/38b–39b.

55. RCPLHK, 2/45a.

56. Hummel, *Eminent Chinese*, p. 475.

57. RCPLHK, 2/53a–69a.

58. NP, 2/75b–76a.

59. Fang Bao, *Fan Bao ji*, p. 687.

60. Hummel, *Eminent Chinese*, p. 203–5.

61. Quan Zuwang, *Jiqi ting waibian* (Additions to the Collected Writings from the Studio in Jiqi Mountain) (n.p., 1776), 44/16a–17b.

Chapter Three. General Theory

1. On the intellectual lineages of these two wings, see Thomas A. Wilson, *The Genealogy of the Way: The Consruction and Uses of the Confucian Tradition in Late Imperial China* (Stanford: Stanford University Press, 1995).

2. The oft-mentioned early Qing proponents of practical learning, such as Gu Yanwu, Huang Zongxi, and Wang Fuzhi, did reject what they perceived to be empty speculation on the metaphysics nature and the mind. But Gu proclaimed his allegiance to the Cheng-Zhu tradition, and Huang to the Lu-Wang one, while Wang restructured Song–Ming philosophy by largely staying within its metaphysical universe. See, for instance, my "Toward an Interpretaion," pp. 35–49, and Allison Harley Black, *Man and Nature in the Philosophical Thought of Wang Fu-chih* (Seattle: University of Washington Press, 1989), pp. 6–56.

3. Elman, *From Philosophy*.

4. This essay constitutes fascicle (*zhuan*) 8 of the *Rongcun quanji* (Anthology of Li Rongcun's Essays) (hereafter cited as RCQJ). This work is included in *Rongcun quanshu* (Complete Works of Li Rongcun) (n.p., preface 1829). All of Li Guangdi's writings cited in this book are found in this voluminous collection.

5. *Knowledge Painfully Acquired: The K'un-chih chi by Lo Ch'in-shun*, translated, edited, and with an introduction by Irene Bloom (New York: Columbia University Press, 1987), p. 69. The original Wade-Giles romanizations in this translation are here converted to Pinyin ones.

6. Ibid., p. 124.

7. Ibid., p. 58. For an excellent general examination of Luo's thought, see Bloom, pp. 13–22. See also Rong Zhaozu, *Mingdai sixiangshi* (A History of Ming Thought) (Taipei: Kaiming, 1966), pp. 183–96.

8. RCQJ, 8/1b–2a.

9. RCQJ, 8/1a–b.

10. *Rongcun yulu* (Collected Sayings of Li Rongcun) (hereafter cited as RCYL), 26/1a–b.

11. RCYL, 26/1b–2a.

12. RCYL, 26/2b–a.

13. RCYL, 26/3a.

14. This work constitutes *zhuan* 6 and 7 of RCQJ.

15. RCQJ, 7/11b.

16. RCOJ, 7/12a.

17. RCQJ, 7/23a–b.

18. RCQJ, 8/2b.

19. RCQJ, 8/3a.

20. RCQJ, 7/12a.

21. RCQJ, 7/21a–b.

22. RCQJ, 7/22b.

23. RCQJ, 7/22b–23a.

24. RCQJ, 7/12b–13a.

25. RCQJ, 7/12b–13a.

26. RCQJ, 8/4a.

27. RCQJ, 8/4b.

28. RCQJ, 8/6a.

29. RCQJ, 7/21a.

30. RCQJ, 2/15b.

31. RCQJ, 7/21a.

32. RCOJ, 8/15a–b.

33. RCOJ, 8/3a–b. For an overview of the question of the mind-heart in the philosophical tradition of Confucianism, see my "An Early Qing Critique," and Chin-shing Huang, *Philosophy*, pp. 4–24.

34. RCQJ, 7/8b–9a.

35. RCQJ, 7/9a–b.

36. Tillman, *Confucian Discourse*, pp. 9–10.

37. On the intimate relationship between philosophy and action in Neo-Confucian thought, see Judith Berling, "Embodying Philosophy:

Some Preliminary Reflections from a Chinese Perspective," in Frank Reynolds and David Tracy, eds., *Discourse and Practice* (Albany: State University of New York Press, 1992), pp. 233–60. It is also pertinent to note in this context Lee Yearley's characterization of Confucianism as a "locative religion," pointing to the Confucian belief that individuals found their location in the enveloping cosmos through the human institutions created by the ancient sages. See his "A Confucian Crisis: Mencius' Two Cosmogonies and Their Ethics," in Robin W. Lovin and Frank E. Reynolds, eds., *Cosmogony and Ethical Order: New Studies in Comparative Ethics* (Chicago: University of Chicago Press, 1985), pp. 310–327.

38. This is the theme of Ivanhoe's *Confucian Moral Self Cultivation* (New York: Peter Lang, 1993).

39. Lee H. Yearley, *Mencius and Aquinas: Theories of Virtue and Conceptions of Courage* (Albany: State University of New York Press, 1990), pp. 175–79.

40. See James Legge, trans., *The Chinese Classics* (Hong Kong: The University of Hong Kong Press, 1960), v.1, p. 407.

41. *Zhongyong zhangduan*,14a.

42. *Zhongyong yulun*, 8a.

43. Yearley, *Mencius*, pp. 13–14.

44. RCQJ, 8/7a.

45. RCQJ, 8/7a–b.

46. RCQJ, 6/17a–b.

47. Zhu Xi, in his *A Discourse on Humaneness* (Ren shuo), describes humaneness as "the virtue of the mind-heart" (*xin zhi de*) which, coming from heaven, is all-encompassing. See *Zhuzi wenji* (Collected Writings of Master Zhu) (Taipei: Shangwu, 1966 reprint), pp. 466–67.

48. RCQJ, 6/19a.

49. RCQJ, 6/19b.

50. RCQJ, 6/19a.

51. RCQJ, 6/19b–20a. In his *Chapters and Verses of the Doctrine of the Mean*, Guangdi provides another explanation of the priority of wisdom over humaneness: "As for the origin of humaneness, it is the mind-hearts of heaven and earth which are at work when they beget things. Therefore, in order to know humanity, one cannot not know heaven. Knowing heaven and knowing humanity is wisdom. Such wisdom is the origin of humaneness, rightness and propriety. It is as what Master Dong [Zhongshu] said, 'Heaven's nature must be understood before humaneness and rightness can be understood. Knowing humaneness and rightness, there is then the emphasis on propriety and tradition.'" (13b).

52. RCQJ, 6/18b–19a.
53. RCQJ, 6/20a.
54. RCQJ, 6/1a.
55. "Chengming" is the title of chapter six of Zhang's *Zhengmeng* (Correcting Youthful Ignorance). See *Zhang Zai ji* (Anthology of Zhang Zai's Writings) (Beijing: Zhonghua, 1985), pp. 20–24.
56. RCQJ, 6/20a.
57. RCQJ, 6/20a–b.
58. For a succinct definition of praxis, see Richard J. Bernstein, *Praxis and Action: Contemporary Philosophies of Human Activity* (Philadelphia: University of Pennsylvania Press, 1971), pp. ix–xiii, and Calvin O. Schrag, *Communicative Praxis and the Space of Subjectivity* (Bloomington: Indiana University Press, 1989), pp. 17–23. Note that in the Aristotelian sense, *theoria* and *praxis* are not meant to be antagonistically in opposition, but dialectically form two dimensions of a full human life.
59. Thomas Kasulis, "Philosophy as Metapraxis," in Reynolds and Tracy, *Discourse*, pp. 173–75.
60. Here, Guangdi is paraphrasing a statement from the *Classic of Documents*, which Zhu quoted. In the *Zhuzi yulei*, Zhu is recorded to have said, "The *Documents* states, 'To know is not difficulty, but to act on what is known is especially difficult.'" See *Zhuzi yulei* (Classified Sayings of Master Zhu) (Beijing: Zhonghua, 1986), v.1, p. 223.
61. RCQJ, 8/8b.
62. Note that this statement is borrowed by Wang from the *Analects*, BK.I, CH.VIII. See Legge, vol. 1, p. 141.
63. RCQJ, 8/9a–b.
64. RCQJ, 8/9b–10a.
65. RCQJ, 8/10a–b.
66. *Analects*, BK.VII, CH.IX, according to Legge's translation.
67. This piece comprises the second fascicle of the RCQJ.
68. RCQJ, 2/17a–b.
69. RCQJ, 2/27b.
70. RCQJ, 8/11a.
71. RCQJ, 8/11a.
72. RCQJ, 8/11a–b.
73. *Lunyu zhaji*, 1/22b.
74. *Lunyu zhaji*, 1/8b.
75. RCQJ, 8/11b–12a.
76. RCQJ, 8/12b.
77. RCQJ, 8/13b.
78. RCQJ, 6/3a.
79. RCQJ, 6/3b.

80. RCQJ, 2/17a. This statement is from his *Written Notes on the Classics*.

81. Donald Munro, *The Concept of Man in Early China* (Stanford: Stanford University Press, 1969), pp. ix, 48–58.

Chapter Four. The Ontology of *Xing* and Its Meta-practical Import

1. On the life and thought of Lu Shiyi, see Ge Rongjin and Wang Jincai, *Lu Shiyi pingzhuan* (A Critical Biography of Lu Shiyi) (Nanjing: Nanjing daxue, 1996).

2. *Sibianlu jiyao* (Selected Notes on Reflections and Disputations) (Taipei: Guangwen, 1977 reprint), v2.1/8b–9a. Hereafter cited as SBLJY. Note that this work is divided into the *qianji* (the first collection) and the *houji* (the second collection). For citation purposes, the former is identified as v1, and the latter as v2.

3 *Lunxue chouda* (Exchanges of Learning and Rewarding Responses), 2/3b–4a. This work is a collection of correspondence between Lu Shiyi and his friends, included in *Lu Futing xiansheng yishu ershi'er zhong* (The Bequeathed Works of Mr. Lu Futing in Twenty-two Titles) (Beijing,1889). Hereafter cited as *Yishu*.

4. "Taiji tushuo jiangyi" (An Explication of the Meanings of *The Discourse on the Diagram of the Great Ultimate*), an essay found in *Lu Futing xiansheng wenji* (Collected essays of Mr. Lu Futing), 1/12a–b. The collection of essays is hereafter cited as *Wenji*. The *Wenji* is collected in *Yishu*.

5. *Wenji*, 1/13b.

6. SBLJY, v2.1/5a–b.

7. *Wenji*, 1/15a–b.

8. SBLJY, v.2.4/1a.

9. SBLJY, v2.4/8b.

10. SBLJY, v2.9/6a.

11. "Xingshan tushuo," 1a–3a. This essay is found in *Yishu*.

12. RCQJ, 2/2a–b.

13. *Zhouyi guanxiang* (A Scrutiny of the Images of the *Classic of Changes*),12/2a.

14. "Zhengmeng yi" (The Meanings of [Zhang Zai's] "Correcting Youthful Ignorance"), 47a.

15. RCQJ, 6/2a.

16. RCYL, 25/11a.

17. RCQJ, 7/10a–11b.

18. *Zhouyi guanxiang*, 10/7b.

19. RCQJ, 1/15a.
20. RCQJ, 7/18b.
21. RCYL, 26/7a–b.
22. RCYL, 26/7b.
23. RCQJ, 16/2b.
24. RCQJ, 1/18a.
25. RCYL, 25/8a.
26. "Mengzi zhachi shang" (Detailed Recordings of the *Mencius*, Part One), 15b.
27. "Song liuzi" (Six Song Masters), in RCYL, 18/2a–3b.
28. SBLJY, v2.5/10a.
29. SBLJY, v1.2/10b.
30. *Lunxue chouda*, 2/5a–b.
31. SBLJY, v1.3/1a–b.
32. *Lunxue chouda*, 2/5b.
33. *Lunxue chouda*, 2/28b.
34. SBLJY, v1.8/1a.
35. SBLJY, v1.2/9b.
36. SBLJY, v1.2/9b.
37. SBLJY, vl.2/8b–9a.
38. SBLJY, v1.2/9a.
39. *Lunxue chouda*, 2/18a.
40. SBLJY v1.3/3b–4a.
41. SBLJY, v1.3/4a.
42. SBLJY, v1.2/13a.
43. SBLJY, v2.6/16b–17a.
44. "Huaiyun wenda jicun" (A Collection of the Surviving Fragments of *Questions and Answers at Huaiyun*), 12b. This essay is found in the *Yishu*.
45. SBLJY, v1.1/9a.
46. SBLJY, v1.1/8b.
47. SBLJY, v1.1/13b.
48. SBLJY, v1.4/3a–5b.
49. RCYL, 25/8a.
50. RCYL, 25/10a.
51. RCYL, 20/1b.
52. *Zhongyong yulun* (Additional Discussions on the *Mean*), 2a–b.
53. Ibid., 11a.
54. RCYL, 7/20a.
55. RCYL, 6/1a–2b.
56. On this classical Confucian dichotomy, see A. C. Graham, "The Background of the Mencian Theory of Human Nature," in his *Studies in*

Chinese Philosophy and Philosophical Literature (Singapore: The Institute of East Asian Philosophy, 1986), pp. 54–56.

57. RCYL, 26/4b–5a.
58. RCYL, 1/19a.
59. RCYL, 1/16b.
60. RCQJ, 6/9a.
61. *Daxue guben shuo* (Discourse on the Ancient Edition of the *Great Learning*), 4a.
62. RCQJ, 6/11a–b.
63. *Zhongyong yulun*, 14b–15a.
64. *Xiaojing zhu* (Annotations of the *Classic on Filial Piety*), 2a–b.
65. Wing-tsit Chan, "Ch'eng-Chu," p. 560.
66. Ying-shih Yü, "Preliminary Observations," pp. 105–36.
67. RCYL, 8/15b–16a.
68. RCYL, 8/17a.
69. RCYL, 8/17b–19b.
70. RCQJ, 8/19a.
71. RCQJ, 2/17a.
72. RCQJ, 6/20a.
73. *Du Lunyu zazhi* (Notes Taken While Reading the *Analects*), 22b–23a.
74. RCQJ, 6/3a.
75. RCQJ, 6/7a.
76. RCQJ, 6/6a–b.
77. RCQJ, 8/8a–9b.
78. RCYL, 33/3b.
79. Qian Mu, *Jin sanbai nian*, v. 1, p. 13. See also Ng, "Toward an Interpretation," pp. 35–49.
80. SBLJY, v2.4/4b.
81. SBLJY, v2.4/13b.
82. SBLJY, v2.4/14a.
83. *Xingshantu shuo*, 4a.
84. SBLJY, v2.4/12a.
85. SBLJY, v2.5/5a.
86. SBLJY, v2.5/12b.
87. *Xingshantu shuo*, 3a.
88. *Wenji*, 1/23a–b.
89. SBLJY, v2.4/9b.
90. For a concise examination of Han Yu's conception of nature, see Wing-tsit Chan, *Sourcebook*, pp. 450–56.
91. See Han Yu's "An Inquiry of Human Nature" (*Yuanxing*), which is included in Li Guangdi's *Hanzi cuiyan*, 1a–2b.

92. *Hanzi cuiyan*, 8a.

93. *Hanzi cuiyan* (Choice Words of Master Han), 2b–3a.

94. RCYL, 6/14b–15a.

95. Here I follow D. C. Lau's translation of the word *cai* as "native endowment" as it appears in *Mencius*. Wing-tsit Chan and others commonly translate it as "capacity," "ability" or "aptitude." See Lau's translation of *Mencius* (Penguin, 1970), especially book VI.

96. RCYL, 6/21a.

97. RCYL, 6/19b–20a.

98. RCYL, 6/15a–b.

99. RCYL, 6/21b–22a.

100. RCYL, 6/22a.

101. RCYL, 18/11b.

102. RCYL, 6/24a.

103. RCQJ, 8/16a. On the meaning of *zhong*, see Wing-tsit Chan, *Sourcebook*, pp. 95–99. See also Tu Wei-ming, *Centrality and Commonality* (Albany: State University of New York Press, 1989), p. 16.

104. Graham, "Mencian Theory," in *Studies*, pp. 8, 43.

105. Ames, "The Mencian Conception," p. 144.

106. Ibid., pp. 150, 165. For an opposing interpretation that stresses the givenness of *xing*, see Bloom, "Mencian Arguments." Her position is best summed up by this quote from her essay: "*Hsing* is complex in two senses: (1) it is in part given by Heaven and in part realized or enacted by us, that is, partly within and partly beyond our control; and (2) it is a complex of dispositions, moral as well as appetitive, that is, intelligible in both normative and descriptive terms" (p. 44).

107. On the contents of the Mencian theory and other theories on human nature before Cheng-Zhu, see Graham, "Mencian Theory," especially pp. 54–59. On the question of the innovative elements in the Ch'eng-Chu scheme of conceiving human nature, see A. C. Graham, "What was New in the Ch'eng-Chu Theory of Human Nature?" in Graham, *Studies*, pp. 412–35.

108. Donald Munro, *Images of Human Nature: A Sung Portrait* (Princeton: Princeton University Press, 1988), p. 9.

Chapter Five. Reading the Classics

1. Roger Ames, "Foreword," in Hoyt Cleveland Tillman, *Ch'en Liang on Public Interest and the Law* (Honolulu: University of Hawaii Press, 1994), p. x.

2. John B. Henderson, *Scripture, Canon, and Commentary: A Compar-*

ison of Confucian and Western Exegesis (Princeton: Princeton University Press, 1991), pp. 3–4.

3. Steven Van Zoeren, *Poetry and Personality: Reading, Exegesis and Hermeneutics in Traditional China* (Stanford: Stanford University Press, 1991), p. 2.

4. Daniel K. Gardner, "Confucian Commentary and Chinese Intellectual History," *Journal of Asian Studies* 57.2(May 1998):397.

5. I borrow the term from Brice R. Wachterhauser, "Introduction," in Brice R. Wachterhauser, ed., *Hermeneutics and Truth* (Evanston, Ill.: Northwestern University Press, 1994), p. 1.

6. On the "contemporary" hermeneutic implications of traditional Chinese exegesis, see Van Zoeren, pp. 3–7.

7. See for instance, Jean-Francois Lyotard, *The Post-Modern Condition: A Report on Knowledge*, translated by G. Bennington and B. Massumi (Minneapolis: University of Minnesota Press, 1984); Michel Foucault, "What Is an Author?" in D. Bouchard, ed., *Language, Counter-Memory, Practice* (Ithaca, N.Y.: Cornell University Press, 1977); Jacques Derrida, *Of Grammatology*, translated by Gayatri Chakravorty Spivak (Baltimore: Johns Hopkins University Press, 1976) and "Structure, Sign and Play in the Discourse of the Human Science," in R. Macksey and E. Donato, eds., *The Languages of Criticism and the Sciences of Man* (Baltimore: Johns Hopkins University Press, 1970); Roland Barthes, "The Death of the Author," in *Image, Music, Text*, translated by S. Heath (New York: Hill and Wang, 1977).

8. For a discussion on the fundamental differences between the French deconstructionist and the German hermeneutic thinking, see Nathan Scott Jr., "The House of Intellect in an Age of Carnival: Some Hermeneutic Reflections," *Journal of the American Academy of Religion* 55.1(Spring 1987):8–13.

9. Ibid., p. 13.

10. David Tracy, *The Analogical Imagination: Christian Theology and the Culture of Pluralism* (New York: Crossroads, 1981), p. 134.

11. Ibid., p. 108.

12. Robert M. Grant, with David Tracy, *A Short History of the Interpretation of the Bible*, 2nd ed. (Philadelphia: Fortress Press, 1984), p. 186.

13. On these central ideas in Tracy's systematic theology, see also his *Blessed Rage for Order: The New Pluralism in Theology* (New York: Seabury Press, 1975) and *Plurality and Ambiguity: Hermeneutics, Religion, Hope* (San Francisco: Harper & Row, 1987). A succinct overview can also be found in chapters sixteen through eighteen, in Tracy, *Short History*.

14. Huston Smith, "Postmodernism and the World's Religions," in Walter Truett Anderson, ed., *The Truth about the Truth* (New York: Tarcher/Putnam Book, 1995), p. 205.

15. Cf. David Tracy's statement on the hermeneutic history of the Bible: "The problem of interpretation becomes a central issue in cultural periods of crisis. So it was for the Stoics and their reinterpretation of the Greek and Roman myths. So it was for those Jews and Christians who developed the allegorical methods. And so it is for Jews and Christians since the emergence of historical consciousness." See his *Short History*, p. 154.

16. For a detailed discussion on Zhu Xi's hermeneutics, see Daniel Gardner, *Learning to Be a Sage: Selections from the Conversation of Master Chu, Arranged Topically* (Berkeley: University of California Press, 1990), pp. 42–54, 79–80, Van Zoren, *Poetry*, pp. 230–49, and Matthew Levy, "Chu Hsi Reading the Classics: Reading to Taste the Tao," paper presented at the International Conference on the Chinese Hermeneutical Traditions, Rutgers University, October 1996.

17. Wing-tsit Chan, *Sourcebook*, p. 97.

18. Note that Tu Wei-ming translates *yong* as commonality. Note also that Wm. Theodore de Bary, in his *The Liberal Tradition in China* (New York: Columbia University Press, 1983), translates the term *xinfa* as "The Method or System of the Mind-and-Heart." F. W. Mote has objected to this translation. See his "The Limits of Intellectual History?" *Ming Studies* 19 (Fall 1984):17–25. On Zhu Xi's compilation, see Qian Mu, *Zhuzi xinxue'an* (A New Study on the Learning of Master Chu), 3 vols. (Chengdu: Bashu shushe, 1987), vol. 2, pp. 1355–88.

19. Quoted in Qian Mu, *Zhuzi*, p. 1379.

20. Quoted in ibid.

21. RCYL, 7/1a.

22. RCYL, 15/7a.

23. "Zhongyong yulun" (Further Thoughts on the *Mean*), 1a–b.

24. RCYL, 7/5a–b.

25. RCYL, 8/2b.

26. RCYL, 8/2b–3a.

27. RCYL, 8/4b–5b.

28. Li Guangdi, *Sishu jieyi* (Explaining the Meanings of the Four Books), "fafan" (Explanatory Statement), 2a.

29. *Zhongyong zhangduan* (Chapters and Sections of the *Mean*), "xu" (preface), 1a–b.

30. Ibid., 3b.

31. Ibid., 3b.

32. Ibid., 19b.

33. Ibid., 1a.

34. On Zhu Xi's modification of the *Great Learning*, see Daniel Gardner, *Chu Hsi and the Ta-hsueh* (Cambridge, Mass.: Harvard University

Press, 1986), pp. 36–37. On the general history of the textual revisions of the Classic, see Huang Chin-shing, "Lixue," pp. 351–91.

35. Zhu Xi, *Sishu zhangju jizhu* (Annotations to the *Sishu zhangju*) (Taipei: Zhonghua, 1983), p. 3.

36. Wang Mouhong, *Zhuzi nianpu* (A Biographical Annals of the Life of Zhu Xi) (Taipei: Shangwu, 1982), p. 226.

37. Zhu Xi, *Sishu*, pp. 6–7.

38. See Zhu Xi, *Zhuzi yulei*, p. 421.

39. "*Daxue guben shuo*," "jiuxu" (the original preface), 1a–b.

40. RCYL, 1/10b. Here, without much explanation, Guangdi seemed to imply that Zhu Xi took "the clear character" to mean "the mind-heart." He was not being quite fair to Zhu. Even though Zhu did use the mind-heart (*xin*) to explain the clear character, he also saw the latter as the fundamental substance (*benti*). See *Zhuzi yulei* (Topically Arranged Conversations of Master Zhu) (Beijing: Zhonghua, 1986), pp. 374–79.

41. RCYL, 1/17a–b.

42. RCYL, 1/13b.

43. RCYL, 1/14a, 16b.

44. RCYL, 1/16b.

45. RCYL, 1/19a.

46. RCQJ, 6/9a.

47. RCQJ, 6/11a–b.

48. *Analects*, BK.I, CH. XV. See Legge, vol. 1, p. 144. Legge's translation modified here.

49. Zhu Xi, *Sishu jizhu* (Anthology of Annotations of the Four Books) (Sichuan: Bashu, 1986), 1/7a.

50. *Lunyu zhaji*, 1/6b.

51. *Sishu jizhu*, 9/1b–2a.

52. *Lunyu zhaji*, 2/23a–24a.

53. *Analects*, BK.VII, CH.VI. See Legge, vol. 1, p. 196. Legge's translation modified.

54. *Lunyu zhaji*, 1/22b.

55. *Analects*, BK.XIV,CH.XLV. See Legge, vol. 1, p. 292. Legge's translation modified.

56. *Lunyu zhaji*, 2/14b.

57. *Analects*, BK.XVI, CH.VIII. See Legge, vol. 1, p. 313.

58. *Lunyu zhaji*, 2/30a–b.

59. *Analects*, BK.II, CH.III. See Legge, vol.1, pp. 146–47.

60. *Lunyu zhaji*, 1/8b–9a.

61. On Guangdi's exegetical studies of the *Changes*, see Zeng Qunhai, "Li Guangdi de Yixue chutan" (A Preliminary Inquiry into Li

Guangdi's Study of the *Changes*), in *Qing tai jingxue guoji yantaohui lunwenji* (A Collection of Essays from the International Conference on Classical Learning in the Qing Period) (Taipei: Zhongyang yanjiuyuan Zhongguo wenzhe yanjiusuo, 1994), pp. 193–214. While this work is excellent in providing a general outline of Guangdi's study of the *Changes* in the exegetical vein, it does not probe the philosophical import and purport of Guangdi's hermeneutics.

62. On Guangdi's compilation of this text, see, for instance, Chen Jinkun, "Zhouyi zhezhong 'mingbenyi' 'zhidayi' de Yixue sixiang" (The Ideas of "Knowing the Original Meanings" and "Knowing the Profound Meanings" in the *Zhouyi zhezhong*) in Yang Guozhen et al., *Li Guangdi*, pp. 252–63. See also Zeng Qunhai, pp. 205–8.

63. RCYL, 9/9b.

64. *Zhouyi tonglun*, 1/7a–b.

65. Paul Ricoeur, "The Hermeneutical Function of Distanciation," in *Paul Ricoeur: Hermeneutics and the Human Sciences*, edited and translated by John B. Thompson (Cambridge: Cambridge University Press, 1981), p. 131.

66. *Zhouyi tonglun*, 2/31b–32a.

67. The *Wenyan* constitutes one of the so-called Ten Wings (*Shiyi*) of the *Changes*, which are exegetical materials attached to the main text of the Classic.

68. *Zhouyi tonglun*, 4/11b–12a.

69. *Zhouyi tonglun*, 4/12a.

70. *Zhouyi tonglun*, 3/9a–b.

71. *Zhouyi tonglun*, 3/10a–b.

72. On the *Fu* hexagram, see Richard John Lynn, trans., *The Classic of Change: A New Translation of the I Ching as Interpreted by Wang Bi* (New York: Columbia University Press, 1994), pp. 285–92. See also Richard Wilhelm, trans. (rendered into English by Cary Baynes), *The I Ching or the Book of Changes* (Princeton: Princeton University Press, 1977), pp. 97–100.

73. *Zhouyi tonglun*, 2/35a–35b.

74. On the *Wu Wang* hexagram, see Lynn, pp. 293–98, and Wilhelm, pp. 100–103.

75. *Zhouyi tonglun*, 2/36a–b.

76. Martin Buber, *The Prophetic Faith*, translated by C. Witten-Davis (New York: Harper and Row, 1960), p. 58.

77. Tracy, *Plurality and Ambiguity*, p. 12.

78. Tracy, *Analogical Imagination*, pp. 132–34.

79. Northrop Frye, *The Great Code: The Bible and Literature* (New York: Harcourt Brace Jovanovich, 1982), pp. xvi–xix.

80. Ibid., pp. 32–34.

81. Frank Kermode, *The Classic* (New York: Viking Press, 1975), pp. 44–45.

82. Tracy, *Analogical Imagination*, p. 102. This idea of "excess of meaning" may be understood as analogous to Lévi-Strauss's theory of a "surplus of signifier" regarding shamanism. The shaman provides not a direct cure but rather a general language of symbols and rituals that enable the ready expression and release of psychic states which may otherwise be suppressed. See Kermode, pp. 135–36.

83. Tracy, *Analogical Imagination*, pp. 118–22. See also David Couzens Hoy, *The Critical Circle: Literature and History in Contemporary Hermeneutics* (Berkeley: University of California Press, 1978), pp. 41–78. Hoy's characterization of the hermeneutic procedures is based on his understanding of Gadamer's methods.

84. Tracy, *Analogical Imagination*, p. 103.

85. Buber, *Prophetic Faith*, p. 165.

86. Martin Buber, "Biblical Humanism," in *On the Bible*, edited by N. Glatzer (New York: Schocken, 1982), p. 213. See also *Prophetic Faith*, p. 169.

87. *Zhongyong zhangduan*, preface, 1b.

88. RCYL, 1/1b.

89. RCYL, 1/3b.

90. Gadamer, *Truth*, pp. 184–97.

91. On Gadamer's objection to such programmatic hermeneutics, see Hans-Georg Gadamer, *Truth and Method*, 2nd rev. ed., translated by Joel Weinsheimer and Donald Marshall (New York: Continuum, 1994), pp. 173–218. See also Georgia Warnke, *Gadamer: Hermeneutics, Tradition and Reason* (Cambridge, U.K.: Polity Press, 1987), chapter one.

92. On the contents, nature, and goals of Qing *kaozheng* learning, see Elman, *From Philosophy*, especially pp. 37–137.

93. "Li xu" (The Preface by Li), in *Sishu jieyi*, 1a–2b.

94. On Dilthey, see Gadamer, *Truth*, pp. 231–42.

95. RCYL, 9/2a.

96. RCYL, 9/8b–9a.

97. Paul Ricoeur, "Explanation and Understanding," in *The Philosophy of Paul Ricoeur* (New York: Beacon, 1978), p. 165. On this point, see also Steven Kepnes, *The Text as Thou: Martin Buber's Dialogical Hermeneutics and Narrative Theology* (Bloomington: Indiana University Press, 1992), pp. 37–40.

98. Gadamer, *Truth*, p. 358.

99. Ibid., p. 288.

100. Ibid., pp. 265–71, 291–300.

101. Ibid., pp. 300–307.

102. Martin Buber, "Education," in *Between Man and Man*, edited by Maurice Friedman, translated by R. G. Smith (New York: Macmillan, 1965), p. 97.

103. Gadamer, *Truth*, pp. 378–79.

104. RCYL, 1/1a.

105. On the Neo-Confucian belief in the oneness of all minds and its epistemological implications, see Daniel Gardner, "Modes of Thinking and Modes of Discourse in the Sung: Some Thoughts on the *Yü-lu* ('Recorded Conversations') Texts," *Journal of Asian Studies* 50.3(August 1991):574–603.

106. *Daxue guben shuo*, 4a.

107. Tracy, *Plurality*, p. 9.

108. Gadamer, *Truth*, p. xxxi.

Chapter Six. Vita Activa

1. RCYL, 33/3b. Quoted in chapter four.

2. On Aristotle's definition of praxis, see Calvin Schrag, pp. 18–21.

3. "What Does Humanism Mean?" David Stewart, trans., in David Stewart and Joseph Bien, eds., *Political and Social Essays* (Athens: Ohio University Press, 1974), p. 79.

4. Hannah Arendt, *Between Past and Present* (London: Penguin, 1978 reprint), pp. 3–4.

5. Wm. Theodore de Bary, *The Trouble with Confucianism* (Cambridge, Mass.: Harvard University Press, 1991), pp. 17–23. For a discussion specifically devoted to the Confucian "utilitarian" orientation toward the direct organization of the state and society as the means to fulfill the Way, see Tillman, *Utilitarian Confucianism*, and *Ch'en Liang*.

6. On the Confucian emphasis on action in the sociopolitical domains, apart from the works cited in note 5, see the following: Yü Ying-shih, "Qingdai sixiangshi zhongyao guannian tongshi" (General Explanations of the Important Concepts in Qing Intellectual History), in Yü Ying-shih, *Zhongguo sixiang chuantong de xiandai quanshi* (Contemporary Interpretations of Traditional Chinese Thought) (Taipei: Lianjing, 1987), pp. 418–31, Hao Chang, "Neo-Confucian Moral Thought and Its Modern Legacy," *Journal of Asian Studies* 39.2(February 1980):199–203, Hao Chang, "On the *Ching-shih* Ideal," Hao Chang, "SongMing yilai rujia jingshi sixiang shishi" (A Tentative Interpretation of Confucian Thought on Statecraft since the Song and Ming), in Zhongyang yanjiuyuan jindaishi yanjiuso, ed., *Jinshi Zhongguo jingshi sixiang yantaohui lunwenji* (Proceedings of the Conference on the Theory of Statecraft in Modern China)

(Taipei: Zhongyang yanjiuyuan, 1984), pp. 3–19, Tu Wei-ming, *Way, Learning, and Politics*, especially pp. 1–28, and Benjamin Schwartz, "Some Polarities in Confucian Thought," in David Nivison and Arthur Wright, eds., *Confucianism in Action* (Stanford: Stanford University Press, 1959), pp. 50–62.

7. De Bary, *Trouble*, p. 22.

8. Ibid., p. xii.

9. RCYL, 27/1a.

10. RCYL, 27/5a.

11. RCYL, 27/6a–b.

12. RCYL, 27/12b.

13. "Dushu bilu" (Notes Taken While Reading), in RCQJ, 2/24a.

14. Hao Chang, "On the *Ching-shih* Ideal," pp. 38–46.

15. Metzger, *Escape from Predicament*, pp. 15, 196–210.

16. "Shangshu judu," in RCQJ, 4/4b–5a.

17. RCQJ, 4/10a–b.

18. RCQJ, 4/11a.

19. RCQJ, 4/11b.

20. These nine virtues are enumerated in the chapter entitled "The Counsels of Gaoyao" (*Gaoyao mo*). Here in "Establishing Government," they are simply referred to without elaboration. See Legge, *Chinese Classics*, vol. 3, p. 71.

21. RCQJ, 4/14b–15b.

22. RCQJ, 4/18a–b.

23. RCQJ, 4/21b–22a.

24. *DaQing shichao shengxun: Shengzu renhuangdi* (Imperial Instructions of the Ten Reigns of the Great Qing Dynasty: The Reign of Kangxi) (Taipei: Wenhai, 1965 reprint), 7/2b.

25. Hao Chang, "On the *Ching-shih* Ideal," pp. 45–50.

26. "Lunyu zhaji," 2/7a.

27. RCYL, 22/17b.

28. RCYLXJ, 8/17b.

29. RCYLXJ, 9/3a.

30. RCYLXJ, 9/1a.

31. RCYL, 27/11b.

32. Thomas Metzger has described the Qing bureaucratic corruption as a "massive phenomenon," of which the Qing officials themselves were quite aware. See Metzger, pp. 167–72.

33. For a description of the activities of the unscrupulous lower gentry, see T'ung-tsu Ch'u, *Local Government in China under the Ch'ing* (Stanford: Stanford University Press, 1969), pp. 185–90. The transgressions listed by Guangdi were apparently quite commonplace, according to

Ch'u's study. On the practice of the sale of ranks in the Kangxi period, see Lawrence Kessler, *K'ang-hsi and the Consolidation of Ch'ing Rule, 1661–1684* (Chicago: University of Chicago Press, 1976), pp. 156–58.

34. RCQJ, 26/9b–17b.

35. RCYL, 27/7b–8a.

36. RCYL, 27/11b.

37. RCYL, 27/14b.

38. RCQJ, 20/2b–5a.

39. RCYL, 14/15a–b.

40. RCQJ, 20/2b. Interestingly, Guangdi sometimes also used mathematics to interpret the *Classic of Changes*. For instance, the statement on the second line (*yao*) of the *Kun* hexagram reads: "He is straight (*zhi*), square (*fang*), and great (*da*), so without working at it, nothing he does here fails to be fitting." Guangdi glosses the meaning and significance of this statement as follows: "All mathematics begin with a point. In the beginning, there is only a point which, when extended and lengthened, becomes a line. When four lines of equal length join to form a square, there is a surface. With the layering of surfaces comes a structure. 'Straight, square and great' mean precisely this. Straight refers to the line, square the surface, and great the structure. Only with straightness can there be a square; only with squareness can something become great. . . . Therefore, [the commentary of the image of the hexagram] says, 'With the establishment of reverence and rightness, one keeps oneself from isolation.'" Guangdi here interprets the mathematical connections as the moral nexus between reverence and rightness. See RCYL, 9/25a–b. On the introduction of Western mathematics in the late Ming and early Qing, see Kessler, pp. 146–47.

41. RCQJ, 14/19b.

42. RCQJ, 14/21b.

43. *Nianpu*, 1/17b–18a.

44. *Nianpu*, 2/1a–b.

45. RCYL, 27/13b.

46. "Zhouguan biji," in RCQJ, 5/5b.

47. *Kangxi zhengyao* (Highlights of the Administration of the Kangxi Reign), compiled by Wang Youli (Taipei: Huawen, 1969), 1/6a–b.

48. RCYL, 27/5a.

49. RCQJ, 27/3a–4b. See also *Nianpu*, 2/9b–13b. Note that one of his memorials on flood control can be found in the famous *Anthology of Writings on Statecraft in the Imperial Dynasty* (Huangchao jingshi wenbian), compiled by He Changling et al. (Taipei: Wenhai, 1971), 110/13a–b.

50. RCQJ, 27/12a–13a.

51. RCYL, 27/2a.

52. "Guanlan lu" (Notes Recorded While Watching the Waves), in RCQJ, 1/25a.

53. "Guanlan lu," 1/26b–27a.
54. RCYL, 27/1b.
55. *Nianpu*, 2/9b–11b.
56. RCQJ, 27/6b.
57. RCQJ, 26/6b–7a.
58. RCQJ, 27/7b–11b.
59. RCQJ, 27/13b–15a.
60. RCQJ, 27/15a–b. On the establishment and operation of granaries in the Qing, see Kung-chuan Hsiao, *Rural China: Imperial Control in the Nineteenth Century* (Seattle: University of Washington Press, 1960), pp. 144–59. Note that one of Guangdi's memorials concerning the need to maintain grain and rice reserve in the granaries can be found in the *Huangchao jingshi wenbian*, 39/7a–b.
61. RCQJ, 26/17b–20a.
62. RCQJ, 26/4a–6b.
63. RCQJ, 26/20b–22b.
64. RCYL, 27/3a–b.
65. Metzger, pp. 169–70.
66. J. G. A. Pocock, *Politics, Language and Time: Essays on Political Thought* (New York: Atheneum, 1971), pp. 44, 46.
67. Kai-wing Chow, pp. 44–46. See also John D. Langlois Jr., "Chinese Culturalism and the Yüan Analogy: Seventeenth-Century Perspectives," *Harvard Journal of Asiatic Studies* 40.1(June 1980):355–98.
68. RCYL, 27/15b–16a.
69. RCQJ,1/9a.
70. RCYL, 27/16b–17a.
71. RCYL, 27/18b.
72. RCQJ, 1/9a.
73. RCQJ, 6/22a–b.
74. "Zhouli sande liude shuo" (On the *Rites of Zhou*'s Ideas of the "Three Categories of Virtues" and the "Six Virtues"), in RCQJ, 16/16a–18b.
75. RCYL, 3/2b.
76. RCYL, 2/8b–9a.
77. Cf. Pocock, pp. 43–46, 78–79.
78. Kai-wing Chow, pp. 71–128.
79. "Jiamiao jixiangli lüe," in RCQJ, 5b.
80. RCQJ, 21/4a–9a. See also RCYL, 27/19b–22b.
81. "Shizu ciji li lüe," in *Rongcun xuji*, 6/14a–16b.
82. RCYL, 27/23b–24a. Note that three essays by Guangdi on the rituals concerning lineage can be found in the *Huangchao jingshih wenbian*, 66/1b–2a, 5a–6a, 6a–7a.
83. This is the main thesis of Kai-wing Chow's monograph.

84. *Huangchao jingshi wenbian*, 60/6b–7a.

85. An excellent examination of the formation and development of the Confucian temple can be found in Huang Chin-shing, *Youru shengyu*, pp. 125–325. See also Thomas Wilson, "The Ritual Formation of Confucian Orthodoxy and the Descendants of the Sage," *Journal of Asian Studies* 55.3 (August 1996):559–84, and John K. Shryock, *The Origin and Development of the State Cult of Confucius* (New York: Paragon Book Reprint Corp., 1932, reprint 1966).

86. On the evolution of this institution, see Huang Chin-shing, *Youru shengyu*, p. 226–311.

87. On the Ming reform, see ibid., pp. 133–48.

88. RCQJ, 21/1a–3b.

89. *Nianpu*, 2/50a–b. See also RCYL, 27/17a–18b.

Concluding Reflections

1. Ivanhoe, *Confucian*, pp. 98–99. See also his "Character Consequentialism: An Early Confucian Contribution to Contemporary Ethical Theory," *Journal of Religious Ethics* 19.1(Spring 1991):55–70.

2. Anne Birdwhistell, *Li Yong (1627–1705) and Epistemological Dimensions of Confucian Philosophy* (Stanford: Stanford University Press, 1996).

3. Bernard Williams, *Ethics and the Limits of Philosophy* (Cambridge, Mass.: Harvard University Press, 1985), pp. 1–21, 197–202, and Julia Annas, *The Morality of Happiness* (New York: Oxford University Press, 1993), pp. 27–34. Note that for Williams, philosophy, especially that which is indentured to the imposition of rationality through reductive theory, has its limits in proffering truly meaningful answers, because its theoretical reflection often falls shorts of squaring with practice.

4. Richard Norman, *The Moral Philosophers: An Introduction to Ethics* (Oxford: Clarendon Press, 1983), pp. 1–3.

5. Schwartz, *World*, pp. 51–52.

6. See, for instance, his *Confucian Thought: Selfhood as Creative Transformation* (Albany: State University of New York Press, 1985), especially pp. 19–33, 131–46.

7. Rodney Taylor, "The Sage as Saint: The Confucian Tradition," in Richard Kieckhefer and George Bond, eds., *Sainthood: Its Manifestations in World Religions* (Berkeley: University of California Press, 1988), p. 220.

8. Mary Evelyn Tucker, "Religious Dimensions of Confucianism: Cosmology and Cultivation," *Philosophy East and West* 48.1(January 98):14.

9. On-cho Ng, "Mystical Oneness and Meditational Praxis: Religiousness in Li Yong's (1627–1705) Confucian Thought," *Journal of Chinese Religions* 22(Fall 1994):75–102.

10. Mihaly Csikszentmihalyi, *Flow: The Psychology of Optimal Experience* (New York: Harper and Row, 1990).

11. A concise and convenient summation of flow can be found in the sequel, Mihaly Csikszentmihalyi, *The Evolving Self: A Psychology for the Third Millennium* (New York: HaperCollins, 1993), pp. xiii–xviii. On transcender, see pp. 207–49.

Glossary of Transliterations

airan 靄然
ban 頒
baolan 包攬
Benchao renwu 本朝人物
benti 本體
benxin 本心
bumian er zhong 不勉而中
buren 不仁
busi er de 不思而得
buza 不雜
buzheng shi 布政使
buzhuan 補傳
cai 才
caiqing 才情
caixing 才性
changping cang 長平倉
Chen Menglci 陳夢雷
Chen Que 陳確
Chen Xianzhang 陳獻章
cheng 誠
chengming 誠明
chengming zhi xue 誠明之學
chengshen 誠身
chengwu 成物
chengyi 誠意
Chengyi zhang 誠意章
chijing 持敬
chishou 持守
chuandao 傳道
chuanjing 傳經
Chuxia lu 初夏錄
cise 辭色
congsi 從祠
cun 存
cun shixin 存實心
cuncheng 存誠
cunxing 存性
da zongfa 大宗法
dade 大德
dafa 大法
Dai Mingshi 戴名世
danggu 黨錮
dangran 當然
dangran zhi li 當然之理
dangran zhi ze 當然之則
dao qi shun 道其順
dao wenxue 道問學
daotong 道統
daoxin 道心
daoxue 道學
daru 大儒
dati 大體
Daxue bian 大學辨
Daxue guben shuo 大學古本說
Daxue zhangju 大學章句
Dazhuan 大傳
de zhi ben 德之本
dexing 德性

di 地
ding yu yi 定於一
dong 動
duan 端
dungen 鈍根
duowen duojian 多聞多見
dushu fa 讀書法
erxing 二性
fa (issuance) 發
fa (law, method) 法
Fan Bao 方苞
fangxin 放心
fen 分
Fu 復
fu 賦
Gao Panlong 高樊龍
genben 根本
Geng Jingzhong 耿精忠
gewu 格物
gezhi 格致
gijutsu 技術
gong (public) 公
gong (tribute) 貢
gongfu 功夫
Gu Xiancheng 顧憲成
guan 貫
Guan Zhidao 管志道
guben 古本
gueishen 鬼神
guyi 古意
Hanxue 漢學
hanyang 涵養
hanyong 涵泳
he 和
heng 亨
houzhu shenpei 厚聚深培
Huang Daozhou 黃道周
Huangchao jingshi wenbian 皇朝經世文編
Huang Qing jingjie 皇清經解
Huang Qing jingjie xubian 皇清經解續編
ji 極
ji gaoming 極高明
ji juexue 繼絕學
Jiamiao jixiang li lüe 家廟祭享禮略
jiangxue 講學
jianwen 見聞
jiao 教
jiexia 浹洽
jing (classics) 經
jing (equanimity, tranquility) 靜
jing (reverence) 敬
jingshi 經世
Jingshu biji 經書筆記
jingtian 敬天
jingyan 經延
jinxue 進學
jishan chengxing 繼善成性
jissen 實踐
Jiudi 九諦
jue 覺
jueyu 絕欲
jujing 居敬
jujing qiongli 居敬窮理
junzi benti 君子本體
juren 舉人
kaozheng xue 考証學
keisei chiyô no gaku 經世致用の學
keishi 經史
kueikong 虧空
Kun 坤
lei 類
li (furthering) 利
li (principle) 理
li (ritual-propriety) 禮
li (studious action) 力
Li Guangdi 李光地
li ji qi 立其氣
Li zheng 立政
liangneng 良能
liangxin 良心
liangzhi 良知
liangzuo 良佐

licheng 立誠
Lifa 立法
ligen 利根
linggen 靈根
liu xing 六行
Liu Zongzhou 劉宗周
liuyi 六藝
lixing 立性
liyi fenshu 理一分殊
lizhi 立志
Lu Longqi 陸隴其
Lu Shiyi 陸世儀
Lunyu zhaji 論語劄記
Mei Wending 梅文鼎
miao 妙
miaohe 妙合
ming 命
ming mingde 明明德
ming shili 明實理
ming zhi ti 命之體
ming zhi yong 命之用
mingcheng 明誠
mingshan zhixing 明善知性
mingxing 明性
minqing 民情
minsheng 民生
mou 畝
Nanshan ji ou chao 南山集偶鈔
neige 內閣
neisheng 內聖
peixiang 配享
pian 偏
pin 品
ping tianxia 平天下
qi 氣
qi ji li 氣即理
Qian 乾
Qian Dehong 錢德洪
Qian Yiben 錢一本
qianyuan 乾元
qibing 氣禀
qing 情
qing zhi xing 情之性
qingtan 清談
qiongli 窮理
qizhi 氣質
qizhi zhi xing 氣質之性
quan 權
Quan Zuwang 全祖望
ren 仁
ren zhi ben 仁之本
rencai 人才
rendao 人道
renji 人極
renlun 人倫
renxin 人心
renxing 人性
renyu 人欲
renzheng 仁政
rijiang 日講
Rongcun pulu hekao 榕村譜錄合考
Rongcun shuwu 榕村書屋
rongmao 容貌
san de 三德
san jun 三俊
san xing 三行
san zhe 三宅
sangang 三綱
sanpin 三品
shan 善
shangdi 上帝
Shangshu judu 尚書句讀
shannian 善念
she cang 社倉
shen 神
shendu 慎獨
shenduan qifou 神短氣浮
sheng 生
shengwu 生物
shengxian zhi xue 聖賢之學
Shengxue zongyao 聖學宗要
shengyuan 生員
shengzhi 生知
shi 實

shi er jin xing 實而盡性
Shi Lang 施琅
Shi wo 時我
shiren 侍人
shiti 實體
shiwu 時務
shizhe 十哲
shizu 始祖
Shizu ciji li lüe 始祖祠祭禮略
shuaixing 率性
shui 税
shunyou 純佑
si 私
Sibianlu jiyao 思辨錄輯要
side 四德
siduan 四端
siju jiao 四句教
sipei 四配
siwu 四無
siyou 四有
Songxue 宋學
Suan fa 算法
Sun Shenxing 孫慎行
suoyi 所以
suoyiran 所以然
suran 肅然
taiji 太極
taixu 太虛
Tanggao 湯誥
tanggu 黨詘
tanhua 探花
ti 體
ti qi jian 體其健
tiandao 天道
tiande 天德
tiandi zhi de 天地之德
tiandi zhi xing 天地之性
tianli 天理
tianming 天命
tianming zhi xing 天命之性
tianren heyi 天人合一
tianren yili 天人一理
tiaomu 條目
tonglei 同類
tongnian 同年
tongsheng 童生
tongti 統體
tongti de yitaiji 統體的一太極
tongzheng shi 通政使
Tuanci 彖辭
Tuanzhuan 彖傳
waiwang 外王
wang fa 王法
Wang Ji 王畿
wanshu 萬殊
wanwu yiti 萬物一體
wei 威
weidao 為道
weifa 未發
weishan 為善
weitian 畏天
weiyi 威儀
wen 文
Wenmiao peixiang siyi 文廟配享私議
Wenyan 文言
wu'e 無惡
wu (emptiness) 無
wu (enlightenment) 悟
wu (things) 物
Wu Wang 無妄
wuchang zhi ben 五常之本
wudui 無對
wuji 無極
wuqing wuxin 無情無心
wushan wu'e 無善無惡
wuwu zhi taiji 物物之太極
wuxing 五行
wuyi wuwo 無意無我
xi 習
xianhou 先後
xianzu 先祖
xiao 孝
xiao zongfa 小宗法

xiaokang 小康
xiaoxin 小心
Xiaoxin zhai 小心齋
xiaren 下人
Xici zhuan 繫辭傳
xin (mind-heart) 心
xin (trustworthiness) 信
Xin xing shuo 心性説
xin zhi lingming 心之靈明
xin zhi ti 心之體
xinde 心德
xinfa 心法
xing (action, practice) 行
xing (nature) 性
xing shan 性善
xing shishi 行實事
xing zhi ben 性之本
xing zhi de 性之德
xing zhi qing 性之情
xing zhi shili 性之實理
xing zhi xing 性之性
Xingjie 性解
Xingli jingyi 性理精義
xingqi 形器
Xingshan tushuo 性善圖説
xingshang 形上
xingti 性體
xingxia 形下
xinxue 心學
xinzheng 新政
xinzhi 心知
xiushen 修身
xu 虚
xu er shunli 虚而順理
Xu Fuyuan 許孚遠
Xu Qianxue 徐乾學
xue 學
xuewen 學問
xungu 訓詁
yangxing 養性
yangyang 洋洋
yao 爻
Yao Yue 堯曰
yi (disposition) 彝
yi (rightness) 義
yi (will, purport) 意
yide 懿德
yifa 以發
yiguan xingshan 一貫性善
yili 義理
yili zhi xing 義理之性
yili zhi xue 義理之學
yishu 遺書
yizhi yineng 已知已能
yong (commonality) 庸
yong (courage) 勇
yong (utility, function) 用
you 右
youyou 遊遊
yu 欲
Yu Chenglong 于成龍
yuan 元
zhangju 章句
zhen (authenticity) 真
zhen (perseverence) 貞
zheng 正
Zheng Chenggong 鄭成功
Zheng Jing 鄭精
Zhengmin 蒸民
zhengxin 正心
zhengxin chengyi 正心誠意
Zhengxing bian 証性編
zhengxue 正學
zhi (highest) 至
zhi (orderly rule) 治
zhi (to extend to the utmost) 致
zhi (wisdom, knowledge) 知
zhi guangda 致廣大
zhi liangzhi 致良知
zhi yu zhishan 止於至善
zhi zhi zhi 知之致
zhiben 知本
zhicheng 至誠
zhicheng jinxing 知誠盡性

zhidao 治道
zhide 治德
zhiguo 治國
zhishan 至善
zhixing 知行
zhiyi shang 質疑上
zhiyi xia 質疑下
zhizhi (completion of knowledge) 知至
zhizhi (extension of knowledge to the utmost) 致知
zhong (centrality) 中
zhong (loyalty) 忠
zhong (moral gravity) 重
Zhongyong zhangduan 中庸章段
Zhongyong zhangju 中庸章句
Zhou Rudeng 周汝登
Zhouyi tonglun 周易通論
Zhouyi zhezhong 周易折中
zhujing 主敬
zhusheng 諸生
Zhuzi daquan 朱子大全
ziran 自然
zishou 自守
zisi 自思
zong 宗
zongzhi 宗旨
zongzi 宗子
Zuiyan 罪言
Zun dexing 尊德性
Zun Zhu yaozhi 尊朱要旨
zunchen zhi yi 尊臣之義
zuo 左

Selected Bibliography of Works Cited

Ames, Roger. "Foreword," in Hoyt Cleveland Tillman, *Ch'en Liang on Public Interest and the Law*. Honolulu: University of Hawaii Press, 1994. Pp. ix–xiv.

Ames, Roger. "The Mencian Conception of *Ren Xing*: Does It Mean 'Human Nature'?," in Henry Rosemont, ed., *Chinese Texts and Philosophical Contexts: Essays Dedicated to Angus C. Graham*. La Salle, Ill.: Open Court, 1991. Pp. 143–75.

Annas, Julia. *The Morality of Happiness*. New York: Oxford University Press, 1993.

Arendt, Hannah. *Between Past and Present*. London: Penguin, 1978 reprint.

Barthes, Roland. "The Death of the Author," in Roland Barthes, *Image, Music, Text*. Translated by S. Heath. New York: Hill and Wang, 1977.

Berling, Judith. "Embodying Philosophy: Some Preliminary Reflections from a Chinese Perspective," in Frank E. Reynolds and David Tracy, eds., *Discourse and Practice*. Albany: State University of New York Press, 1992. Pp. 233–60.

Bernstein, Richard J. *Praxis and Action: Contemporary Philosophies of Human Activity*. Philadelphia: University of Pennsylvania Press, 1971.

Birdwhistell, Anne. *Li Yong (1627–1705) and Epistemological Dimensions of Confucian Philosophy*. Stanford: Stanford University Press, 1996.

Black, Allison Harley. *Man and Nature in the Philosophical Thought of Wang Fu-chih*. Seattle: University of Washington Press, 1989.

Bloom, Irene, trans. and ed. *Knowledge Painfully Acquired: The K'un-chih chi by Lo Ch'in-shun*. New York: Columbia University Press, 1987.

Bloom, Irene. "Mencian Argument on Human Nature (*Jen Xing*)," *Philosophy East and West* 44.1(January 1994):19–53.

Buber, Martin. "Biblical Humanism," in Martin Buber, *On the Bible*. Edited by N. Glatzer. New York: Schocken, 1982.

Buber, Martin. "Education," in Martin Buber, *Between Man and Man*. Edited by Maurice Friedman and translated by G. Smith. New York: Macmillan, 1965.

Buber, Martin. *The Prophetic Faith*. Translated by C. Witten-Davis. New York: Harper and Row, 1960.

Busch, Heinrich. "The Tung-lin Academy and Its Political and Philosophical Significance," *Monumenta Serica* 14(1949–1955):1–63.

Cai, Guanle. *Qingdai qibai mingren zhuan* (Biographies of Seven Hundred Eminent Personages in the Qing Period). Beijing: Zhongguo shudian, 1984 reprint.

Ch'ien, Edward T. *Chiao Hung and the Restructuring of Neo-Confucianism in the Late Ming*. New York: Columbia University Press, 1986.

Ch'u, T'ung-tsu. *Local Government in China under the Ch'ing*. Stanford: Stanford University Press, 1969.

Chan, Wing-tsit. "The *Hsing-li ching-i* and the Ch'eng-Chu School of the Seventeenth Century," in Wm. Theodore de Bary, ed., *The Unfolding of Neo-Confucianism*. New York: Columbia University Press, 1975. Pp. 543–79.

Chan, Wing-tsit. *A Sourcebook in Chinese Philosophy*. Princeton: Princeton University Press, 1963.

Chang, Hao. "Neo-Confucian Moral Thought and Its Modern Legacy," *Journal of Asian Studies* 39.2(February 1980):199–203.

Chang, Hao. "On the *Ching-shih* Ideal in Neo-Confucianism," *Ch'ing-shih wen-t'i* 3.1(November 1974):38–46.

Chang, Hao. "SongMing yilai rujia jingshi sixiang shishi" (A Tentative Interpretation of Statecraft in Confucianism Since the Song and Ming), in Zhongyang yanjiuyuan jindaishi yanjiusuo, ed., *Jinshi Zhongguo jingshi sixiang yantaohui lunwenji* (Proceedings of the Conference on the Theory of Statecraft in Modern China). Taipei: Zhongyang yanjiuyuan, 1984.

Chen, Jinkun. "Zhouyi zhezhong mingbenyi zhidayi de Yixue sixiang" (The Ideas of "Knowing the Original Meanings" and "Knowing the Profound Meanings" in the *Zhouyi zhezhong*), in Yang Guozhen et al., *Li Guangdi yanjiu* (Studies on Li Guangdi). Fujian: Xiamen daxue, 1993. Pp. 252–63.

Chen, Que. *Chen Que ji* (Collected Works of Chen Que). Beijing: Zhonghua, 1979.

Cheng, Chung-ying. "Practical Learning in Yen Yuan, Chu Hsi and Wang Yang-ming," in Wm. Theodore de Bary and Irene Bloom, eds.,

Principle and Practicality. New York: Columbia University Press, 1979. Pp. 37–67.

Chow, Kai-wing. "The Development of Sung Learning in Ch'ing Thought," *Chinese Studies* (Hanxue yanjiu) 13.2(December 1995):47–76.

Chow, Kai-wing. *The Rise of Confucian Ritualism in Late Imperial China: Ethics, Classics, and Lineage Discourse*. Stanford: Stanford University Press, 1994.

Csikszentmihalyi, Mihaly. *Flow: The Psychology of Optimal Experience*. New York: Harper and Row, 1990.

Csikszentmihalyi, Mihaly. *The Evolving Self: A Psychology for the Third Millennium*. New York: HarperCollins, 1993.

Da Qing Shengzu Ren Kangxi huangdi shilu (The Veritable Records of the Reign of the Kangxi Emperor). Taipei: Huawen, 1964.

Da Qing shichao shengxun Shengzu renhuangdi (Imperial Instructions of the Ten Reigns of the August Qing Dynasty: The Reign of Kangxi). Taipei: Wenhai, 1965 reprint.

de Bary, Wm. Theodore. *Neo-Confucian Orthodoxy and the Learning of the Mind-and-Heart*. New York: Columbia University Press, 1981.

de Bary, Wm. Theodore. *The Liberal Tradition in China*. New York: Columbia University Press, 1983.

de Bary, Wm. Theodore. *The Message of the Mind in Neo-Confucianism*. New York: Columbia University Press, 1989.

de Bary, Wm. Theodore. *The Trouble with Confucianism*. Cambridge, Mass.: Harvard University Press, 1991.

de Bary, Wm. Theodore. *Self and Society in Ming Thought*. New York: Columbia University Press, 1970.

de Bary, Wm. Theodore, and John Chaffee, eds. *Neo-Confucian Education: The Formative Stage*. Berkeley: University of California Press, 1989.

Derrida, Jacques. "Structure, Sign and Play in the Discourse of the Human Sciences," in Richard Macksey and Eugenio Donato, eds., *The Structuralist Controversy: The Languages of Criticism and the Sciences of Man*. Baltimore: Johns Hopkins University Press, 1970. Pp. 247–64.

Derrida, Jacques. *On Grammatology*. Translated by Gayatri Chakravorty Spivak. Baltimore: Johns Hopkins University Press, 1976.

Diggins, John Patrick. *The Promise of Pragmatism: Modernism and the Crisis of Knowledge and Authority*. Chicago: University of Chicago Press, 1994.

Donglin shuyuan zhi (Records of the Donglin Academy). Taipei: Guangwen, 1968 reprint.

Fang, Bao. *Fang Bao ji* (Collection of [the Writings of] Fang Bao). Shanghai: Guji, 1983.

Foucault, Michel. "What Is an Author?" in D. Bouchard, ed., *Language, Counter-Memory, Practice*. Ithaca, N.Y.: Cornell University Press, 1977.

Frye, Northrop. *The Great Code: The Bible and Literature*. New York: Harcourt Brace Jovanovich, 1982.

Gadamer, Hans-Georg. *Truth and Method*. 2nd rev. ed. Translated by Joel Weinsheimer and Donald Marshall. New York: Continuum, 1994.

Gao, Panlong. *Gaozi yishu* (Bequeathed Writings by Master Kao). Siku quanshu edition. Taipei: Shangwu, 1983.

Gardner, Daniel K. "Confucian Commentary and Chinese Intellectual History," *Journal of Asian Studies* 57.2(May 1998):397–422.

Gardner, Daniel K. "Modes of Thinking and Modes of Discourse in the Sung: Some Thoughts on the *Yü-lu* ('Recorded Conversations') Texts," *Journal of Asian Studies* 50.3(August 1991):574–603.

Gardner, Daniel K. *Chu Hsi and the Ta-hsueh*. Cambridge, Mass.: Harvard University Press, 1986.

Ge, Rongjin, and Wang Jincai. *Lu Shiyi pingzhuan* (A Critical Biography of Lu Shiyi). Nanjing: Nanjing daxue, 1996.

Graham, A. C. "What Was New in the Ch'eng-Chu Theory of Human Nature?" in A. C. Graham, *Studies in Chinese Philosophy and Philosophical Literature*. Albany: State University of New York Press, 1990. Pp. 412–35.

Graham, A. C. "The Background of the Mencian Theory of Human Nature," in A. C. Graham, *Studies in Chinese Philosophy and Philosophical Literature*. Albany: State University of New York Press, 1990. Pp. 7–66.

Grant, Robert M., and David Tracy. *A Short History of the Interpretation of the Bible*. Philadelphia: Fortress Press, 1984.

Gu, Qingmei. "Gu Jingyang Gao Jingyi sixiang zhi bijiao yanjiu" (A Comparative Study of the Thoughts of Gu Xiancheng and Gao Panlong). Ph.D. diss., National Taiwan University, 1979.

Gu, Qingmei. "Liu Jieshán dui Yangming zhiliangzhi shuo zhi jicheng yu fazhan" (Liu Zongzhou's Continuation and Development of Wang Yangming's Teachings on the Idea of the Innate Knowledge of the Good), in Gu Qingmei, *Mingdai lixue lunwenji* (Collection of Essays on Confucianism in the Ming Period). Taipei: Da'an, 1990. Pp. 237–48.

Gu, Xiancheng. *Gu Duanwengong yishu* (Bequeathed Writings by Gu Xiancheng). N.p., 1877 edition.

Gu, Xiancheng. *Xiaoxinzhai zhaji* (Notebook from the Studio of the Prudent Heart). Taipei: Guangwen, 1975 reprint.

He, Yousen. "Qingdai jingxue sichao" (The Tides of Thought of Classical Learning in the Qing Period), in Institute of Literature and Philosophy, ed., *Qingdai jingxue guoji yantaohui lunwenji* (The Conference Proceedings of the International Meeting on Classical Learning in the Qing Period). Taipei: Institute of Literature and Philosophy, Academia Sinica, 1994. Pp. 15–29.

He, Youshen. "Qingdai Han Song zhi zheng pingyi" (A Balanced Discussion of the Debate Between Han Learning and Song Learning in the Qing), *Wen shi zhe xuebao* 27(December 1978):97–113.

Henderson, John B. *Scripture, Canon, and Commentary: A Comparison of Confucian and Western Exegesis*. Princeton: Princeton University Press, 1991.

Holmes, Oliver. *Human Reality and the Social World: Ortega's Philosophy of History*. Amherst: University of Massachusetts Press, 1975.

Hou, Wailu. *SongMing lixue shi* (A History of Confucianism in the Song and Ming). Beijing: Renmin, 1987.

Hoy, David Couzens. *The Critical Circle: Literature and History in Contemporary Hermeneutics*. Berkeley: University of California Press, 1978.

Hsiao, Kung-chuan. *Rural China: Imperial Control in the Nineteenth Century*. Seattle: University of Washington Press.

Hu, Shi. *Dai Dongyuan de zhexue* (The Philosophy of Dai Zhen). Shanghai: Commercial Press, 1927.

Huang, Dezhao. *Qingdai keju zhidu* (The Examination System in the Qing Period). Beijing: Zhonghua, 1984.

Huang, Chin-shing. "Lixue kaozhengxue yu zhengzhi: yi Daxue gaiben de fazhan wei lizheng" (Learning of Principle, Evidential Learning and Politics: Using the Developments of the Textual Alterations of the *Great Learning* as an Example), in Huang Chin-shing, *Youru shengyi* (Entering the Sage's Sanctuary). Taipei: Yunchen, 1994. Pp. 351–92.

Huang, Chin-shing. *Philosophy, Philology, and Politics in Eighteenth-Century China: Li Fu and the Lu-Wang School under the Ch'ing*. Cambridge: Cambridge University Press, 1995.

Huang, Daozhou. *Huang Zhangpu ji* (The Collected Works of Huang Daozhou). N.p.: n.d.

Huang, Daozhou. *Rongtan wenye* (The Enterprise of Inquiry and Learning in a Fuzhou Academy). Taipei: Guangwen, 1975 reprint.

Huang, Zongxi. *Mingru xue'an* (Records of the Ming Scholars). Beijing: Zhonghua, 1985.

Huang, Zongxi. *The Records of the Ming Scholars.* Edited by Julia Ching. Honolulu: University of Hawaii Press, 1987.

Huangchao jingshi wenbian (Anthology of Writings on Statecraft in Our Imperial Dynasty). Compiled by He Changling et al. Taipei: Wenhai, 1971 reprint.

Hummel, Arthur, ed. *Eminent Chinese of the Ch'ing Period.* Taipei: Ch'eng Wen Publishing Company, 1970 reprint.

Ivanhoe, P. J. "Character Consequentialism: An Early Confucian Contribution to Contemporary Ethical Theory," *Journal of Religious Ethics* 19.1(Spring 1991):55–70.

Ivanhoe, P. J. "On the Metaphysical Foundations of Neo-Confucian and New Confucianism," *Journal of Chinese Philosophy* 22(1995):81–89.

Ivanhoe, P. J. *Confucian Moral Self Cultivation.* New York: Peter Lang, 1993.

Jasper, Karl. *The Great Philosophers.* Translated by Ralph Manheim. New York: Harcourt, Brace & World, 1962.

Kangxi zhengyao (Highlights of Politics and Goverment During the Kangxi Reign). Compiled by Zhang Shen. Taipei: Huawen, 1969 reprint.

Kasulis, Thomas. "Philosophy as Praxis," in Frank Reynolds and David Tracy, eds., *Discourse and Practice.* Albany: State University of New York Press, 1992. Pp. 169–96.

Kepnes, Steven. *The Text as Thou: Martin Buber's Dialogical Hermeneutics and Narrative Theology.* Bloomington: Indiana University Press, 1992.

Kermode, Frank. *The Classic.* New York: Viking Press, 1975.

Kessler, Lawrence. *K'ang-hsi and the Consolidation of Ch'ing Rule, 1661–1684.* Chicago: University of Chicago Press, 1976.

Langlois, John D., Jr. "Chinese Culturalism and the Yuan Analogy: Seventeenth-Century Perspectives," *Harvard Journal of Asiatic Studies* 40.1(June 1980):355–98.

Lau, D. C., trans. *Mencius.* London: Penguin, 1970.

Legge, James, trans. *The Chinese Classics.* 5 vols. Hong Kong: The University of Hong Kong Press, 1960.

Li, Guangdi. *Rongcun quanshu* (Complete Works of Li Guangdi). N.p., preface 1829. This collection of Li Guangdi's works includes the following major titles:

Rongcun quanji (Anthology of Writings by Li Guangdi).

Rongcun yulu (Recorded Sayings of Li Guangdi).

Rongcun yulu xuji (A Sequel to the *Recorded Sayings of Li Guangdi*).

Li, Qingfu. *Rongcun pulu hekao* (An Investigation into the Events Recorded in Li Guangdi's *Biographical Annals* and *Recorded Sayings*). Appended to *Rongcun quanshu.*

Li, Qingzhi. *Wenzhen gong nianpu* (Biographical annals of Li Guangdi). Taipei: Guangwen, 1971 reprint.

Li, Yong. *Erqu ji* (Anthology of [Li] Yong's [Writings]). Beijing: Zhonghua, 1996.

Liang, Ch'i-ch'ao. *Intellectual Trends in the Ch'ing Period*. Translated by Immanuel C. Y. Hsu. Cambridge, Mass.: Harvard University Press, 1959.

Liu, Zongzhou. *Liuzi quanshu* (Complete Works of Master Liu). Kyoto: Chubun, 1981 reprint.

Lu, Shiyi. *Lu Futing xiansheng yishu ershi'er zhong* (The Bequeathed Works of Lu Shiyi in Twenty-Two Titles). Beijing, 1899.

Lu, Shiyi. *Sibianlu jiyao* (Selected Notes of Reflections and Disputations). Taipei: Guangwen, 1977 reprint.

Lynn, Richard John, trans. *The Classic of Change: A New Translation of the I Ching as Interpreted by Wang Bi*. New York: Columbia University Press, 1994.

Lyotard, Jean-Francois. *The Post-Modern Condition: A Report on Knowledge*. Tanslated by G. Bennington and B. Massumi. Minneapolis: University of Minnesota Press, 1984.

McMorran, Ian. "Wang Fu-chih and the Neo-Confucian Tradition." In Wm. Theodore de Bary, ed., *The Unfolding of Neo-Confucianism*. New York; Columbia University Press, 1975. Pp. 413–69.

Metzger, Thomas. *Escape from Predicament: Neo-Confucianism and China's Evolving Political Culture*. New York: Columbia University Press, 1976.

Mink, Louis O. *Mind, History, and Dialectic: The Philosophy of R. G. Collingwood*. Bloomington: Indiana University Press, 1969.

Mote, Frederick W. "The Limits of Intellectual History?" *Ming Studies* 19(Fall 1984):17–25.

Mou, Zongsan. *Xinti yu xingti* (The Reality of the Self's Nature and the Reality of the Mind's Nature). Taipei: Zhengzhong, 1968.

Munro, Donald. *Images of Human Nature: A Sung Portrait*. Princeton: Princeton University Press, 1988.

Munro, Donald. *The Concept of Man in Early China*. Stanford: Stanford University Press, 1969.

Ng, On-cho. "An Early Qing Critique of the Philosophy of Mind-Heart (*Xin*): The Confucian Quest for Doctrinal Purity and the '*Doxic*' Role of Chan Buddhism," *Journal of Chinese Philosophy* 26.1(March 1999):89–120.

Ng, On-cho. "*Hsing* (Nature) as the Ontological Basis of Practicality in Early Ch'ing Ch'eng-Chu Confucianism: Li Kuang-ti's (1642–1718) Philosophy," *Philosophy East and West* 44.1(January 1994):79–109.

Ng, On-cho. "Is Emotion (*Qing*) the Source of a Confucian Antinomy?" *Journal of Chinese Philosophy* 25.2(June 1998):169–90.

Ng, On-cho. "Mystical Oneness and Meditational Praxis: Religiousness in Li Yong's (1627–1705) Confucian Thought," *Journal of Chinese Religions* 22(Fall 1994):75–102.

Ng, On-cho. "Toward an Interpretation of Ch'ing Ontology," in Richard J. Smith and D.W.Y. Kwok, eds., *Cosmology, Ontology and Human Efficacy: Essays on Chinese Thought*. Honolulu: University of Hawaii Press, 1993. Pp. 35–58.

Norman, Richard. *The Moral Philosophers: An Introduction to Ethics*. Oxford: Clarendon Press, 1983.

Okada, Takehiko. "Wang Chi and the Rise of Existentialism," in Wm. Theodore de Bary, ed., *Self and Society in Ming Thought*. New York: Columbia University Press, 1970. Pp. 121–44.

Ortega y Gasset, José. *History as a System*. Translated by William Atkinson. New York: W.W. Norton, 1941.

Paul Ricoeur, "Explanation and Understanding," in Paul Ricoeur, *The Philosophy of Paul Ricoeur*. Boston: Beacon, 1978.

Pocock, J. G. A. *Politics, Language and Time: Essays on Political Thought*. New York: Atheneum, 1971.

Qian, Daxin. *Qianwentang wenji* (Collected Writings from the Qianwen Studio). Shanghai: Commercial Press, 1935.

Qian, Mu. *Zhongguo jin sanbainian xueshushi* (The History of Chinese Learning in the Past Three Hundred Years). Taipei: Shangwu, 1937.

Qian, Mu. *Zhuzi xin xue'an* (A Record of the Learning of Zhu Xi). 3 vols. Chengdu: Bashu, 1987.

Qian, Yiji. *Beizhuan ji* (Anthology of Tomb Inscriptions and Biographical Sketches). N.p., preface 1826.

Qing shi gao (A Draft Dynastic History of the Qing). Taipei: Guofang yanjiu yuan, 1961.

Quan, Zuwang. *Jiqi ting waibian* (Additions to the Collected Writings from the Studio in Jiqi Mountain). N.p., 1776.

Ricoeur, Paul. "The Hermeneutical Function of Distanciation," in John B. Thompson, ed. and trans., *Paul Ricoeur: Hermeneutics and the Human Sciences*. Cambridge: Cambridge University Press, 1981.

Ricoeur, Paul. "What Does Humanism Mean?" in David Stewart and Joseph Bien, eds., *Political and Social Essays*. Athens: Ohio University Press, 1974.

Rong, Zhaozu. *Mingdai sixiangshi* (A History of Ming Thought). Taipei: Kaiming, 1966.

Schirokauer, Conrad, and Robert Hymes, eds. *Ordering the World: Approaches to State and Society in Sung Dynasty China*. Berkeley: University of California Press, 1993.

Schrag, Calvin O. *Communicative Praxis and the Space of Subjectivity*. Bloomington: Indiana University Press, 1989.

Schwartz, Benjamin I. "Some Polarities in Confucian Thought," in David Nivison and Arthur Wright, eds., *Confucianism in Action*. Stanford: Standford University Press, 1959. Pp. 50–62.

Schwartz, Benjamin I. *The World of Thought in Ancient China*. Cambridge, Mass.: Harvard University Press, 1985.

Scott, Nathan, Jr. "The House of Intellect in an Age of Carnival: Some Hermeneutic Reflections," *Journal of the American Academy of Religion* 55.1(Spring 1987):8–13.

Shryock, John K. *The Origin and Development of the State Cult of Confucius*. NewYork: Paragon Book Reprint Corp., 1966 reprint.

Smith, Huston. "Postmodernism and the World's Religions," in Walter Truett Anderson, ed., *The Truth about the Truth*. New York: Tarcher/Putnam Book, 1995. Pp. 204–14.

Tang, Chün-i. "Liu Tsung-chou's Doctrine of the Moral Mind and Practice and His Critique of Wang Yang-ming," in Wm. Theodore de Bary, ed., *The Unfolding of Neo-Confucianism*. New York: Columbia University Press, 1975. Pp. 305–32.

Tang, Chün-i. "The Development of the Concept of Moral Mind from Wang Yang-ming to Wang Chi," in Wm. Theodore de Bary, ed., *Self and Society in Ming Thought*. New York: Columbia University Press, 1970. Pp. 93–120.

Tao, Qing. *Ming yimin jiu dajia zhexue* (The Philosophies of the Nine Great Ming Loyalists). Taipei: Hongye, 1997.

Taylor, Rodney. "Meditation and Ming Neo-Orthodoxy," in Rodney Taylor, *The Religious Dimensions of Confucianism*. Albany: State University of New York Press, 1990. Pp. 93–114.

Taylor, Rodney. "The Sage as Saint: The Confucian Tradition," in Richard Kieckhefer and George Bond, eds., *Sainthood: Its Manifestations in World Religions*. Berkeley: University of California Press, 1988. Pp. 218–42.

Tillman, Hoyt Cleveland. *Ch'en Liang on Public Interest and the Law*. Honolulu: University of Hawaii Press, 1994.

Tillman, Hoyt Cleveland. *Confucian Discourse and Chu Hsi's Ascendancy*. Honolulu: University of Hawaii Press, 1992.

Tillman, Hoyt Cleveland. *Utilitarian Confucianism: Ch'en Liang's Challenge to Chu Hsi*. Cambridge, Mass.: Harvard University Press, 1982.

Tracy, David. *Blessed Rage for Order: The New Pluralism in Theology*. New York: Seabury Press, 1975.

Tracy, David. *Plurality and Ambiguity: Hermeneutics, Religion, Hope*. San Francisco: Harper & Row, 1987.

Tracy, David. *The Analogical Imagination: Christian Theology and the Culture of Pluralism*. New York: Crossroads, 1981.

Tu Wei-ming. *Centrality and Commonality*. Albany: State University of New York Press, 1989.

Tu, Wei-ming. "Perceptions of Learning (*Hsüeh*) in Early Ch'ing Thought," in Tu Wei-ming, *Way, Learning, and Politics: Essays on the Confucian Intellectual*. Albany: State University of New York Press, 1993. Pp. 117–40.

Tu, Wei-ming. "Subjectivity in Liu Tsung-chou's Philosophical Anthropology," in Donald Munro, ed., *Individualism and Holism: Studies in Confucian and Taoist Values*. Ann Arbor: University of Michigan Press, 1985. Pp. 215–38.

Tu, Wei-ming. *Confucian Thought: Selfhood as Creative Transformation*. Albany: State University of New York Press, 1985.

Tucker, Mary Evelyn. "Religious Dimensions of Confucianism: Cosmology and Cultivation," *Philosophy East and West* 48.1(January 1998):5–45.

Van Zoeren, Steven. *Poetry and Personality: Reading, Exegesis and Hermeneutics in Traditional China*. Stanford: Stanford University Press, 1991.

Wachterhauser, Brice R. "Introduction," in Brice R. Wachterhauser, ed., *Hermeneutics and Truth*. Evanston, Ill.: Northwestern University Press, 1994. Pp. 1–24.

Wakeman, Frederic, Jr. *The Great Enterprise: The Manchu Reconstruction of Imperial Order in Seventeenth-Century China*. Vol. 2. Berkeley: University of California Press, 1985.

Wang, Mouhong. *Zhuzi nianpu* (A Biographical Annals of the Life of Zhu Xi). Taipei: Shangwu, 1982.

Wang, Yangming. *Instructions for Practical Living and Other Neo-Confucian Writings*. Translated with notes by Wing-tsit Chan. New York: Columbia University Press, 1962.

Warnke, Georgia. *Gadamer: Hermeneutics, Tradition and Reason*. Cambridge: Polity Press, 1987.

Weintraub, Karl. *Visions of Culture*. Chicago: University of Chicago Press, 1966.

Wilheim Richard, trans. *The I Ching or the Book of Changes*. Rendered into English by Cary Baynes. Princeton: Princeton University Press, 1977.

Williams, Bernard. *Ethics and the Limits of Philosophy*. Cambridge, Mass.: Harvard University Press, 1985.

Wilson, Thomas A. "The Ritual Formation of Confucian Orthodoxy and the Descendants of the Sage," *Journal of Asian Studies* 55.3(August 1996):559–84.

Wilson, Thomas A. *The Genealogy of the Way: The Construction and Uses of the Confucian Tradition in Late Imperial China*. Stanford: Stanford University Press, 1995.

Wyatt, Don J. "A Language of Continuity in Confucian Thought," in Paul Cohen and Merle Goldman, eds., *Ideas Across Cultures: Essays on Chinese Thought in Honor of Benjamin I. Schwartz*. Cambridge, Mass.: Harvard University Press, 1990. Pp. 50–57.

Yamanoi, Yû. "Mimmatsu Shinsho ni okeru chiyô no gaku," in Yamanoi Yû, *Min Shin shishô shi kenkyû* (A Study of the History of Ming–Qing Thought). Tokyo: Chubun, 1980.

Yang, Guozhen, et al. *Li Guangdi yanjiu* (Studies on Li Guangdi). Fujian: Xiamen daxue, 1993.

Yearley, Lee H. "A Confucian Crisis: Mencius' Two Cosmogonies and Their Ethics," in Robin W. Lovin and Frank E. Reynolds, eds., *Cosmogony and Ethical Order: New Studies in Comparative Ethics*. Chicago: University of Chicago Press, 1985. Pp. 310–27.

Yearley, Lee H. *Mencius and Aquinas: Theories of Virtue and Conceptions of Courage*. Albany: State University of New York Press, 1990.

Yü, Ying-shih. "Cong SongMing ruxue de fanzhan lun Qingdai sixiang-shi" (A Discussion of Qing Intellectual History in Light of the Developments of Song-Ming Confucianism), *Zhongguo xueren* 2(September 1970):19–41.

Yü, Ying-shih. "Qingdai sixiangshi de yige xinjieshi" (A New Explication of Qing Intellectual History), in Yü Ying-shih, *Lishi yu sixiang* (History and Thinking). Taipei: Lianjing, 1976. Pp. 121–56.

Yü, Ying-shih. "Qingdai sixiangshi zhongyao guannian tongshi" (General Explanations of the Important Concepts in Qing Intellectual History), in Yü Ying-shih, *Zhongguo sixiang chuantong de xiandai quanshi* (Contemporary Interpretations of Traditional Chinese Thought). Taipei: Lianjing, 1987. Pp. 418–31.

Yü, Ying-shih. "Some Preliminary Observations on the Rise of Ch'ing Confucian Intellectualism," *Tsing-hua Journal of Chinese Studies* 10.1–2(December 1975):105–36.

Zeng, Qunhai, "Li Guangdi de Yixue chutan" (A Preliminary Inquiry into Li Guangdi's Study of the *Changes*), in *Qingdai jingxue guoji yantaohui lunwenji* (A Collection of Essays from the International Conference on Classical Learning in the Qing Period). Taipei: Zhongyang yanjiuyuan Zhongguo wenzhe yanjiusuo, 1994. Pp. 193–214.

Zhan, Haiyun. *Qingchu xueshu lunwenji* (Anthology of Essays on the Learning and Scholarship of the Early Qing). Taipei: Wenjin, 1992.

Zhang, Dainian. *Zhongguo zhexue dagang* (An Outline of Chinese Philosophy). Beijing: Zhongguo kexue, 1982.

Zhang, Zai. *Zhang Zai ji* (Anthology of [the Writings of] Zhang Zai). Beijing: Zhonghua, 1985.

Zhu Xi, *Sishu zhangju jizhu* (Annotations to the *Sishu zhangzhu*). Taipei: Zhonghua, 1983.

Zhu, Xi. *Zhuzi wenji* (Collected Writings of Zhu Xi). Edited by Wang Yunwu. Taipei: Commercial Printing Press, 1966 reprint.

Zhu, Xi. *Zhuzi yulei* (Conversations of Master Zhu, Arranged Topically). Beijing: Zhonghua, 1986.

INDEX